HER PAST AROUND US

INTERPRETING SITES FOR WOMEN'S HISTORY

The statue of Dr. Elizabeth Blackwell by Ted Aube is at William Smith College, Geneva, NY, site of Geneva Medical College where Blackwell received the first medical degree conferred on a woman in the United States—with Kathleen Tocke on her graduation day. (*Photo by Eileen Eagan.*)

HER PAST AROUND US

INTERPRETING SITES FOR WOMEN'S HISTORY

Edited by

Polly Welts Kaufman
&
Katharine T. Corbett

KRIEGER PUBLISHING COMPANY
Malabar, Florida
2003

Original Edition 2003

Printed and Published by
KRIEGER PUBLISHING COMPANY
KRIEGER DRIVE
MALABAR, FLORIDA 32950

Library of Congress Cataloging-in-Publication Data

Her past around us : interpreting sites for women's history / edited by Polly Welts Kaufman & Katharine T. Corbett.
    p. cm. — (Public history series)
  ISBN 1-57524-130-7 (hardcover : alk. paper)
   1. Women—History. 2. Women—historiography. 3. Local history. 4. Historic sites. 5. Local geography. I. Kaufman, Polly Welts, 1929- II. Corbett, Katharine T. III. Series.

HQ1121 .H46 2003

2002029848

10   9   8   7   6   5   4   3   2

CONTENTS

CONTRIBUTORS

LESLIE BROWN teaches African American history and African American studies at Washington University, St. Louis. Her Ph.D. is from Duke University. Her research interests are exploring the connections between race, gender, and class in the urban south. She is currently working on a community study of Durham, NC, in the period between 1890 and 1940.

KATHARINE T. CORBETT, the former director of interpretation at the Missouri Historical Society, was in charge of research and interpretation for two NEH-funded award-winning exhibits. She taught women's history and the history of St. Louis at the University of Missouri-St. Louis and University College, Washington University and has served on the board of the National Council on Public History. Her latest book is *In Her Place: A Guide to St. Louis Women's History* (1999).

EILEEN EAGAN is a member of the History Department faculty and on the Women's Studies' Council at the University of Southern Maine. She teaches twentieth-century U.S. history and the history of women in the U.S. Her research and publications include studies of peace movements, Irish and Irish-American women in Maine, parks, and women in popular culture. She has participated in developing history trails of workers and women in Portland, Maine. She is currently working on a history of Irish immigration to Maine.

BARBARA J. HOWE is director of women's studies at West Virginia University and the former director of the public history program. She has served as chair of the National Council on Public History, as a member of the governing council of the American Association for State and Local History, and as co-chair of the West Virginia advisory committee for the report of the Institute for Women's Policy Research on the Status of Women in West Virginia. Her research interests include the history of West Virginia wage-earning women in the nineteenth century.

CANDACE A. KANES teaches history and women's studies at the Maine College of Art in Portland, Maine. She is interested in women's economic activities in the nineteenth and early twentieth centuries, and particularly in the work of business women. She also has taught at Bates College and the University of New England. She holds a Ph.D. from the University of New Hampshire in modern American history and is a former newspaper reporter and editor.

POLLY WELTS KAUFMAN teaches history at the University of Southern Maine. She was a founder of the Boston Women's Heritage Trail and project director for women's history trails in Portland and Brunswick, Maine. During her recent year as a Fulbright roving scholar in American studies in Norway, she was the project director for a walking trail to statues of named women in Oslo, printed in both Norwegian and English. Her most recent book is *National Parks and the Woman's Voice: A History* (1996).

BONNIE HURD SMITH is a special projects consultant to the Peabody Essex Museum in Salem, Massachusetts. She was the author of the Salem Women's Heritage Trail and previously served as director of the Boston Women's Heritage Trail. Smith is the former president of the Sargent-Murray-Gilman-Hough House Museum board in Gloucester and the author of *From Gloucester to Philadelphia in 1790: Observations, Anecdotes, and Thoughts from the Letters of Judith Sargent Murray*. She is currently transcribing Murray's letter books for future publication.

MARGARET LYNCH-BRENNAN is an associate with the New York State Education Department where she serves as co-state coordinator for "High Schools That Work," an education reform initiative. She is a Ph.D. candidate in American history at SUNY, Albany, writing her dissertation on "Ubiquitous Biddy: Irish Immigrant Women in Domestic Service in America, 1840–1930."

PAMELA K. SANFILIPPO is the park historian at Ulysses S. Grant National Historic Site, where she developed the educational program. She is a doctoral student in history and education at the University of Missouri in St. Louis, combining her history background with an emphasis on curriculum and instruction. She has written several articles and developed curriculum projects on the people and property of White Haven, the estate at Grant NHS.

TARA TRAVIS resides at Canyon de Chelly and is a historian with the National Park Service. The third generation of her family to work on the Navajo reservation, Travis was the primary investigator of a project to document the historic Navajo landscape of Canyon del Muerto. She is a Ph.D. candidate in history at Arizona State University and is writing her dissertation on a Navajo history of Canyon de Chelly. She was a historian for the Southern Arizona Office of the NPS and the Indian Arts Research Center at the School of American Research in Santa Fe.

ANNE M. VALK teaches at Southern Illinois University at Edwardsville where she offers courses in public history, oral history, and U.S. women's history. She is currently working on a book about women's activism and feminism in Washington, D.C. in the 1960s and 1970s. Her other research interests include local history, African American life during segregation, and gay and lesbian history.

NANCY MAYER WETZEL writes and lectures on turn-of-the-twentieth century garden history and the notable plantswomen of that period. She is a landscape gardener with a speciality in the design and care of perennial flower gardens. Wetzel's practice includes the gardens of the Sarah Orne Jewett House, a property of the Society for the Preservation of New England Antiquities in Berwick, Maine.

INTRODUCTION

Women's work and voluntary activities provide essential strands in the fabric of every community. Whether they managed shops on Main Street, taught in schoolrooms, presided over kitchens, worked in factories, served on volunteer boards, or were elected to public office, women have contributed to the well-being of communities. *Her Past Around Us: Interpreting Sites for Women's History* is a guide to finding and presenting places that reveal women's stories and illuminate their goals. Some of these sites, such as city hall, are not generally associated with women; some are sites of long-forgotten women's activities; while others, such as kitchens, usually assumed to be women's domain, reflect unexpected complexities of meaning.

This collection of essays is designed to be useful to teachers and historical societies searching their own communities for new sites significant to the history of women. The essays also will be of interest to anyone who wants to use local and national historic sites as windows into women's history. Because the focus is on the tangible and the specific, the essays offer useful resources for helping connect the public to its past.

Recent studies suggest that Americans seldom relate to history through passive techniques traditionally offered in classrooms. The public is most likely to make connections to the past through specifics: by researching family histories, by visiting historic sites and museums, by watching television programs on historical topics, or by surfing the Internet. People become intrigued by colorful ancestors, by nearby historic buildings or personalities, or by the history of a local ethnic community. Instead of asking broad historical questions, David Glassberg says, "The public begins with a place it cares about, and then asks what happened there."[1]

Too often the answers to "what happened there" are about men, even though women lived or worked in a site and influenced its function and appearance. Lately, however, historians have begun reinterpreting many traditional sites as well as identifying new places significant for women's history. On a national level, public historians have put many women's history sites on the map. In the late 1980s, a group of women's historians found that only 2.5 percent of the nation's two thousand National Historic Landmarks focused on women. They organized the Women's History Landmark Project and added fifty new landmarks. They brought public attention to such significant places where women worked and lived as the Triangle Shirtwaist Factory Building in New York where 146 young women workers died in a fire in 1911 and the New England Hospital for Women and Children, built and staffed by women, that opened in Boston in 1862. Earlier, women activists, both inside and outside the National Park Service, helped establish such new national historic sites as Women's Rights National Historical Park, Eleanor Roosevelt National Historic Site, and Mary McLeod Bethune Council House National Historic Site. Other national parks began to research and present women's history programs to the visiting public.[2]

1

On the local level, however, a large number of the places the public cares about are not designated as historic sites, much less sites identified with women's history. In fact, no place is more "historic" than another until someone—perhaps through community memory or scholarly research—has found a story in it and linked that story to larger questions of historical significance. When we locate places in the community where people can see the material evidence of women's history for themselves, we are responding to the public's desire for the specific and experiential. These sites may be familiar places that have not been previously identified as women's spaces. They may even be places associated with women that have not been interpreted to reveal the complexities of women's activities there. By drawing on current scholarship in women's studies and in public history, we can exploit these historic places to raise important, less tangible, issues about women's experience.[3]

Her Past Around Us is a guide to finding, interpreting, and promoting places that reveal women's stories and enrich our understanding of their lives. In every community one only has to look and ask questions. The eleven chapters explore possibilities for using women's history and feminist analysis to look at familiar places through the lens of gender. They offer a variety of approaches to exploring the places of women's activities that bring new visibility to women's lives.

For the most part the authors make no attempt to be comprehensive, but instead develop case studies to be used as guides for interpreting or reinterpreting similar places. The sites analyzed here include homes, gardens, factories, cemeteries, business districts, and even entire communities. They are places to learn about women running millinery shops, surviving in a new country by working in another woman's kitchen, stripping tobacco leaves in a factory in the South, laboring for slave owners, commemorating achievement, and mourning their dead.

In asking, "Who walked before me?" Polly Welts Kaufman takes women's history directly to the streets. Her guide to developing and presenting women's history tours and walking trails begins with the necessity for creative scholarship that poses questions useful for probing for the significance of women's places. She urges readers to explore their own neighborhoods not only to identify women's spaces, but also to determine the reasons women chose particular locations for their activities. The members of the New England Woman Suffrage Association, for example, selected an office in a building half a block from the Massachusetts State House where their presence and their cause could not be ignored. Kaufman's practical suggestions for involving students and volunteers in research and planning support her conviction that women's history is a cooperative endeavor.

While most essays suggest new ways of looking at familiar places, Eileen Eagan asks us to look for something missing from most communities: statues in public places commemorating specific women and their achievements. Her comprehensive national survey of statues to named women reveals that unlike men, women have seldom been honored with individual statues. They were more often represented as symbols or ideals. Eagan traces the history of public statues of women in the United States, linking symbolic monuments such as the ubiquitous

"Pioneer Mother" to prevailing attitudes about gender and nationalism. She explains why some women were honored in bronze while many others await their places on the public landscape.

The centrality of the role of Native American women in maintaining cultural continuity for their people in periods of great change is the theme of Tara Travis's essay. Travis examines the role of women in two Southwestern history sites: Canyon de Chelly National Monument and Hubbell Trading Post National Historic Site. Throughout their history, Navajo families have clustered around a head mother and her extended kin. The head mother has been the center of the homestead, the basic unit of Navajo society. Despite the severe disruptions to the lives of Navajo people by the invading Americans which caused changes in settlement patterns, Travis explains, the women preserved the Navajo culture by maintaining and protecting traditional homestead units.

Although a home is a domestic space, a woman's place, in the past most homes designated as historic sites recognized the public achievements of the male owners and the interpretation focused on male activity. Administrators of historic homes are widening their research and refocusing their public programming to include the experiences of women associated with their sites. In her essay, Bonnie Hurd Smith examines how public historians, curators, and volunteers are listening for women's voices at sites in the Northeast. The Society for the Preservation of New England Antiquities (SPNEA), for example, changed the official name of its Harrison Gray Otis House to the Otis House, to acknowledge that the majority of the occupants were women leading active lives.

Pamela Sanfilippo uncovers women's history embedded in a home preserved because it belonged to a president of the United States: the Ulysses S. Grant National Historic Site in Missouri. She contrasts the domestic experiences of Julia Dent Grant, the president's wife, with those of the women and children enslaved by the Dent family by analyzing clues in the house itself, the arrangement of rooms, and in that most traditional of women's spaces, the kitchen. Weaving together evidence from artifacts, the architecture, and manuscripts, she reveals the interplay between the women who lived in shadows and those in sunlight at White Haven. Her essay is a model for searching out the history of enslaved women who made life comfortable for white women and their families in what are now historic houses.

Some of the essays in this collection bring new questions to sites that are already connected with women's history. Margaret Lynch-Brennan asks who was working in the kitchens of middle and upperclass homes in nineteenth-century northern cities. She finds immigrant women who moved off trans-Atlantic ships into the attic rooms of Victorian houses that are today open to the public. She looks at one of these homes from the servant's point of view, contrasting the domestic life a young Irish woman left behind with the one she encountered in the United States as a domestic servant. Her chapter offers a number of resources and interpretive strategies for making these hidden women come alive for visitors.

Nancy Wetzel takes us out of the house and into the garden. Arguing that the

Colonial Revival of the late nineteenth century inspired women to recreate and preserve the gardens of their grandmothers' generation, she describes how their domestic gardens functioned as private spaces and as opportunities for semipublic expressions of creativity. She moves from the restoration of a neglected estate garden to the twentieth century when women expanded their vision and became preservationists, professional gardeners, botanists, and landscape designers.

For much of this nation's history, the context for women's work and social roles was primarily domestic. Houses and their grounds are, therefore, logical places to start searching for clues not only to what they did, but also to what they, and those around them, thought about it. Clothing, home furnishings, the tools of house work, personal possessions, even the use of rooms are evidence of cultural attitudes about gender. Public places are also sites for learning about societal values. Churches, schools, workplaces all reflect the ideas of the people who built them. Katharine Corbett takes us to a St. Louis cemetery influenced by the Rural Cemetery Movement and suggests that nineteenth-century domestic ideals, which shaped the lives of middle-class women, are revealed in the design of the cemetery and its monuments. She also finds cemeteries to be good places for introducing the public to local women's history.

An emphasis on domesticity can lead to the erroneous belief that women worked only in homes, either their own or someone else's. Other women's workplaces, buildings still standing in the retail and industrial areas of our cities and towns, are often familiar local places with hidden histories. Candace Kanes finds women entrepreneurs on Main Street, as early as the Colonial era, operating their own grocery stores, lunchrooms, dressmaking, millinery, and hairdressing shops. Starting with city maps and the records of the Buffalo chapter of Zonta, a national organization of businesswomen that cut across lines of class and ethnicity, Kanes uncovered evidence of women's business activities that led her to investigate additional sources in Buffalo and other communities. Organizational records, city directories, and historical society resources all contained information she could use for reading visual clues to women's work lives on the urban landscape.

The word "place" carries a double meaning for all women, but for African American women in the urban South attitudes about proper place and expected roles translated into race and gender segregation intended to confine them within proscribed physical spaces. Leslie Brown and Anne Valk reveal that in Durham, North Carolina, black women dominated their own spaces by claiming as "our territory" the places they were assigned to and the places they established themselves. African American women made these places into arenas for racial and gendered struggles, expanding their terrain as they actively asserted themselves to meet personal and community needs. Using a wide variety of resources, including oral interviews, Brown and Valk put African American women's agency firmly on the map of Durham. This case study, which uses a whole city as a women's history site, demonstrates ways of researching and interpreting complex issues of race, class, and gender embedded in the history of every community.

Barbara Howe also looked at public space and found something missing. Too often community celebrations and public events ignored the scholarship in women's history that would have enriched the experiences for all participants. She identifies useful sources and offers concrete suggestions for local observances of significant events in women's history, using as an example "Celebrate '98" which commemorated the 150th anniversary of the Seneca Falls women's rights convention. She urges public historians, scholars, teachers, administrators, and others concerned with women's history to become involved in the planning process for all sorts of community events. By bringing a feminist perspective to the table, planners can influence content and promote activities that include women as both subjects and participants.

A feminist perspective underlies each of the essays in *Her Past Around Us*. The authors not only employ feminist analysis, but they also understand that knowledge leading to action is the most useful kind. Dolores Hayden claims that people who find their own history in the public landscape of their neighborhoods and cities develop different, more meaningful, connections to the past. She worked with other women to identify places in Los Angeles where an ex-slave midwife had practiced and where Latina women organized dressmakers and cannery workers. They went on to found a community-based group to create walking tours, erect public art, and sponsor programming that made these places visible on the urban landscape. Each of the chapters in *Her Past Around Us* includes suggestions for action. They point to creating women's history trails, revising the interpretation of historic houses and sites, influencing local school curricula, compiling oral history collections, creating women's history exhibits, and integrating women's roles into existing and future exhibits and community programs.[4]

Teachers of United States history and women's studies will find tangible examples in this collection for helping students understand abstract concepts such as gendered racism and the ideology of domesticity. Sending students who have read essays on historic house interpretation to visit local house museums can lead to lively classroom discussions. Embedded in each chapter are many topics for future research. Students can uncover the hidden stories of local women, their work, their organizations, their place in the community. Research projects that link topics in local history to such larger themes as slavery, industrialization, urbanization, and immigration enhance a student's ability to understand national history.

Public historians who interpret historic houses will find many suggestions for research and presentation in this collection of essays. Those responsible for public programming at museums and historical societies can enrich their offerings by building on their audiences' interest in the past around them. Looking at houses, gardens, workplaces, cemeteries, sculpture, and city streets through the lens of gender adds a new perspective that can aid in refocusing established programs for greater appeal. The suggested references included in each chapter will be helpful in finding creative ways to include current women's history scholarship in program development.

Her Past Around us encourages collaboration among historians, curators, teachers, students, and volunteers in creating public awareness of women's history in their communities. It will be most successful if teachers and their students contact women (and men) in the neighborhood to help plan a women's history trail, if historians interest citizens in looking for public ways of remembering women who made a difference in their communities, and if visitors hear the stories of all the women who lived within the walls of the houses we so carefully preserve. Evidence of women's experience is all around us, hidden in old street patterns, old buildings, and old memories. When two St. Louis graduate students followed the trail from archival strike photographs, to long-closed clothing factories, to the doors of retired garment workers, they were greeted with what users of *Her Past Around Us* can also expect to hear: "What took you so long?"[5]

* * *

A general acquaintance with U.S. women's history helps the researcher in local women's history set the stories they find in a broader context. Readers especially interested in specific areas will want to investigate resources in particular topics. Each chapter in *Her Past Around Us* includes a suggested list of sources pertaining to the subject presented. Some recommended publications are discussed below.

There are now many choices for both general and specific books on U.S. women's history. Two standard one-volume surveys that will help researchers fit the stories of women in their local communities into the country's history of women are Sarah Evans, *Born for Liberty: A History of Women in America* (New York: Oxford University Press, 1997) and Nancy F. Cott, editor, *No Small Courage: A History of Women in the United States.* (New York: Oxford University Press, 2000). A version of the latter work is available for younger readers by the same publisher as *The Young Oxford History of Women in the United States* in eleven illustrated short paperbacks. Volume 11 includes brief biographies of notable women and lists museums and historic sites presenting women's history. The standard four-volume historical encyclopedia of women's biographies available in most libraries is *Notable American Women, 1607–1950, A Biographical Dictionary* edited by Edward T. James, Janet Wilson James, and Paul S. Boyer (Cambridge, MA: Harvard University Press, 1971) and *Notable American Women, the Modern Period* edited by Barbara Sicherman and Carol Hurd Green (Cambridge, MA: Harvard University Press, 1980). The American Historical Association published two guides to women's history: Karen Anderson, *Teaching Gender in U.S. History* (1997) and Linda Gordon, *U.S. Women's History* (1999).

Although there are several one-volume collections of articles on U.S. women's history, one that covers a wide diversity of women is Ellen Carol DuBois and Vicki L. Ruiz, *Unequal Sisters: A Multi-Cultural Reader in U.S. Women's History* (New York: Routledge, 2000). A useful one-volume collection of articles is contained in Linda K. Kerber and Jane Sherron DeHart, *Women's America: Refocusing the Past.* (New York: Oxford, 1999). For a collection of documents, rather than articles, see Ruth Barnes Moynihan, Cynthia Russett, and Laurie Crumpacker, *Second to None: A Documentary History of American Women* (Lincoln: University of Nebraska Press, 1994) in two volumes.

Collections of first-hand accounts of women's experiences in specific areas will provide models for researching women's similar experiences in a local community. For women and their work in a variety of locations, see Rosalyn Baxandall and Linda Gordon, *America's Working Women: A Documentary History* (New York: W.W. Norton & Company, 1995). For immigrant women, see Maxine Schwartz Seller, *Immigrant Women* (New York: State University of New York Press, 1994) and Peter Morton Coan, *Ellis Island Interviews in Their Own Words* (New York: Checkmark Books, 1997). The Coan collection includes men as well. An example of a book on teachers' lives is Mary Hurlbut Cordier, *Schoolwomen of the Prairies and Plains: Personal Narratives from Iowa, Kansas, and Nebraska, 1860s to the 1920s* (Albuquerque: University of New Mexico Press, 1992). Studs Terkel, *Hard Times:An Oral History of the Great Depression* (New York: Pantheon, 1970), includes firsthand accounts of women's experiences during the 1930s.

Every community can add to the women's history of their area by documenting the activities of past and present women's voluntary associations. The early women's club movement is chronicled in Karen Blair, *The Clubwoman as Feminist: True Womanhood Redefined, 1868–1914* (New York: Holmes and Meier, 1980). Ann Firor Scott looked at women's work in voluntary organizations in *Natural Allies: Women's Associations in American History* (Chicago: University of Illinois Press, 1992). For a study of Catholic women in religious orders, see Carol K. Coburn and Martha Smith, *Spirited Lives: How Nuns Shaped Catholic Culture and American Life* (Chapel Hill: University of North Carolina Press, 1999).

A comprehensive one-volume history of African American women is Darlene Clark Hine and Kathleen Thompson, *A Shining Thread of Hope: The History of Black Women in America* (New York: Broadway Books, 1998). A work that emphasizes the power of the African American women's club movement is Paula Giddings, *When and Where I Enter: The Impact of Black Women on Race and Sex in America* (New York: Morrow, 1984). For the stories of individual African American women, see *Black Women in America, An Historical Encyclopedia* (Bloomington: Indiana University Press, 1994) in two volumes collected by Darlene Clark Hine, Rosalyn Terborg-Penn, and Elsa B. Brown. Howell Raines included many women's oral histories of the Civil Rights Movement in his *My Soul is Rested: The Story of the Civil Rights Movement in the Deep South* (New York: Penquin, 1983).

Some cities, states, and regions have published histories of women in their geographical areas that provide a beginning for the community researcher. The most recent studies present a multicultural approach. Among them are Susan Armitage and Elizabeth Jameson, eds., *The Women's West* (Norman: University of Oklahoma Press, 1987); Katharine T. Corbett, *In Her Place: A Guide to St. Louis Women's History* (St. Louis: Missouri Historical Society, 1999); Christie Anne Farnham, ed., *Women of the American South: A Multicultural Reader* (New York: New York University Press, 1997); and Linda Williams Reese, *Women of Oklahoma, 1890–1920* (Norman, University of Oklahoma Press, 1997). Vicki Ruiz looks at Mexican-American women in the Southwest in *From Out of the Shadows, Mexican Women in Twentieth Century America* (New York: Oxford University Press, 1998).

A model for using material culture to interpret the lives of Native American women is the result of a collaboration between native people and the staff of a museum. Together they produced an exhibit and the richly illustrated book: Barbara A. Hail, ed., *Gifts of Pride and Love, Kiowa and Comanche Cradles* (Providence, RI: Brown University, Haffenreffer Museum of Anthropology, 2000).

The field of public history offers both guides to finding and utilizing local history and discussions on the nature of public perceptions of the past. Dolores Hayden in *The Power of Place: Urban Landscapes as Public History* (Cambridge, MA: MIT Press, 1995) offers a creative approach to finding change over time in the urban landscape that celebrates the work of women and minorities. In *Nearby History: Exploring the Past Around You* (Walnut Creek, CA: Alta Mira Press, 2000), David E. Kyvig and Myron A. Marty show the researcher how to find and interpret photographs, documents, buildings, and artifacts and how to create oral histories and archives. Both Roy Rozenzweig and David Thelen in *The Presence of the Past: Popular Uses of History in American Life* (New York: Columbia University Press, 1998) and David Glassberg in *Sense of History:The Place of the Past in American Life* (Amherst: University of Massachusetts Press, 2001) can help the researcher find out what the public expects history to be about and how to work with differing—sometimes controversial—perceptions, memories, and traditions.

Two comprehensive collections of essays on women's historic landmarks and buildings provide both information and models for research on women's history in the built environment. Women's history landmarks in such fields as architecture, arts, education, religion, and work are described in Page Putnam Miller, ed., *Reclaiming the Past: Landmarks of Women's History* (Bloomington: Indiana University Press, 1992). Essays on how to identify, interpret, and preserve women's historic sites are included in Gail Dubrow and Jennifer Goodman, eds., *Restoring Women's History Through Historic Preservation* (Baltimore: Johns Hopkins University Press, 2002). Two encyclopedias list scores of actual women's history sites, state by state. They are Marion Tinling, *Women Remembered: A Guide to Landmarks of Women's History in the United States* (Westport, CT: Greenwood Press, 1980) and Lynn Sherr and Jurate Kazickas, *Susan B. Anthony Slept Here: A Guide to Women's Landmarks* (New York: Random House, 1994).

The publications of the National Park Service and the Organization of American Historians offer specific suggestions on interpreting women's historic sites. Two of the Park Service's Cultural Resource Management bulletins are particularly useful: "Creative Teaching with Historic Places" (Vol. 23, No. 8, 2000) and "Placing Women in the Past " (Vol. 20, No. 3, 1997). Issues of the *OAH Magazine of History* published by the Organization of American Historians contain suggestions and examples for curricula and interpretative programs on a variety of subjects including women's history, notably: "The Stuff of Women's History" (v. 12 , Fall 1997).

Primary sources are available from the archives and special collections of community and university libraries. Many have special collections devoted to women's history, including the Schlesinger Library at the Radcliffe Institute in Cambridge, Massachusetts, and the Sophia Smith Collection at Smith College in Northhampton, Massachusetts.

Several museums devoted to women's history contain not only exhibits but also archives and active web sites. They include:

National Cowgirl Museum and Hall of Fame, 1720 Grady Street, Forth Worth, TX, <www.cowgirl.net>. The museum is in a new building and includes exhibits and programs about the women of the American West.

National Museum of Women in the Arts, 1250 New York Avenue, N.W., Washington, DC 20005-3970, <www.nmwa.org>. This museum displays the works of women artists both in its permanent collection and in changing exhibits.

National Women's Hall of Fame, 76 Fall Street, Seneca Falls, NY 13148, <www.greatwomen.org>. The facility honors nearly 200 notable women with exhibits and archives.

Women's Museum: An Institute for the Future, 3800 Parry Avenue, Dallas, TX 75226, <www.thewomensmuseum.org>. The museum is housed in a restored building built for the Texas Centennial Exposition and offers programs and exhibits.

Women of the West Museum, now part of the Autry Museum of Western Heritage, 4700 Western Heritage Way, Los Angeles, CA 20027. Use either <www.wowmuseum.org> or <www.autry-museum.org>.

Women's history museums under development include:

National Women's History Museum, Washington, D. C., <www.nmwh.org>.

International Museum of Women, San Francisco, CA, <www.imow.org>.

New web sites are continually being created and readers should use key words to keep up-to-date. Some of the most useful long-standing ones are listed below:

Jewish Women's Archives: <www.jwa.org/main.htm>

National Collaborative for Women's History Sites: <ncwhs.oah.org/>

National Register of Historic Places: Places Where Women Made History:
   <www.cr.nps.gov/nr/travel/pwwmh/>

National Women's History Project: <www.nwhp.org>

Native American Women:
   <www.library.wisc.edu/libraries/WomensStudies/native.htm>

President's Commission on the Celebration of Women in American History:
   <www.gsa.gov/staf/pa/whc.htm>

Women and Social Movements (1830–1930): <//womhist.binghamton.edu>

Women in Congress: <//bioguide.congress.gov/congresswomen/alpha.asp>

Women in Government (state by state): <www.gendergap.com>

Women's Rights National Historical Park: <www.nps.gov/wori>

*   *   *

The editors would like to thank the chapter authors for their contributions of creative scholarship and practical suggestions for enriching public presentations of women's history. We are grateful as well to Barbara Howe for the idea of a book that encourages readers to look at familiar places with fresh eyes. Mary Roberts and Elaine Rudd of Krieger Publishing Company helped to make that idea a reality.

NOTES

1. Roy Rosenzweig and David Thelen, *The Presence of the Past: Popular Uses of History in American Life* (New York: Columbia University Press, 1998); David Glassberg, *Sense of History: The Place of the Past in American Life* (Amherst: University of Massachusetts Press, 2001); John R. Stilgoe, *Outside Lies Magic: Regaining History and Awareness in Everyday Places* (New York: Walker, 1998).
2. Page Putnam Miller, ed., *Reclaiming the Past: Landmarks of Women's History* (Bloomington: Indiana University Press, 1992); Polly Welts Kaufman, *National Parks and the Woman's Voice: A History* (Albuquerque: University of New Mexico Press, 1998), 221–31. For a list of national parks interpreting women's history, see pp. 307–12.
3. Pierce Lewis, "Looking down the Velvet Rope: Cultural Geography and the Human Landscape," in Jo Blatti, *Past Meets Present: Essays About Historic Interpretation and Public Audiences* (Washington, DC: Smithsonian Institution Press, 1987).
4. Dolores Hayden, *The Power of Place: Urban Landscapes as Public History* (Cambridge, MA: MIT Press, 1995). See also: *Women's History is Everywhere: 10 Ideas for Celebrating in Communities: A How-to Community Handbook,* prepared by the President's Commission on the Celebration of Women in American History (Washington, DC, 1999), available from U.S. General Services Administration, Department of Communications, 1800 F St., N.W., Washington, DC 20405.
5. Katharine T. Corbett, "St. Louis Women Garment workers: Photographs and Memories," *Gateway Heritage,* vol. 2., no. 2, 1981.

Chapter 1

WHO WALKED BEFORE ME?
CREATING WOMEN'S HISTORY TRAILS

Polly Welts Kaufman

In every community structures important to women's history wait for visitors to unlock their stories. A street corner in San Francisco connects two women's history sites; the place chosen by a Boston women's suffrage organization for their offices reveals the depth of their ambitions; the location of a women's settlement house in Chicago demonstrates the authenticity of their goals; the location of a residence for aspiring women movie stars in Hollywood leads to new understandings of their struggles; and the site of a women's workplace near a commercial waterfront in Portland, Maine, provides a glimpse into the quality of their lives.

By adding geography to women's history, by letting history walk out of the pages of books onto the streets of communities, serendipitous connections and contrasts bring new insights. Creators and followers of women's history trails not only come to realize that history is about actual people who once walked on those streets, but they also discover why the location of a women' s home or workplace matters when interpreting women's experiences.

The two San Francisco sites show change over time in the same community — Chinatown. The first building is the Donaldina Cameron House at 920 Sacramento Street. Established as a refuge for Chinese women in 1873 by the Woman's Board of Foreign Missions, the home was supervised by Cameron from 1900 to 1934. There Cameron and her associates offered shelter and training for between a thousand and two thousand Chinese girls and women, many of whom had been victims of the slave trade. Today, the Presbyterian Church runs a community center in the same place. At 965 Clay Street, right around the corner, is the original Chinese YWCA designed by architect Julia Morgan to reflect Chinese culture and opened in 1930. By then, it was Chinese-American women who were the community activists. Involved from the beginning in the founding of the YWCA, Chinese-American women constituted virtually the entire board of directors and determined what programs would be offered.[1]

In Boston and Chicago the chosen location of women's organizations proves the seriousness of their goals. The New England and American Woman Suffrage Association, publishers of the *Woman's Journal* for the half a century before

Figure 1-1. Boston Public School fifth grader Cherrell Smuler joins her classmates in a protest march to demand that the role of the women who funded the construction of the Bunker Hill Monument be included in the National Park Service's interpretation of the site. (*Courtesy of the* Boston Herald. *Photo by Ted Fitzgerald.*)

women achieved the right to vote, voted for high visibility. They met in rented rooms at 5 Park Street opposite the Boston Common—an office less than a block from the Massachusetts State House, the seat of power—instead of in women's private drawing rooms. The present visitor to Hull House in Chicago who views an exhibit that recreates the original neighborhood on large panels, house by house and street by street, is immediately convinced that Jane Addams and her associates had indeed "settled" themselves securely in the immigrant community they wished to serve.[2]

Contrasts among the lives of different women become apparent to the present-day walker by looking at the geography of woman's history. A particularly poignant example is the former Hollywood Studio Club built on flat land well below Hollywood Boulevard at the corner of Lodi Place and Lexington Avenue. The Club was another YWCA designed by Julia Morgan. Opened in 1926 and sponsored in part by a committee including Constance deMille, wife of the director, and movie star Mary Pickford, the club served as a residence—a shelter—for more than forty-five years for nearly ten thousand young women hoping to be-

Figure 1-2. Contrasting sites in Hollywood: Movie star Mary Pickford's estate, Pickfair, in Beverly Hills stands high above the former Hollywood Studio Club, located on the flats below Hollywood Boulevard. Opened in the 1920s as a YWCA for star-struck young actresses, the Studio Club was designed by Julia Morgan and sponsored by Mary Pickford and Constance De Mille. (*Photos by Roger W. Kaufman.*)

come movie stars. Although the residents did include Marilyn Monroe and Kim Novak, the majority of them never reached the kind of stardom that allowed Mary Pickford to build a mansion on the uphill side of Hollywood Boulevard in Beverly Hills. In Portland, Maine, two early twentieth-century sites near the waterfront provide evidence of the contrast between the lives of women workers and their employers. Across from the waterfront is the factory that employed young women to pack matches (who sometimes suffered from "phossy jaw"); on the hill above is the substantial home of the factory owner.[3]

Women's history trails can take many forms, but what they have in common is that they impart an immediacy to the visitors' experience. The sites are meant to be visited. For people who think history happened to someone else in a faraway place, a walk on a history trail can help them connect their lives to the past. In a city, town, or neighborhood the trails can be walking trails, offered in advertised walks and in self-guiding booklets. Driving tours can be presented for a whole state. Women's history trails can focus on such sub-subjects as women's work or art, or they can concentrate on a particular era of history.

How does one get started? The first rule is to let serendipity do its work. It is like going for a nature walk—not knowing ahead what birds or plants you will find along the way. For tours of towns or cities, trail creators can select the downtown area as a beginning point. Public buildings lead to questions. At the city or town hall, apparent questions are: what women were elected to office? who was the first? has there been change over time? At churches: what roles did women's groups play there? has there been a woman minister or is there an order of sisters religious? Other questions come up as the tour continues along Main Street: where did women work? who were the women milliners and dressmakers? what businesses are run by women today? what organizations did women run? At the public library: who were the local women authors and artists? At schools: who were the woman principals and are there any schools named for women? At hospitals: when did nursing become a profession? who were the first women doctors? In some towns, gravestones in a local cemetery yield some answers or raise more questions.

If trail creators are acquainted with the broad outlines of U.S. women's history, they will be able to place the first sites they find in a context that will lead to new insights. Although it is obvious, for example, that women who worked in shipyards all over the country were replacing men during World War II, the complexities of their personal lives during the Great Depression preceding the war as well as the pressures on women to return to the kitchen after the war, may be less easy to understand without some background.

Besides looking for traditional sites that one might find in many places, trail creators should also ask the question—what is distinctive or even unique about the town, city, or neighborhood chosen for the trail? A knowledge of local and state history will enable them to characterize the city or town. What comes to mind when that place is mentioned and how are women connected to it? A women's history trail of Hollywood would emphasize the film industry, but include not only

Figure 1-3. Contrasting sites in San Francisco: The Chinese YWCA on Clay Street, designed by Julia Morgan and opened in 1925, was directed by Chinese-American women by the early 1930s. In contrast is the former Chinese Mission Home (now a community center) around the corner on Sacramento Street where, at the end of the nineteenth century, Presbyterian women missionaries brought young Chinese women they rescued from forced prostitution. (*Photos by Roger W. Kaufman.*)

homes (and sidewalk footprints) of the hopeful and successful stars, but film studios and the workplaces of women costume and set designers, musicians, theater managers, hairdressers, photographers, and publicists. Different parts of a city or town present different themes. In San Francisco, a National Park Service guide at the Presidio described the influence of women on the military base over a period of two hundred years from Spanish occupation through World War II. In another part of the city, a walk in Chinatown could present sites to illustrate the change over time of the roles of Chinese-American women. Stories could be included about early women immigrants to "Gold Mountain" who came as merchants' wives and in some cases as prostitutes. Sites could present women community organizers, garment workers, telephone operators, teachers, performing artists, fine artists, and ceramicists.[4]

On the other hand, some places consider themselves too strongly identified with a particular image and can use a women's history trail to broaden the community's view of itself. Salem, Massachusetts, has been known for three hundred years as the place that executed fourteen women as witches in 1692. Although the Salem's Women's Heritage Trail includes the monument honoring these women, it is only one of fifty sites that demonstrate an active and well-respected women's community over a period of 350 years.[5]

Perhaps the most important step in creating a women's history trail is involving a broad base of community people. A steering committee representing women from a variety of backgrounds is essential. When the Boston trail was in its early stages, the organizers called a public meeting and were pleasantly surprised at the response from women all over the city from a wide diversity of backgrounds. The proposed trail doubled in size in one evening. Other trail developers have called meetings at community centers or at residences for elderly citizens. Individual oral histories provide useful information.

Once a committee decides to produce a trail, one practical question that needs to be addressed is who is going to do all the follow-up research that is generated by the growing list of sites. Because a major goal of a women's history trail is to develop an appreciation of women's history within a community, it may be members of that community who can help with the research. Community women under the direction of the staff of the local historical society researched the Brunswick, Maine, women's history trail. Another group of available researchers are students in college or high school history classes.

Print sources abound. They provide answers to questions and open up new sites. The archives and indexes to people and newspapers in the local public and/or state library and in the local historical society and/or museum reveal many answers. City, town, and state directories and histories are essential sources. Some libraries keep a local history room with files of names, organizations, and events. The architectural surveys conducted by state historic preservation committees can yield information about individual buildings planned as sites.

While the creators of trails will want to include notable women like Jane Addams and well-known organizations like the YWCA, stories of representative women in many walks of life and from different social and ethnic backgrounds should be included, with or without names. Examples from the Portland, Maine, Women's History Walking Trail provide some suggestions for finding representative women.

The committee that developed the Portland trail wanted to include women workers. In this case, it was print sources that led researchers to sites. The State of Maine Bureau of Industrial and Labor Statistics published frequent reports beginning in 1886 containing statistics about both women and men workers. Similar reports are available in most states. At the time, as Carroll Wright stated in his classic study, *The Working Girls of Boston* (1889), Progressive reformers had begun to question "the moral, sanitary, physical, and economical conditions of the working girls."[6] In Portland, the two women settlement house workers who surveyed women workers in 1907 for the state were thorough. They interviewed teachers in the same year. Another woman researcher questioned women who clerked in stores in 1915–16. The researchers in 1907 found women in a surprising number of occupations and estimated that more than one in five women over sixteen years old worked for wages. Their report details the wages and hours of saleswomen, florists, typists, telephone operators, bookbinders, librarians, milliners, musicians, nurses, and laundry workers; shoe, garment, and hat makers; women who worked for canneries, who made gum and candy, and finally who worked in the match factory. The women interviewers included information on where the women workers lived and what women's organizations offered housing. Their concern about women's housing led to a comment that still rings true for trail walkers and connects them with the past. "If some arrangement could be devised," the women surveyors stated, "to leave a larger margin between the amount of wages received and the price paid for living expenses, the problem of the women wage-earners of Portland would be greatly simplified."[7]

Coupled with the *Portland City Directory,* the surveys proved to be a gold mine for placing women workers on the women's history trail. What is more, the committee and the undergraduates who did the legwork were able to add the workers' actual opinions about their jobs because the 1888 labor report included anonymous interviews with women workers in specific jobs. Women spoke frankly, complaining about poor ventilation, lack of convenient toilets, low wages, and the uncertainty of steady work.[8]

By placing some of the women's workplaces on the map of the city, it became apparent that the sites were scattered throughout the city; they tended to be fairly small and were quite varied. At its peak in 1907, nearly a hundred Portland women worked in a chewing gum factory (now a furniture store), making wages that were half of what the few male workers made. Other women assembled paper boxes in a company still operating and now owned by a woman who supplied the researchers with old newspaper stories. The match factory building still stands. A woman factory inspector's report in 1888 described the effects of the phosphorus on the workers, called phossy jaw. She reported that several of them had lost almost all their teeth and a few suffered from the early stages of bone loss in their jaws.[9]

A find that revealed an unexpected source of the names of Portland professional women in the first half of the twentieth century came from a student's scouring of the *Portland City Directory*. She located a building that served as an office building for women during that period. Among their professions were: dermatologist, osteopath, dressmaker, milliner, music teacher, beautician, chiropodist, chiropractor, and even a psychic. This discovery led to the records and meeting places of the Portland Business and Professional Women's Club, another source for the story of women's work. Other women's work sites on the Portland trail are department stores, hotels, the shipyards of World War II, and a new bridge. Front-page newspaper articles provided the story of the Portland "hello girls" who joined the other New England telephone operators for a strike in April 1919 outside the same building used as a telephone exchange today.[10]

Another major classification of representative women is ethnicity. Portland has a rich background in immigrant groups that continues today. An island in Portland Harbor, House Island, served as an immigrant station from 1906–1923, much the way Ellis Island did in the same era. The researchers found a culturally rich part of the city where the diversity of the city's population over time could be represented. Close together in one neighborhood are a predominantly Italian-American Catholic Church, the former Shaarey Tphiloh Synagogue, and an African Methodist Episcopal Church. Not far is the Roman Catholic Cathedral and the site of the former girls' Cathedral High School. It was operated by the Sisters of Mercy, an order that attracted many Irish-American women. The researchers conducted community meetings and interviews to find representative women to include on the trail. When there was no other apparent location, the committee chose the synagogue and the churches themselves as the sites for presenting the representative women.

In the process of looking for representative women, trail makers will turn up notable women, some of whom are well known and some of whom have been forgotten with the passage of time. Some favorites turn up in several different states. It seems that each place Laura Ingalls Wilder described in her books that are so popular with young women appears as a women's history landmark. They include sites in at least six states: a restored homestead in De Smet, South Dakota; a reconstructed log cabin and plaque in Independence, Kansas; a replica of her birthplace in Pepin, Wisconsin; a dugout at Walnut Grove, Minnesota; the home where she lived for sixty years in Mansfield, Missouri; and the hotel museum at Burr Oak, Iowa, where she lived for a year as a child. The latter is listed on a map of an Iowa trail of women's landmarks. All of these sites make good centers for state and local women's history trails.[11]

Most community people can name their most notable women, but recent generations of social historians have discovered new examples. Allotting a trail site to a newly discovered woman is one way to restore an outstanding woman's story to the public consciousness. Members of a public history project at West Virginia University mapped sites of twenty-three notable women, ranging from nineteenth-century journalist Anne Royal to the modern operatic soprano Phyllis

Curtin. The committee followed it up with a second annotated map of seventeen artists and writers.[12]

One of the results of the Civil Rights Movement was the addition of notable African American women from the past to the historical record; African American women historians were finally heard. Perhaps the most dramatic find in Boston during that period was the rediscovery of Phillis Wheatley, the first published African American poet. Arriving in Boston in 1761 on a slave ship as a child, Wheatley became famous in Revolutionary Boston for her remarkable poetry. Yet after she gained her freedom and lost the patronage of the Wheatley family, she failed in her struggle for survival and died in poverty at the age of thirty-one.[13] Phillis Wheatley's story so captured the imagination and consciences of modern Bostonians that the trustees of the University of Massachusetts at Boston named a building for her in 1985. A committee of Massachusetts women chose Wheatley to join Abigail Adams and suffrage leader Lucy Stone in a new women's group statue on Boston's Commonwealth Avenue Mall. Wheatley also appears on three loops of the Boston Women's Heritage Trail.

At some point in the development of a women's history trail, the committee will face special issues. One is whether or not to include controversial sites. Actually, controversial sites should not be avoided, in fact, they add depth to trails that too often present women as heroic or flawless figures. Some students and faculty members criticized the University of Iowa when they named its center for women and politics after a famous graduate, Carrie Chapman Catt, Class of 1880. Although Catt was the influential head of the National American Woman Suffrage Association when American women finally achieved the right to vote, many of her speeches were racist and classist. She publicly decried the fact that immigrant men could vote while educated daughters of long-term citizens could not. Although a women's guidebook to Washington, D.C., includes such notable African American women as Mary McLeod Bethune, Ida B. Wells, Marian Anderson, and Mary Church Terrell, when it comes to Mount Vernon, the guidebook neglects the work of enslaved women, even though the site managers at Mount Vernon had some slave quarters reconstructed. In San Francisco, the question of whether or not Donaldina Cameron exercised too much social control while running the refuge for Chinese women can lead to good discussions. Although Eleanor Roosevelt is now generally accepted as one of America's most important women, if not the most important, in the twentieth century, her ubiquitousness made her controversial as a president's wife. Interpreters at her Hyde Park, New York, home, Val-Kill, now a national historic site, offer cartoons that illustrate the controversy. She is shown unexpectedly emerging from a coal mine and visiting the men in a CCC camp.[14]

Another issue that particularly applies to women's history trails is the problem of chronology. While it is not difficult to explain the change over time for women workers during the period of a century in Portland, sites layered with changing historical events can be confusing to the walker. For this reason, some trails include time lines. On the other hand, layered history can also offer exciting opportunities to see how changes in land use and time period affect women's lives. The Boston Women's Heritage Trail covers four centuries of history in five loops; walkers travel over many layered sites. When leaders take students from the local schools on walks of the North End of Boston, they have to point out that Paul Revere's children did not play with little Rose Fitzgerald Kennedy, later mother of President John F. Kennedy. She was born across the street from the much-visited Revere House, but more than one hundred years later.

Perhaps the most unusual example of layered history in Boston is the Phillis Wheatley landing site. The waters of the South Cove of Boston Harbor once reached the shore at Beach Street. Now the harbor is a half a mile away. Avery's Wharf stretched south into the harbor from Beach Street along what is now Tyler Street. Built on filled land, Tyler Street is now the heart of Chinatown. But in 1761, it was at Avery's Wharf that the schooner *Phillis* discharged its cargo of seventy-five slaves for auction, including the future Phillis Wheatley, who was then seven or eight years old. The Wheatley family purchased her and named her Phillis for the ship. The land that was once a pier has three other sites on the Boston trail. Two are organizations established by early immigrants to help their own newcomers: the New England Chinese Women's Association, founded in 1942, and the Lebanese-Syrian Ladies' Aid Society founded in 1917. A few doors down is a former mission of the Maryknoll Sisters, an international Catholic order founded by a Boston woman, Mother Mary Joseph Rogers.[15]

Another challenge posed by women's history trails is the problem of the space between sites. Not all women's history trails can fit in the package of walking cities like Boston, Chicago, or Portland, Maine. Each of those trails is divided into separate loops taking between an hour or two hours to complete. A published guide to women in Seattle and King County, *Woman's Place,* has more than 250 sites spread throughout the entire city and county, divided into eleven driving trails. The guidebook showcases women in every kind of activity, demonstrating that the women of the Pacific Northwest can literally do anything. It presents women's work in forest preservation and exploration; immigrant women from Japan, Scandinavia, China, and Ireland; Native American women; hospital founders and temperance leaders; farmers; a mayor and a governor; airplane mechanics; shipyard and lumberyard workers; cooks in mining camps; teachers, mail carriers, and library founders; women artists, pharmacists, actors, socialists, scientists, a governor, jazz musicians, union organizers, prostitutes, and nurses. New York State published a driving trail to women's history sites pictured on a large map of the state. It locates sites to eighty-three prominent women ranging from the women who organized the first women's rights convention at Seneca Falls in 1848 to Eleanor Roosevelt, African American suffragist Sojourner Truth, and socialist Emma Goldman. A guide to women in Philadelphia includes three walking and one driving tour of the city followed by a listing of other women's history sites in the Delaware Valley.[16]

On the other hand, such compact entities as colleges and universities can easily produce women's history walking trails. At the oldest university in the country, Harvard University in Cambridge, Massachusetts, a woman history professor was tired of teaching in buildings and using libraries with only portraits "of long-dead men" looking down at her. Inspired by *A Room of One's Own,* in which Virginia Woolf described her feelings at not being admitted to the Bodleian Library in Oxford, she undertook a quest to find women's history sites on the Harvard campus. Although the eventual tour included the campus of Radcliffe, the former women's college at Harvard, she and the graduate student who worked with her wanted to locate places on the Harvard College campus, once only opened to men. Women's places were easy to find. They included the statue of Charles Sumner by the Bostonian sculptor, Anne Whitney; the men's rooms where for generations women called "Goodies" cleaned; the library donated by a woman; the dormitory named for the poet Longfellow's daughter (not for him); the Harvard Observatory where several women astronomers scanned the skies; and the first coeducational college residence. Seattle's *Woman's Place* includes eight sites at the University of Washington, including the former women's building at the Alaska-Pacific Exposition in 1908, now housing the Northwest Center for Research on Women.[17]

Once the committee finishes a draft of a trail, it is time to produce the printed trail guidebook. Funding for trail guides can come from a variety of sources. State humanities councils, chambers of commerce, state tourist offices, museums, and private businesses all have funded trail guidebooks. Desktop publishing makes producing women's history guidebooks more possible for everyone. Key elements in a guidebook include readable maps and directions. For each site, the Washington, D.C., *Women's History Guide* notes the subway stop. Because so many of the sites in the nation's capital are public buildings, the guidebook includes phone numbers, hours, and a section called "Amenities" which describes cafeterias, gift shops, and explains how to get tickets of admission if necessary. It also includes information on what to look for inside the public buildings: paintings by women artists, statues of women, exhibits of costumes and artifacts. The best women's history guidebooks include historic pictures of places and women along with the text. Designers find and photograph such sources as portraits and statues of women, paintings and sculptures by women, book covers representing women authors, and significant newspaper headlines. Indexes and bibliographies are helpful to users of guidebooks.[18]

Although virtual history does not replace walking on asphalt, brick, or dirt trails, many women's history trail committees are creating useful web sites. At the National Park Service, the staff of the National Register of Historic Places prepared an Internet travel itinerary connecting women's history sites in Massachusetts and New York as a start. To find web sites, enter "women's history trail" or "women's heritage trail" (keeping the quotation marks) in a search engine on the Internet. The entries are constantly changing, but in addition to the National Park Service site, some of the most longstanding are the Boston Women's Heritage Trail, the Connecticut Women's Heritage Trail, and Women of the West (Programs).[19]

After a trail is completed, the committee's work is not finished. Members need to work to build a continuing audience. The opening of the trail should be the occasion for a special program or event. The local historical society launched the Brunswick, Maine, women's history trail with an exhibit featuring the history of local women's activities. A girls' basketball uniform from the 1920s was popular and provided the impetus for a discussion about the significance of changing basketball rules. The Harvard women's history tour opened with a women's history exhibit (also displaying a basketball uniform, among other items) at the Harvard Information Center at Harvard Square where it attracted the general public. Curators at the Rhode Island School of Design organized an exhibit around two Italian-American women dressmakers who built a business with a clientele of elite Providence women during the first half of the twentieth century. The curators displayed the dressmakers' designs and located their work in the art and design movements of the times. On the opening day, they sponsored a symposium and a walking tour of the dressmakers' neighborhood.[20]

If women's history trails are to be kept alive and current, they also need to engage in continuous public programming. Exhibits, lectures, and announced guided walks should be available in addition to printed guides. Newspaper notices draw the general public but offering tours to such organizations as Girl Scouts, civic groups, and schools assures a continuing audience. Making the trail walk a women's history month event will give a trail publicity and attaching a walk to a convention's program will draw an out-of-town audience. Having some kind of an institutional base helps a women's history trail to continue to have a lasting influence on the community. It can be the local museum or library, a college or university, or a public school system.

Traditional methods of engaging the group on a walk are useful but some additional techniques include bringing enlargements of pictures of the people and places presented, handing out women's words for walkers to read at selected sites, helping participants understand the changes in the landscape over time, and making connections between sites. Students dressed up as historic women can meet the group at particular sites and introduce the person they portray. Above all, if participants are local, they will have stories and insights to add and the trail will continue to grow. Community people are often enthusiastic about their own women's history site. Sometimes when the Portland walkers stop at the former chewing gum factory, one of the present furniture company owners rushes out with a mounted photograph of the former women workers.[21]

Projects with schools can be particularly rewarding. The Women of the West Museum in Colorado worked with 120 fourth and fifth grade students at the Dora Moore school in Denver to develop a women's history trail in the historic Capitol Hill area where their school is located. Museum staff deputized the students as "history detectives" and commissioned them to scour their neighborhood for clues. Students conducted research in a variety of sources, developed biographies, made a map, banners, and signs. On opening day, twenty-seven students took the 120 guests on the tour. The project called, "Walk a Mile in Her Shoes," attracted

Figure 1-4. Denver sixth-grade history detectives from the Dora Moore School lead visitors on their new women's history trail, "Walk a Mile in Her Shoes," sponsored by the Women of the West Museum. (*History Detectives from the Dora Moore School, Denver, Colorado 1999 © 2001. Courtesy of the Women of the West Museum, Denver, Colorado.*)

so much attention that the Governor declared the day of the walk, "Women's History Trail Day."[22]

The Boston Women's Heritage Trail has collaborated with the Boston Public Schools since its beginning in 1990. It was originally funded by a grant to the Boston Public Schools from the Women's Educational Equity Act. Elementary school students have created six mini-trails throughout the city, funded to teachers through service learning grants. Third-graders at the Blackstone School "blazed" *Herstory,* their trail of Boston's South End, carrying banners and wearing specially designed T-shirts. On opening day, individual students each told the story of a particular woman, such as Myrna Vasquez, an actress and community activist who was born in Puerto Rico. A local television reporter recorded the event for the evening news. The Boston Women's Heritage Trail also sponsors the Perseverance Project for eighth graders. Students in participating schools are each given a book that tells the story of a young woman who did not give up. The project committee offers curriculum guides, a conference for teachers, and an oral essay contest where students from each school read their own essays on perseverance in their lives. Many of their accounts are just as moving as the stories they have read.[23]

Once a trail is established, it can become an influence on the interpretation of local and even national history. As a minimum, women's sites can be integrated

into other historic walking trails. Like several other cities, Boston is known for
walking trails. Its most famous one is the Freedom Trail, presenting Revolutionary Boston. A red line embedded in the sidewalks serves as a guide for walkers.
The published trail is still largely a dead white man's trail, but when women lead
walks, they can add to the interpretation. They can identify the woman tavern
owner who hosted "Boston Tea Party" activists; read Abigail Adams's description in her own words (while keeping her own spelling) of hearing the "proclamation for independance read and proclamed" at the old State House, and describe
the Boston Common as the place where Revolutionary women set up spinning
wheels to produce thread in protest of British taxes on textiles. When fifth grade
trail makers at an elementary school near the Bunker Hill Monument found that
the National Park Service did not acknowledge the contribution of Sarah Josepha
Hale who organized a women's fair to raise funds to complete the monument, they
stormed the hill and demanded (successfully) that Hale's name be added to the
Park Service's interpretation and brochure.

Another way women's trail committees can influence local and national history
is by becoming active in local historic preservation issues. The Women's History
Landmark Project in the early 1990s doubled the number of National Historic
Landmarks related to women. Because of their efforts sites now designated as
landmarks include the Triangle Shirtwaist Factory Building in New York City
where 146 young women perished in a fire in 1911 and the Nannie Helen Bur-

Figure 1-5. Three Boston students from the Dearborn School dress as the women they researched in an activity inspired by the Boston Women's Heritage Trail. Portrayals from left
are art museum founder Isabella Stewart Gardner, African American poet Phillis Wheatley, and Helen Keller's teacher Annie Sullivan. (*Courtesy of Impact II. Photo by Ellen
McGill.*)

roughs's National Training School for Women and Girls, founded in 1901 in Washington, D.C. When committees work on trails and discover a significant historic building that may be threatened, they can contact their state historic preservation officer to find out what steps need to be taken to save it. Among local historic buildings often associated with women are schools, including the one-room schools all over the country where thousands of women taught. Many citizens have already saved former schools by establishing living history school museums or recycling the building into a new use.[24]

While a yellow line on the sidewalk may not be appropriate for a women's history trail (because the yellow line would have to follow every street), plaques and markers are. Trail committees can approach local historical societies for help with markers. Generally permission is needed from the local municipality and the owner of the building. In San Francisco the Women's Heritage Museum organized an exhibit in conjunction with their successful drive to honor Juana Briones, a Mexican-American pioneer settler of Yerba Buena, with a bench and a plaque in Washington Square Park. It was the first state historic plaque dedicated to a woman in San Francisco. Briones was a single mother, a rancher, and a healer. At the dedication, children from the Juana Briones school depicted a day in the life of Ranchera Juana, and Mayor Willie Brown and Congresswomen Nancy Pelosi participated in the program.[25]

Because women's history trails are about place, some of the sites can also present an opportunity for installing public art. The Biddy Mason project in central Los Angeles is an outstanding example of the use of public art to mark a women's history site. It sprang from Dolores Hayden's history tour, *The Power of Place,* designed to represent the economic history of Los Angeles by mapping the early work sites of the major ethnic groups who settled there. On her map she included the auditorium where militant Latina garment workers organized a strike in 1933 and Little Tokyo, the place Japanese-American women returned to after living in World War II internment camps. One site she chose to develop was the alley and parking lot where the homestead once stood that belonged to Biddy Mason, an African American woman who was a Los Angeles pioneer. By working with city organizations, community people, and artists, Hayden used public art to renew the site and present the story of the development of Los Angeles from a tiny Mexican town to a major city.

Biddy Mason's story itself is remarkable. She arrived in California in 1851 as a slave with her three daughters. She won her own freedom through a court case. Working as a nurse and midwife, she was the first African American woman to own property in Los Angeles on which she eventually built a two-story brick building, renting the downstairs and living upstairs. She was a community leader who founded an orphanage and child care center and helped organize Los Angeles's first African American church in her own home.

Hayden recruited artists and found funding for the project. Among the installations is an 81-foot wall framing a pedestrian walkway between buildings designed by Sheila Levrant de Bretteville. The wall depicts events from Biddy Mason's life and serves as the foreground for the Los Angeles skyline. The project had a ripple effect. Members of the Los Angeles AME Church that Biddy Mason helped found organized a motorcade to celebrate marking Mason's grave with a new stone; the California Afro-American Museum mounted a photographic exhibit on African American midwives; a storyteller developed a performance based on Biddy's life; and local land owners employed two landscape architects to develop a pocket park at the end of the Biddy Mason wall which the city named the Biddy Mason Park.[26]

Women's history trails represent a process. They are never finished, nor should the intention be to complete them. They are about discovery and making connections. They are interactive. Every time a leader takes a group on a trail, walkers share experiences; new sites, understandings, and potential research projects are the result. Children and students enjoy creating neighborhood branches of major trails. Women's stories are everywhere. The major purpose of a trail is to empower the community, especially students, by helping them recognize the roles of women in their neighborhoods, cities, or towns—their places.

One place in Maine where women's stories from the past come through with particular clarity is a point of land reaching out toward Portland Harbor and the islands of Casco Bay called the Eastern Promenade. From one spot, walkers can view several women's history sites: a thousand-year-old burial site of a Native American woman leather maker on an offshore island; the route taken by the ships carrying sea captain's wives on voyages in the nineteenth century; the walk where wives of crews watched for their husbands' return; the lighthouse where self-sufficient wives sustained their family's material needs and helped mitigate problems of isolation; a former summer island resort where women hotel keepers and chambermaids served visitors at the turn of the twentieth century; an island quarantine station where women immigrants first arrived in the United States; and the shipyards where women built liberty ships during World War II. On a foggy day, you can almost hear their voices.[27]

NOTES

1. Peggy Pascoe, *Relations of Rescue: The Search for Female Moral Authority in the American West, 1874–1939* (New York: Oxford University Press, 1991), 13–17, 51–56, 82–85, 93–100, 114–23; Judy Yung, *Unbound Feet: A Social History of Chinese Women in San Francisco* (Berkeley: University of California Press), 35–37, 94–98, et. seq.

2. *Boston Women's Heritage Trail* (Boston, 1999), 11–12; Marilyn A. Domer, Jean S. Hunt, Mary Ann Johnson and Adade M. Wheeler, *Walking with Women through Chicago History* (Chicago, 1981).

3. Sara Holmes Boutelle, *Julia Morgan, Architect* (New York: Abbeville Press, 1988), 113–15; Lynn Sherr and Jurate Kazickas, *Susan B. Anthony Slept Here: A Guide to American Women's Landmarks* (New York: Random House,

1994), 35, 40; *A Women's History Walking Trail of Portland, Maine* (Portland, ME, 1997), 46.

4. Judy Yung, *Unbound Feet;* "The Presidio of San Francisco: Main Post Walk" (San Francisco: National Park Service, Golden Gate NRA, n.d.).

5. Bonnie Hurd Smith, *Salem Women's Heritage Trail* (Salem Chamber of Commerce, Salem, MA, 2000).

6. Carroll D. Wright, *The Working Girls of Boston* (Boston, 1889), 3–5.

7. Eva Shorey, "Women Wage Workers, Portland" in the *21st Annual Report of the Bureau of Industrial and Labor Statistics for the State of Maine* (Augusta, ME, 1907): 138–67; Marion Porter, "Employment of Women in Maine Stores" in the *Third Biennial Report of Labor and Industry for the State of Maine* (Augusta, ME, 1915–16): 50–58.

8. *Second Annual Report of the Bureau of Industrial and Labor Statistics for the State of Maine* (Augusta, ME, 1889), 94–109.

9. Flora E. Haines, "Report of the Special Agent," *Second Annual Report of the Bureau of Industrial and Labor Statistics for the State of Maine* (Augusta, ME, 1889): 138–40.

10. Candace Kanes, "Serious and Ambitious Career Women: The Portland Business and Professional Women's Club in the 1920s" in Marli Weiner, ed., *Of Gender and Place: Women in Maine History* (Orono: University of Maine Press, 2002); *A Women's History Walking Trail in Portland, Maine,* 5, 12, 18, 24, 25.

11. Sherr and Kazickas, *Susan B. Anthony Slept Here,* 496, 249–50, 157, 236; "Women's Landmarks in Iowa," *Des Moines Register,* 25 August 1995: 2T.

12. *Women of West Virginia* (Morgantown: West Virginia Center for Women's Studies, 1987); *West Virginia Women and the Arts* (Morgantown: West Virginia Center for Women's Studies, 1990).

13. Merle Richmond, *Phillis Wheatley* (New York: Chelsea House, 1988).

14. James W. Loewen, *Lies Across America: What Our Historic Sites Get Wrong* (New York: New Press, 1999), 40–41; Jacci Duncan and Lynn Page Whittaker, *The Women's History Guide to Washington* (Alexandria, VA: Charles River Press, 1998).

15. *Boston Women's Heritage Trail,* 45–46; Richmond, *Phillis Wheatley.*

16. Mildred Tanner Andrews, *Woman's Place: A Guide to Seattle and King County History* (Seattle, WA: Gemil Press, 1994); *Where Women Made History: A Traveler's Guide to Historic Sites Honoring the Extraordinary Women of New York State* (New York State Department of Economic Development, 1998); Gayle Brandow Samuels with Lucienne Beard and Valencia Libby, *Women in the City of Brotherly Love . . . and Beyond: Tours and Detours in Delaware Valley Women's History* (Philadelphia, 1994).

17. *A Self-Guided Walking Tour of Harvard Women's History* (Cambridge, MA: Harvard University, 2000). Laurel Thatcher Ulrich, "Harvard's Womanless History," *Harvard Magazine* (December 1999): 51–59; Andrews, *Woman's Place,* 122–29.

18. See especially the work of designer Bonnie Hurd Smith in the *Boston Women's Heritage Trail* and the *Salem Women's Heritage Trail.*

19. Site addresses include: National Register of Historic Places, <www.cr.nps. gov/nr/travel/pwwmh/index.htm>; Boston Women's Heritage Trail, <www. bwht.org>; Connecticut Women's Heritage Trail: <www.cthum.org/home>; Women of the West <www.wowmuseum.org/programs>.

20. "Women's history exhibited," *Harvard College Gazette,* November 2000; "From Paris to Providence: Fashion, Art, and the Tirocchi Dressmakers' Shop, 1915–1947," exhibit, Rhode Island School of Design Museum, 11 January 2001; symposium: "A Day with the Tirocchi Sisters," 10 March 2001.

21. For a useful guide on interpretation, see: William T. Alderson and Shirley Payne Low, *Interpretation of Historic Sites* (Walnut Creek, CA: AltaMira Press, 1996).

22. "Walk a Mile in Her Shoes," Women of the West web site: <www. wowmuseum.org/programs>.

23. Among the paperback books used for the Perseverance Project are: Anne Petry, *Harriet Tubman* (New York: Harper Trophy, 1996); Mildred Taylor, *Road to Memphis* (New York: Puffin, 1996); Katherine Paterson, *Lyddie* (New York: Puffin, 1994); Fran Leeper Buss, *Journey of the Sparrow* (New York: Dell Yearling, 1993); and Cynthia Voigt, *Dicey's Song* (New York: Fawcett, 1995).

24. Page Putnam Miller, *Reclaiming the Past, Landmarks of Women's History* (Bloomington: Indiana University Press, 1992), 1–26; Andrew Guiliford, *America's Country Schools* (Washington, DC: Preservation Press, 1984). For one-room schools, see also the programs of the Blackwell History of Education Museum at Northern Illinois University, DeKalb, IL 60115. Their website is: <www.cedu.niu,edu/blackwell>.

25. *Women's Heritage Museum Newsletter,* San Francisco, CA, February 1998. The Museum is now called the International Museum of Women.

26. Dolores Hayden, Gail Dubrow, and Carolyn Flynn, *The Power of Place, Los Angeles* (Power of Place, Los Angeles, CA, n.d.); Dolores Hayden, *The Power of Place: Urban Landscapes as Public History* (Cambridge, MA: MIT Press, 1995).

27. The burial site is in the process of repatriation under the Native American Graves and Repatriation Act of 1990. *A Women's History Walking Trail in Portland, Maine,* 29–31.

SUGGESTED READINGS

"Creative Teaching with Historic Places," National Park Service, *Cultural Resource Management Bulletin,* 23:8 (2000). In these essays, classroom teachers describe successful history projects with students using national landmarks and national parks as sources.

Page Putnam Miller, ed., *Reclaiming the Past: Landmarks of Women's History.* Bloomington: Indiana University Press, 1992. This useful collection of essays by individual authors covers women's history landmarks in architecture, the arts, education, politics, religion, and work.

Roy Rosenzweig and David Thelen, *The Presence of the Past: Popular Uses of History in American Life*. New York: Columbia University Press, 1998. Based on a survey of hundreds of Americans, the authors found that most Americans feel connected to the past by visiting museums and historic places and through family history but feel unconnected to classroom history.

Lynn Sherr and Jurate Kazickas, *Susan B. Anthony Slept Here: A Guide to American Women's Landmarks*. New York: Random House, 1994. Also available in a video program, this reference is a revision of the original *American Woman's Gazeteer*. The book presents a wide variety of women's history sites and is arranged in alphabetical order by states.

John R. Stilgoe, *Outside Lies Magic: Regaining History and Awareness in Everyday Places*. New York: Walker, 1998. Stilgoe encourages learning history by actively exploring the built environment.

Marion Tinling, *Women Remembered: A Guide to Landmarks of Women's History in the United States*. Westport: CT: Greenwood Press, 1986. This groundbreaking book presents details of women's history sites all over the country. Sites are listed by state within five regions.

WOMEN'S HISTORY TRAIL GUIDEBOOKS, A SAMPLING

Mildred Tanner Andrews, *Woman's Place: A Guide to Seattle and King County History*. Seattle, WA: Gamil Press, 1994.

Boston Women's Heritage Trail. Boston, 1999. Available from Boston Women's Heritage Trail, 22 Holbrook Street, Boston, MA 02130. Web site: <www.bwht.org.>

Jacci Duncan and Lynn Page Whittaker, *The Women's History Guide to Washington*. Alexandria, VA: Charles River Press, 1998.

Gayle Brandow Samuels with Lucienne Beard and Valencia Libby, *Women in the City of Brotherly Love . . . And Beyond: Tours and Detours in Delaware Valley Women's History*. Philadelphia, 1994.

Bonnie Hurd Smith, *Salem Women's Heritage Trail*. Salem, MA: Salem Chamber of Commerce, 2000.

A Women's History Walking Trail of Brunswick, Maine. Brunswick: Pejepscot Historical Society, 1999.

A Women's History Walking Trail in Portland, Maine. Portland, University of Southern Maine, Women's Studies Program, 1997.

Chapter 2

IMMORTALIZING WOMEN: FINDING MEANING IN PUBLIC SCULPTURE

Eileen Eagan

Susan B. Anthony is not one of the figures on Mount Rushmore. In the mid-1930s when carving his mammorth figures of American heroes into the hills of South Dakota, the sculptor briefly agreed to add the suffrage leader's portrait on the west side of the mountain. That plan, proposed by Rose Allen Powell, fell through. The four presidents remain in sole possession of that national icon. However, Powell's campaign for Anthony's inclusion was just part of a long tradition of efforts to give women a place in the national landscape.[1] Forty years later, after a decade of struggle, the National Council of Negro Women erected in Washington, D.C., a statue of educator and activist, Mary McLeod Bethune. The African American women's efforts, like those of Powell on behalf of Anthony, reflected a belief in the importance of both women and monuments.[2]

Examination of statues of women, and the efforts to create them, can illuminate the history of women, their roles in society, and the changing ideas about the meaning of the American past. In this chapter, I am going to look at the use of art and history to honor women's lives and activism and to redefine American history.[3] The chapter concludes with some questions to consider when investigating women's place in public sculpture. A list of statues of women that stand in accessible outdoor locations follows, organized by state and including statues in place in 2001.

Statues are not the only representations of women that can be examined in this manner. There are other ways in which women are commemorated in public spaces.[4] Buildings may be named for women; examples include hospitals and schools (less often armories, perhaps never forts).[5] Women's role in social services has often been recognized in the naming of parks or playgrounds. For example, in 1936, New York City's first "model" playground was named after Dr. Gertrude Kelly; she was an Irish-born physician, philanthropist and supporter of women's suffrage, who ran a clinic for the poor in the Chelsea community.[6] Murals, especially political ones, often have deliberately included women as representative figures. More recently, some murals have portrayed historical female

Figure 2-1. Margaret Haughery, an Irish immigrant who ran a successful baking business in New Orleans, LA, devoted much of her wealth to founding institutions for orphans and poor women. Dedicated in 1884, her statue stands in Margaret Place. (*Photo by Molly Chancey.*)

figures. Harriet Tubman is the subject of a large mural on the outside of Harriet Tubman Elementary School in New Orleans.[7] These forms of recognition—parks, gardens, murals—may be, in some ways, more fitting means to honor women's lives than the appropriation of the traditional (one might say masculine) form of public sculpture, with its focus on individual achievement.

Statues, however, have had an important role in conveying collective definitions of History (with a capital H). As the most visible expression of a consciously defined past, they can generate extensive public debate and controversy over the meaning of history. Such controversies present an excellent opportunity to examine how history is defined and contested, on both the local and national level. Analysis of specific cases can also reveal the ways women, and other groups, use art to attain their goals. Who will be honored with a statue, where should it be placed, and who will fund it are crucial questions. Perhaps the most important issue is who decides the answers to those questions.

A key aspect is the style of representation. In the United States before the twentieth century the most common portrayal of women in public art, aside from that of religious figures, was of women as symbolic figures rather than as actual individuals. This took two forms. The first, the allegory, common in nineteenth-century sculpture, was the use of classical images of women to represent certain virtues. Sculptors used Greek and Roman images of goddesses to represent wisdom, truth, tragedy or justice. The *Statue of Liberty* in New York Harbor is probably the most famous example of this kind of statue. Other symbolic female images can be found on war memorials, cemetery monuments, public buildings and fountains.[8]

A similar but more consciously gendered form can be seen in "ideal" sculpture, generally in marble, that reflected a romantic presentation of fictional and historical subjects. Historian Joy Kasson[9] has noted that in nineteenth-century America this artistic portrayal of females embodied conflicting ideas and feelings about women's roles in society: "Statues of women as captives or queens, victims or avengers, formed an important part of the cultural landscape. . . . " Such "ideal" sculpture was usually located indoors in private homes, gardens or studios; some statues, however, were placed in cemetery lots or displayed in public areas at expositions and world's fairs. Many of the subjects were European. However, this work also included the first statues of American women, including Virginia Dare and Pocahontas, and the first portrayal of Evangeline, based on the poem by Henry Wadsworth Longfellow.[10]

In twentieth-century United States, as the use of monuments for civic and patriotic purposes increased, and as some groups became interested in using public sculpture to teach about the American past, another kind of generalized female figure became more common. These statues were intended to commemorate a particular role that women had played and presumably should continue to play. The most popular of these representative figures was woman as mother.

In the 1920s, the Daughters of the American Revolution (DAR) took the lead in the creation and distribution of statues called *Madonna of the Trail* or, in other cases, *Pioneer Mother*.[11] In 1928 and 1929, as part of their plan for creation and commemoration of a westward trail, the DAR sponsored monuments in twelve states from Maryland to California. Sculptor Auguste Leimbach portrayed a woman carrying a baby and holding another child by the hand. The woman is shown holding a rifle partly hidden by her dress. In this same period, similar statues in tribute to pioneer mothers popped up in other states.

In 1921, as part of a tercentenary celebration, the DAR erected a statue in Plymouth, Massachusetts, called *The Pilgrim Mother,* honoring the women who came over on the *Mayflower*. The inscription on the base describes the value of that role: "They brought up their families in sturdy virtue and a living faith in God without which nations perish." The National Society of New England Women erected a similar statue in Plymouth dedicated to "the Pilgrim Maiden." Its inscription reads:

"To those intrepid English women whose courage, fortitude, and devotion brought a new nation into being, this statue of the Pilgrim maiden is dedicated."[12]

These statues reflect the post-World War I conservative determination to remind people of the Anglo-Saxon virtues. They also present a counterpoint to the *National Monument to the Forefathers* on the summit of the hill in Plymouth. Dedicated in 1889, that eight-one foot tribute to the patriarchs is topped by a female figure of Faith, pointing her finger to heaven and surrounded by other female figures representing Morality, Law, and Liberty. In the same year that the *The Pilgrim Mother* was added to the commemoration scene, the Improved Order of Red Men (a non-native group), in a similarly revisionist gesture, erected the statue, *Massasoit*. The sculpture portrays the head of the Wampanoags whose assistance made possible the English colony's survival and whose land they soon appropriated.[13]

European-American sculptors, and their sponsors, have also commemorated American Indian womanhood. That representation indicates some of the conflicts inherent in views of both women and Native Americans. In Fairmount Park in Philadelphia on a slight hill near the Schuylkill River stands a statue titled *Stone Age in America*. A bronze figure on a granite base depicts an Indian woman who holds a hatchet in her hand while her two children cling to her. At the figure's feet lies a dead bear. Sculptor John Boyle's work, placed in the park in 1888, presents a romantic but fierce view of protective motherhood. Unlike the statue of Hannah Dustin, another female figure portrayed with a weapon (a hatchet she used to scalp Indians), this woman's target was not a human adversary. The sculptor had originally included an eagle at her feet. The Fairmount Park Art Association, apparently believing it would be intolerable to show an Indian woman killing a U.S. national symbol, pressured Boyle into turning the bird into a bear.[14] Despite its ironic title, the statue presents a strong, and in its own way, respectful portrait of a woman and her children.

In later years even more monumental monumental-mothers appeared on the landscape. One of the most imposing of these, a statue based on the famous painting, *Whistler's Mother,* is a prominent feature in Ashland, Pennsylvania.[15] Called *The Mother's Memorial,* it is seven feet high on a granite base. Sponsored by the Ashland Boy's Association, it was erected in 1938. One side is inscribed "Mother" and then "A Mother is the Holiest Thing Alive," a line attributed to the poet Samuel Taylor Coleridge. Larger yet is the ninety-foot high statue, *Our Lady of the Rockies,* completed in 1985, that stands on a mountain overlooking Butte, Montana.[16]

A combination of a representation of motherhood and religious iconography is embodied in the many statues of Mary, the mother of Jesus. When outdoors, they are most often located close to Catholic churches or institutions. Like "Our Lady of the Mountains," their identity is often specific to a place. In some cases, the name ties an American location to a religious location elsewhere. One the most famous of these is the shrine to "Our Lady of Lourdes" built on the campus of the University of Notre Dame in 1896.[17] Modeled on the religious site in France, the shrine has since come to represent, along with the school's football team, the strength of a Catholic culture. It also illustrates the aspect of the Church and culture that emphasizes the importance of women (albeit defined in a particular role and perhaps counterposed to the football team). The combination of a historical figure with iconic significance is also found in the statues of saints that are a significant aspect of women's images in public art.

Throughout the twentieth century allegorical female figures continued to be used in public monuments as representative of community emotions—most often grief and loss. The Marine Memorial in Hampton Beach, New Hampshire, dedicated on Memorial Day in 1957, commemorates New Hampshire sons and daughters lost or buried at sea during World War II.[18] Designed by Alice Cosgrove, a Concord artist, it portrays a woman, holding a wreath in one hand, looking out to sea. The inscription reads, "Breathe soft, ye winds, ye waves in silence rest." Similarly, the 1891 sinking of a Norwegian ship off the coast of Virginia, which took the lives of the captain's wife and son, is commemorated in 1962 by a statue called *The Norwegian Lady* in Virginia Beach.[19] A duplicate was erected that same year in Norway at Moss Harbor. In the summer of 2001, the city of Gloucester, Massachusetts, erected a statue in honor of the wives of fisherman lost at sea.[20]

Although women's maternal role has been the most common subject of such symbolic public sculpture, women's place in the work world has recently received more recognition. In most cases the images are of women in traditional female occupations, or they are presented in a way that defines the woman within a traditional role. The number of statues of nurses and of women in the military has increased. Other activities have also won recognition. There is a 1984 sculpture dedicated to the "Mill Girls" in Lowell, Massachusetts, called *Homage to Women,* near the national park that interprets the textile mills where young women worked in the nineteenth century. The subject of some criticism because of its abstract form, the statue has become an important and popular symbol of the city's history.[21] Its creation, like that of other statues commemorating women's contributions to war and the workplace, was an answer to a call for recognition for women's importance in society.

Heightened consciousness of the importance of public art and historical commemoration has recently resulted in organized efforts for the recognition of the achievements of actual individual women and of groups of women. In the past twenty years the number of such statues has almost doubled and plans for more are on the drawing board. Much of this is a logical result of the women's movement that revived in the late 1960s. Like the movement itself, however, the statues are not without controversy. Who should be honored? Where? In what form? These debates are most extensive—and heated—when the commemoration is to be on the national level and sponsored or endorsed by the government. On the local level, choices reflect local interests but also the interests of specific groups of women who recognize that their own history has been neglected, even by other women. Such statues reflect both national patterns and local stories[22]—the continued importance of regional cultures as well as the development of a kind of feminist canon of significant and emblematic women.

Figure 2-2. *Homage to Women*, a representation of the Lowell Mill Girls at Lowell National Historical Park in Massachusetts by sculptor Mico Kaufman in 1984, is an example of a symbolic public sculpture that recognizes women's contributions in the world of work. (*Courtesy of the National Park Service.*)

Two general categories of women's statues stand out. The first is the commemoration of contemporary women, still living or recently deceased, whose strongest ties were to a local community and who may or may not have had any national impact.[23] In the case of cultural figures, the statue may be a way of asserting the community's claim to a famous person. The second is the creation of monuments of explicitly historical and often political figures. These women usually, but not always, had some connection to the community in which the sculpture is placed, but they are primarily seen as part of national history. The purpose of the statues may be to bring the figures into the narrative of American history or it may be to give new life to their memory and new meaning to their lives.

Although the last twenty years produced a burst of new statues, the idea of commemorating individual women is not new. The creation of monuments to types of women, such as "pioneer mothers," reflected social changes and local conditions. So too, the placement in public of statues to honor specific women has been the result of individual circumstances and the decisions of specific groups. Broader cultural and political interests have also shaped this process. The post-Civil War period brought campaigns in the North and the South to use monuments to commemorate the dead and to shape historical memory. These efforts continued into the first decades of the twentieth century. Indeed, fifty years after the war, there were widespread efforts to commemorate and interpret/re-interpret its meaning.[24]

Although women played a prominent role in the fund raising and promotion of Civil War monuments, as indeed they had played in supporting the war, most female figures on monuments were allegorical. Women's actual role in the war was generally not mentioned.[25] Exceptions were the Confederate Woman's Monument at the state capitol in Columbia, South Carolina (1912) and another to the women of the Confederacy in Ft. Hill, South Carolina (1895). Two tributes to Confederate Woman by a female sculptor, Belle Kenney, still stand in Nashville, Tennessee (1927), and Jackson, Mississippi (1917). The United Daughters of the Confederacy played a key role in these monuments; in some cases they engaged in a controversy over the type of portrayal of women on the monuments.[26]

Although some northern monuments' inscriptions mention the service of women, there was no equivalent tribute to women's work.[27] However, in 1914, the Massachusetts Daughters of Veterans placed inside the State House in Boston a monument to the Army nurses of the Civil War.[28] Bronze on a marble base, the statue portrays a nurse giving water to a soldier.

If the portrayal of women in general was limited, that of African American women was particularly lacking. In *Standing Soldiers, Kneeling Slaves: Race, War, and Monument in Nineteenth-Century America,* historian Kirk Savage analyzes the role of monuments in portraying African Americans and emancipation.[29] While he is not focusing on the issue of representation of African American women, Savage does discuss the role of gender in shaping images of slavery and emancipation. He also gives an example of how people can imbue statues with their own meanings and turn allegorical figures into identifiable individuals. The Rhode Island *Soldiers' and Sailors' Monument,* erected in 1871 in Providence, contains one of the first images of emancipation on a Civil War monument. Sculptor Randolph Rogers used a female figure of a freed slave on a relief panel. He did the same in a 1872 soldiers' and sailors' monument in Detroit using three dimensional figures rather than relief. Although the female *Emancipation* statue was meant to be allegorical, Savage notes, "African American audiences reappropriated it as a portrait of the escaped slave, Sojourner Truth."[30] Still, a specific statue of a historical African American woman would not occur until much later.

By the twentieth century, the role of women nurses and volunteers in the war's relief commissions had become part of the North's historical narrative. Some of the women had published memoirs; other accounts of the war also noted their service. Women's work as nurses and in medical care received particular recognition especially in their home states. The state of Illinois commissioned a statue of Mary Ann Bickerdyke by sculptor Theo Ruggles Kitson and placed it in front of the county courthouse in Galesburg, Illinois, in 1906.[31] It was the first monument to an actual woman active in the Civil War. The figure is holding a wounded soldier and, as in the Boston statue, she is giving him water. Like many other monuments to nurses, this statue draws on the imagery of Michelangelo's *Pieta.* However, as a historian of women sculptors notes,[32] the female figure's "muscular arms, workaday clothes, and active gesture presents a different image of womanhood from the passive, elegant, or classicized female images of the period." There

Figure 2-3. Daughters of Civil War Veterans who were members of the Illinois Chapter of Ladies of G.A.R. surround the statue to" Mother" Bickerdyke, Civil War hospital matron, in Galesburg, IL. Dedicated in 1906, the statue was created by Theo Ruggles Kitson. (*Courtesy of the Galesburg [Illinois] Public Library.*)

was more to Mother Bickerdyke than traditional female virtues of sacrifice and deference. The inscription notes that when a surgeon whom she had fired complained to General Sherman, his response was "She outranks me."

Even though the Civil War and women's role in that national trauma was one focus of commemoration in the postwar period, public art reflected other concerns as well. Three of the earliest statues of women in public places clearly reflect both local and national issues. In 1874 a statue of Hannah Dustin was erected in Boscowan, New Hampshire, on a little island in the Merrimack River. A similar memorial was erected in Haverhill, Massachusetts, in 1879 (in the Grand Army of the Republic Park) to honor Dustin, a survivor and quite aggressive avenger of Indian captivity in 1697.[33] In New Orleans, in 1884, a publicly funded statue was erected of Margaret Gaffney Haughery, an Irish-born businesswoman and philanthropist who helped found asylums and institutions for children and the aged.[34] The fact that she had stood up to Yankee General Benjamin Butler during Reconstruction no doubt added support for the creation of the monument only two years after her death. Although these statues may reflect different political views and cultures in their respective regions—north and south—they both show women who in some ways represented traditional female virtues but who in other ways went strikingly beyond the "female sphere."

At the turn of the twentieth century, the revived women's movement helped shape the images of women presented in public art. Civic art, like the City Beautiful movement, was part of the progressive movement. Many people who believed in the impact of the environment on character and behavior tied this to a belief in the importance of public art. Civic groups officially dominated by men sponsored memorials to the Spanish-American War, and American expansionism in general, to encourage ideals of nationalism. They presented past and present business and civic leaders as exemplars of good citizenship. With perhaps aesthetically and intellectually mixed messages, urban elites promoted European styles and symbols and American historical figures.[35] Expositions and local and national centennials, bicentennials and sesquicentennials were the occasions for monument building. These were not without controversy. In the early 1920s the portrayal of "Vice" as a female figure in a statue dedicated to "Civic Virtue" caused an uproar among women's groups in New York.[36]

Although women did participate in those efforts, some, especially in the women's clubs and in the suffrage movement, organized to include themselves and their stories in public art and American iconography. They worked to make women part of the American body historic as well as the body politic. Women's groups, which sometimes supported representative statues, also organized to recognize individual historical women. In Adrian, Michigan, in 1909, for example, the local Women's Christian Temperance Union (WCTU) chapter helped erect a statue of Laura Smith Haviland, a Quaker abolitionist, educator, and social reformer.[37]

The significance of the WCTU as a force in American society is reflected in the choice of Frances Willard, that group's long-term leader, for inclusion in two national galleries of American heroes: the Statuary Hall in the U.S. Capitol and the newly created "Hall of Fame for Great Americans" in New York City. Willard became the first, and for fifty years the last, woman selected by her state for inclusion in the Capitol.[38] Each state is entitled to two statues of its citizens in the Statuary Hall. As of 2001, there were only six women represented out of a total of ninety-seven statues. Along with educator Mary Lyons, and astronomer Maria Mitchell, Willard entered the Hall of Fame's pantheon, which is sponsored by New York University at its campus in the Bronx, now part of Bronx Community College.[39] There are still only ten busts of women at that location.

A striking intersection of national interests, feminist concerns, and regional views of American history occurred in Portland, Oregon, in 1905 at the Lewis and Clark Exposition. To contribute to the commemoration, the Portland Women's Club raised funds for a statue of Sacajawea, the Shoshone guide on the 1804 expedition. That exposition, and a 1902 book that emphasized Sacajawea's importance, encouraged women's clubs in the West to see her as a model for the public presence of women.[40] Eva Emery Dye, the book's author and a member of the

Figure 2-4. Women suffrage leaders dedicated the monument to Sacajawea, Shoshone Indian guide for Lewis and Clark, in 1905 at the Lewis and Clark Exposition in Portland, OR.
The Portland Women's Club raised the funds for the statue sculpted by Alice Cooper Hubbard. (*Courtesy of the Oregon Historical Society.*)

Oregon State Women's Suffrage Association, helped organize the Sacajawea
Statue Association. Paradoxically, given the element of racism in the women's
rights movement, suffragists adopted Sacajawea as a symbol for their cause; Susan B. Anthony and other activists, whose conference coincided with the unveiling, spoke at the dedication.[41]

In addition to the Portland project, a Woman's Club in Bismarck, North
Dakota, successfully worked to place a statue of Sacajawea at that state's capitol
in 1910. Public school children of the state collected money for the statue. However, Native American women played no role in the campaign.[42] A 1938 statue in
the Oregon State capitol in Salem shows a standing Sacajawea, as usual portrayed
with her baby on her back, pointing the way to Lewis and Clark, both on horse-

back.[43] The Portland and Bismarck statues, however, do not include the expedition leaders. In the 1920s, the success of the Sacajawea statue influenced the DAR's decision to erect the (clearly European-American) statues called *The Madonna of the Trail*.

Also in this period, early America and the "frontier" were popular themes for monuments of women. In Castile, New York, a statue was erected in 1910 of Mary Jemison, a woman whose eighteenth-century captivity by Indians was a story quite different from that of Hannah Dustin. Jemison was adopted by a Seneca family and chose to stay. She twice married Indian men, raised eight children, owned and farmed land, and wrote a memoir in 1824 that spoke positively of her experiences. The statue of Jemison portrays her with a child on her back as she arrives in the rural area now part of Letchworth State Park. Like the Sacajawea statues, this monument resembles the Pioneer Mother statues that became popular in the 1920s. It was, apparently, barely conceivable, for a woman to be portrayed alone.[44]

The 1920s saw more efforts in general to put into concrete (or marble) interpretations of American history, identity, and nationalism. Part of this involved a long-term regional rivalry over the "myths of origin" of the United States, a battle that pitted Plymouth against Jamestown in a competition between Virginia and Massachusetts for historical place.[45] As this conflict lost some of its force, there was more emphasis on the role of women in the national origin stories. This included recognition of the part played by Native American women.

The Pocahontas Association, a group composed of descendants of the daughter of Chief Powhatan, Pocahontas, and John Rolfe, one of the English settlers, successfully campaigned for a statue of Pocahontas in Jamestown.[46] The statue and its 1922 dedication reflect the contradictory attitude toward Indians, and toward women, by presenting as a heroine a woman who gave up her culture and moved to England with her husband. The story of Pocahontas focuses on her role in marriage and childbearing while avoiding the issues of miscegenation that made interracial relationships taboo, indeed often illegal, in the 1920s. However, although the story emphasizes the triumph of European "civilization," it also suggests the creation of a new people. In this respect, the image of Pocahontas is potentially like that of Malinche, the Aztec woman who became Cortez's mistress and in Mexican folklore becomes the powerful mother of a new race.

Like the statues of Sacagawea in the West, the Virginia monuments of the seventeenth-century heroine offered a construction of American womanhood. The inscription on a Jamestown memorial plaque celebrated Pocahontas for her nurturing and collaborationist role: "Gentle and humane, she was the friend of the earliest struggling English colonists whom she nobly rescued, protected and helped."[47] Although Pocahontas is mistakenly shown in Plains Indian style hair and dress, at least one scholar sees her portrayal in that statue as a positive transformation from preceding images—"in command of her surroundings." She can be seen as personifying the assertive women of the groups whose effort to ensure her presence at the Jamestown site was also a struggle to give themselves a part in presenting the nation's history.[48]

While Pocahontas was being recognized in Plymouth, a more rebellious, and more Anglo, model of womanhood appeared on the Boston landscape. The Massachusetts State Federation of Women's Clubs, in cooperation with the Anne Hutchinson Memorial Committee, donated a statue of Anne Hutchinson to the State House in 1922; it was the first, and for many years the only, outdoor statue of a woman in Boston.[49] The statue, by noted sculptor Cyrus Dallin, portrays Hutchinson looking skyward, a Bible in her hand, and her daughter by her side — the very image of religious womanhood. However, the choice of a woman who had been expelled from the colony for speaking out suggests that the Women's Club members may have had a more feminist message in mind.

The successful passage in 1920 of the Women Suffrage amendment to the Constitution led to a more explicitly feminist work by sculptor Adelaide Johnson. Her *Portrait Monument to Lucretia Mott, Elizabeth Cady Stanton, and Susan B. Anthony*[50] shows figures of the three women rising from a large marble carving. The design was meant to symbolize the fact that the leaders had emerged from and were part of a larger movement. The National Women's Party presented the sculpture to Congress in February 1921. After only one day's presentation in the Capitol rotunda, the statue was moved to the crypt in the Capitol basement where it remained for the next seventy-five years.[51]

All these statues can be seen as part of competing definitions of "Americanism" in the 1920s. The post World War l period brought the "Red Scare," increased immigration restriction, and the revival of the Ku Klux Klan in the North. In that climate some ethnic and religious groups formed their own organizations that paralleled those of dominant groups, and asserted both their separateness and their "American" identity. This tension between separatism and assimilation can be seen in the efforts of women as well. In 1924, for example, the Ladies Auxiliary of the Ancient Order of Hibernians, an Irish group, erected a monument, *Nuns of the Battlefield,* at Rhode Island and M Street, NW, in Washington, D.C.[52] The bronze relief panel shows life-size figures of nuns in habits that distinguish several different religious orders whose members served as nurses in the Civil War. The figures on the monument make clear the desire of the Irish group to identify with the cause of peace and patriotism **and** to bring the image of religious women into public space and the historical record.

The 1930s brought two developments in public sculpture in general and in the representation of women in particular. The first was federal funding provided for art by the Works Progress Administration (WPA) through the Federal Art Project. Created to provide employment for artists, the FAP also attempted to relate art to local communities and to their histories.[53] Much of this art, including sculpture, had a mythical character to it. The human figures tended to be idealized representations of workers or farmers and of American manhood and womanhood. However, the project's structure made possible the expression of a variety of views and perspectives on the role of women and of the ways to present them. As historian Barbara Melosh has observed, the interaction among the artists, the project administrators, and the public promoted an element of contention and negotiation about gender images and about ideas about manhood and womanhood. However, despite some focus on women's participation in civic life, they were most often portrayed as mothers and wives, representing a particular image of femininity. A study of specific projects shows that sometimes the public and administrators complained that the women seemed to be too large, taking up too much space.[54]

WPA art put little focus on women as individual historical figures. In the mid-to late 1930s, the Federal Arts Project, in conjunction with local hospital and nurse's associations, did erect statues of Florence Nightingale in San Francisco and Los Angeles.[55] In 1941, the WPA funded a memorial dedicated to Emma Willard in Middlebury, Vermont. A relief carving on marble honored Willard for her pioneering efforts for education for women.[56]

A second influence on public sculpture and the representation of women in the 1930s was the increased popularity of movies. In 1931 movie star Delores Del Rio donated a statue, *Evangeline*, to St. Martinsville, Louisiana, the site of the burial place of Emmeline Labiche,[57] whose life may have been the basis for Longfellow's poem. The New England poet's romantic story told of the Acadians driven from their homes in Nova Scotia by the British in 1755. Del Rio had just starred in the silent movie, *Evangeline* (1929), and her portrayal was the model for the statue's depiction of the Acadian heroine.[58] The memorial therefore represents the fictional heroine of the poem and film and two "real" women—Emmeline Labiche and Delores Del Rio. While conveying a traditional and sentimental image of womanhood, the statue is part of the mythology of Acadian culture and a tribute to its persistence in Louisiana. The Evangeline story is also part of the Acadian heritage in Nova Scotia and, as in Louisiana, has become a focus of cultural tourism. The Canadians erected a statue in 1920 outside a church in what is now the Grand Pré National Historic Site.[59] The statues demonstrate the international nature of history and mythmaking.

There was no major public memorial to women in the Second World War or the Korean War and, despite the iconic image of "Rosie the Riveter," the 1940s and 1950s were periods of minimal attention to women in public art and monuments. The era of the "Feminine Mystique" offered little motivation for recognition of women in public places. Indeed public art lost out to the private world of the gallery or museum, and the public world of the Cold War. At the same time, the art world increasingly viewed representational work and traditional statues as passé.

An exception to this trend was an increasing number of outdoor religious statues, many of women, especially in Catholic areas. Statues of Mary, the mother of Jesus, and of female saints had been important images in churches and shrines in Catholic and ethnic neighborhoods. These often reflected the parishioners' ethnic backgrounds through their portrayal of their patron saints and their Madonnas, for example, Our Lady of Guadalupe in Mexican neighborhoods. Most of these were associated with churches or schools. In addition, small statues and shrines could be found in back or front yards in ethnic neighborhoods. In the 1950s, as the Catholic Church became more visible as cultural force, so did its symbols.

The canonization of the first American saints also was a catalyst for the creation of public statues, posing another kind of controversy. In New Orleans in 1949 an outdoor statue was erected in honor of Mother Frances Xavier Cabrini. Three years earlier, the Catholic Church had canonized the Italian-born nun, who had founded many hospitals, orphanages and other institutions in the United States. The use of public funds to maintain the statue was controversial; a challenge led to a court ruling in 1952 approving the funding. Despite the obvious sectarian aspect of the statue, the role of Mother Cabrini's religious order in providing health care in New Orleans carried the day, assisted perhaps by the Catholic vote. In 1958 a privately funded statue of Mother Cabrini was placed in a Newark, New Jersey, public park.[60]

Other statues followed.[61] The role of Catholic women's religious orders in providing public health care was recognized by the State of Washington's selection of a nun, Mother Joseph of the Sisters of Providence, as its choice for one of two statues in the U.S. Capitol in 1980. A small copy of that statue also stands in Vancouver, Washington. The canonization of Mother Marguerite D'Youville, a French Canadian nun who founded a religious order that created hospitals and schools in the United States as well as Canada, led to statues such as one in front of St. Peter's Home in Manchester, New Hampshire. However, the canonization of Elizabeth Seton, the first American-born saint, in 1975 inspired the largest number of outdoor statues—at least twelve across the country. As the founder of the Sisters of Charity, an order active in creating hospitals and orphanages, Seton is also a symbol of women's role in nursing as well as religion; statues of her are located at hospitals, convents, and schools such as the University of San Diego.

The more public nature of religious statues could have unexpected consequences, including a loss of their specific meaning. In 1985 a helicopter lifted a 90-foot tall Madonna named *Our Lady of the Rockies* to its site near Butte, Montana. Although it was built as thanks for a successful prayer to Mary, many residents think it is not a Catholic religious figure at all, but an undefined woman who can represent everyone.[62] In fact, as a symbol and source of income, the tourist attraction and familiar icon has to some extent replaced the area's mines that have gone out of business.

The turmoil of the 1960s and 1970s created new movements that revived a wider interest in monuments and public art. Activists, including some historians, sought a new American history and new monuments to represent it. The Civil Rights movement, the war in southeast Asia, the antiwar movement, and the revived women's movement all led to increased interest in history and a determination to reshape it and its images. New forms of art and interest in civic space and in art in public places combined with events of the period to create renewed interest in all types of public monuments. The idea of art as political expression revived, as did the idea of a "people's art." The relative affluence of the period also enabled private and public groups to raise the funds for memorials.

The first impact came from the U.S. war in southeast Asia. As with other American wars, an early impulse was commemorative and patriotic and focused on those in military service as an undifferentiated—but presumably masculine—group. Initial impulses were also local, as towns and neighborhoods created their own monuments to victims of the war. Rather than erect a standard doughboy or the Civil War mass-manufactured soldier, people wanted to commemorate individuals. So when First Lieutenant Sharon Lane, an Army nurse, was killed in Vietnam in 1969, her community placed a statue of her outside Aultman Hospital in Canton, Ohio.[63] That monument—erected in 1973—may be the only statue of an individual woman in the military from that war.

The dedication of the *Vietnam Veterans Memorial* in Washington in 1982 unleashed a movement among women veterans for their own specific monument. This sentiment increased after a statue of three servicemen was added to the original, very moving, nonrepresentational sculpture by Maya Lin. In 1993, the *Vietnam Women's Memorial,* by sculptor Glenna Goodacre, joined the other Vietnam memorials.[64] The inclusion of a figure of a wounded serviceman with the three servicewomen suggests that there was still some unease in recognizing women's potential as warriors as well as nurturers. Similarly, the *Pieta* reference of the woman holding the wounded male soldier certainly continued an image from earlier monuments to nurses.[65] With a raised consciousness, women veterans of other wars began to organize for their own inclusion in the historical record and in memorials. That effort culminated in 1997 with the extensive memorial, near Arlington Cemetery, *Women in Military Service in America.*[66]

Retroactive justice was also accomplished for specific groups of military women. The Women Air Force Service Pilots of the Second World War were honored by a sculpture in Ohio at Wright Air Force Base.[67] Interestingly, however, there is no statue anywhere of Jacqueline Cochran, the woman most responsible for the creation and functioning of the WASPs. While these memorials generally resulted from the efforts of servicewomen and veterans, the military itself seized on the idea of a women's monument as a recruiting device. The figure, *Molly Marine,* a statue erected in New Orleans during World War II, became a symbol of the "new military." In 1966, during the war in Vietnam, the concrete statue was rededicated and given a fresh bronze coating. In 1999–2000, copies of the statue were installed with formal dedications at Marine Corp bases in Quantico, Virginia, and Parris Island, South Carolina.[68]

For women's monuments, 1982 was a key year. In addition to the *Vietnam Veterans Memorial,* a new kind of historic park opened honoring the women (and some men) of the women's rights movement. The creation of the Women's Rights National Historic Park commemorated the activists of the nineteenth century who met in Seneca Falls in 1848 and produced their eloquent and forceful "Declaration of Rights" for women.[69] The park encouraged other efforts on the national and local level to recognize historic sites related to women, and to create new monuments and statues, as well as to restore some neglected ones. This kind of official new history-making was a response to the revived feminist movement of the 1970s and 1980s, and a sign of its impact on historians, the National Park Service, and those in Congress who supported the funding of the Park. It also indi-

cates a desire to recognize individual leaders like Susan B. Anthony and Elizabeth Cady Stanton as well as to educate Americans about social change.

Inside the visitor center of the Women's Rights NHP stand nineteen life-sized
bronze statues representing the women, and some men, who attended the 1848
conference. These include Elizabeth Cady Stanton, Frederick Douglass, and others. The collective sculpture combines the role of individual historical figures
with recognition of the importance of the group; it honors anonymous as well as
famous feminists. Sculptor Lloyd Lillie found a way to combine traditional individual representation statues with a design that enabled visitors to sense the
dynamics of the 1848 conference; they can also imagine themselves as being part
of it.

Outdoors in the town of Seneca Falls, another group statue overlooks the river.
Dedicated in 1998, *When Anthony Met Stanton* by sculptor Ted Aube shows
women's rights activist Amelia Bloomer introducing the two women who would
become long-term partners in the struggle for women's suffrage. Not far away, in
Geneva, New York, stands a statue by the same sculptor of another nineteenth-
century pioneer, Elizabeth Blackwell, one of the first women to receive a medical
degree in the United States. The statue sits looking out on the quadrangle of the
campus of Hobart and William Smith College.[70]

Other women's rights activists have returned to public vision and civic life.
Anna Howard Shaw was honored in Michigan in a 1988 statue. Esther Morris of
Wyoming and Jeannette Rankin of Montana, the first female member of Congress,
were both selected by their states for inclusion in the Capitol's Statuary hall. A
copy of the Morris statue stands in front of the Wyoming State capitol in
Cheyenne.[71] Ft. Wayne, Indiana, celebrated the new millennium by dedicating a
group sculpture of three sisters: Agnes Hamilton, an artist and settlement house
worker; Alice, a doctor and pioneer in workplace health issues; and Edith, a
scholar of classical mythology.[72] Sojourner Truth, who fought for African Americans' freedom and for women's rights, is honored by a twelve-foot statue in Battle Creek, Michigan, where she lived the last twenty-five years of her life.

That statue of Sojourner Truth represents the strength of women's activism; it
also reminds us of the continuing tensions within the women's movement. The
problems in combining commemoration and history, of even finding truth in history, can be seen clearly in the controversy over statues of women in two national
capitals: Washington, D.C., and Ottawa, Canada. These debates suggest that the
contest over history can take many forms. The first controversy arose in the late
1990s and involved a group of primarily white feminists in conflict with a group
of African American women over who should be included in the national portrayal of the women's suffrage movement. The second controversy, also in the
late 1990s, arose over the racial ideology of some members of a group of white
Canadian women: "The Famous Five" being honored in a sculpture for their work
in the women's movement in Canada. The cases raised a number of issues. Can
movements and individuals be commemorated in ways that recognize flaws as
well as strengths? How can contemporary values and beliefs be incorporated into

past narratives and their symbols? Are women as historic actors and subjects of monuments being held to higher standards today than were the men whose statues dominate the historic landscape? Is history in stone inherently flawed?

In the 1990s a group of women organized to bring the Adelaide Johnson's statue of Stanton, Anthony, and Mott out of the Capitol basement and up into Rotunda. After considerable resistance from men in Congress, and some conservative columnists, they were successful in getting a congressional resolution passed in 1996 authorizing the move. The *Portrait Monument* was raised from the Crypt and reinstalled in the Rotunda over Mother's Day weekend in 1997.[73] However, the sculptor's 1921 choice of the three women to commemorate, and the statue itself, came under intense criticism from some of African American women. The National Political Congress of Black Women (NPCBW), in particular, criticized Johnson's failure to include Sojourner Truth or any other African American suffragist. Other individuals and groups joined the effort to get a figure of Truth added as a figure in the uncarved area of the statue. The statue's supporters called for an additional statue rather than altering the original sculpture. Meanwhile those opposed to any women's rights leaders statue in the Rotunda enjoyed the conflict. The statue was installed as is and plans made for a statue of Truth.

The conflict, however, showed the deep impact of racism in dividing women. It raised the question of how, and perhaps whether, to commemorate imperfect heroines. The focus on Sojourner Truth, rather than on other African American women activists like Mary Church Terrell or Ida B. Wells Barnett, also speaks to the ways in which particular historical figures come to achieve an iconic and political meaning.[74] The case also revealed quite different views about the integrity and immutability of art objects and monuments themselves.

Meanwhile in Canada, a group of women sought to create a monument honoring a group known as "The Famous Five"—Henrietta Muir Edwards, Louise McKinney, Irene Parlby, Nellie McClung, and Emily Parsons. They were five women from western Canada who had challenged the exclusion of women from political offices in Canada—in particular the Canadian Senate. They lost in the Canadian Supreme Court, but in 1929 won a victory in the British Privy Council. The decision declared that women were included in the definition of "person" for legal purposes under the British North American Act.[75]

Nearly seventy years later, a group primarily of women determined that the five should be commemorated with statues in Calgary—representing their ties to the western provinces—and in the nation's capital in Ottawa.[76] "The Famous Five Foundation" raised funds and commissioned a sculptor. Barbara Paterson created a group portrait of statues of the women seated at a tea party receiving the news of their victory. Like the Seneca Falls statues, the grouping is bold and cheerful, not pompous and heroic, and draws attention to the group of women as a source of strength.

Controversy rose from the right, middle, and the left. The Calgary city government initially turned down the proposal. Opposition came from women concerned about some of the Five's association with eugenics and anti-immigrant and racist

Figure 2-5. The group statue of Canada's "Famous Five" displayed in both Calgary and Ottawa honors the five women from western Canada who in 1929 successfully challenged the exclusion of women from holding seats in the Canadian Senate. Barbara Paterson's scupture depicts the women receiving news of their victory at a tea party. (*Photo by Jean D. Linehan.*)

ideology. Class bias as well as racial bias became issues to be confronted by the statues' supporters.[77] Some of the criticism was harsh; one journal article about it was titled "But She Was a Feminist Racist." However, the controversy became an opportunity to discuss these issues, not just in relation to the five women, but also as part of Canadian history. Once the statues were approved, the solution to the dilemma—how to celebrate the good without seeming to endorse or ignore the bad—took what one might call a distinctly Canadian form.

The dedication ceremonies became opportunities to put the women's achievements into the context of a new, more diverse and open social order. The ceremony in Ottawa, in particular, was designed to broaden the definition of "womanhood" as well as "personhood." As actors played the five women, dancers, musicians, singers from Native and other ethnic groups, performing in their own languages as well as English and French, joined in the event on Parliament Hill. It became in part a way to redefine Canadian history. Among those participating, along with the prime minister and members of Parliament, were the women in government who had helped to make the event possible. These included Hedy Fry, Secretary of State for Multiculturalism, Canadian Heritage Minister Sheila Copps, and the Governor-General of Canada, Adrienne Clarkson, born in Hong Kong, who moved to Canada as a refugee during World War II.

The Canadian ceremony suggests that new ways can be found to make monuments suitable to the needs of a new history, more inclusive and perhaps more human. In California, public commemoration has broadened to include the history of Chinese women and Chicanas in Los Angeles and the celebration of entertainers in Hollywood.[78] In New York, *The Empire State Carousel* depicts, democratically, actual historical people like Eleanor Roosevelt and Susan B. Anthony along with mythical characters.[79]

Not everyone is happy with these new directions, especially the trend toward nonrepresentational sculpture. Although newspaper columnists, and sometimes editors, have turned their attention to the absence of statues of women in their cities, they also have been critical of some of new memorials. The distinctly nonrepresentational sculpture consisting of pieces of limestone and rock used in Chicago to honor Jane Addams and other women struck at least one commentator as unworthy of their subjects. Why, she asked, were women's memorials in the form of rocks, while men commemorated in Chicago received massive statues in their honor? Likewise, a commentator in Detroit commented positively on the larger than life, but life-like, statue of Sojourner Truth erected in Grand Rapids in 1999.[80]

Although sometimes decisions are made on the national level, in most cases public art issues are dealt with on local levels. Indeed, the increase of the number of women's statues reflects efforts to combine national and local history of women. Contemporary women as well as historical figures have become the subject of statues. Sometimes these are a tribute to women's recent political roles such as, for example, statues of Governor Ella Grasso in Connecticut and Congresswoman Milicent Fenwick in New Jersey. Sometimes they are monuments to entertainers, hometown heroines who tie the local to the national. A statue of Kate Smith, a popular singer from the 1930s to the 1950s, stands outside the Spectrum, Philadelphia's sports arena where she (in person or on tape) sang "God Bless America" before each hockey game.[81]

As in the past, the national, local, and sometimes international issues have complex interconnections. Texas is one of the states that has a large number of statues of women among its extensive and diverse public sculpture. One of the largest assemblages of statues of historical figures is located in San Antonio as an outdoor sculpture garden at Sea World, a park owned by Anheuser-Busch, the giant brewing corporation. The "Texas Walk" includes fifteen life size bronze statues of noteworthy Texans. Three of them are women: Congresswoman Barbara Jordan, writer Katharine Anne Porter, and athlete Mildred "Babe" Didrikson Zaharias.[82] All were installed in 1998. The Catholic heritage and population of San Antonio is reflected in the visibility of religious symbols, especially statues of Mary. Incarnate Word College is the site of an "Our Lady of Lourdes Grotto," a 1905 replica of the French shrine, with statues of Mary and St. Bernadette.[83]

Controversy over sculpture in Corpus Christi, Texas, illustrates how efforts to increase recognition of ethnic groups may include demands for monuments to assert their cultural presence in public space and in public memory. Mexican-Americans in that city were determined to see their presence and their history acknowledged. However, a dispute over the 1997 Bayfront statue of the Tejano singer, Selena, showed the difficulty of finding agreement on ethnic representations. It also produced debate about the appropriate portrayal of female figures. As one scholar noted, the controversy over the Selena statue brought to the surface the many, sometimes competing, forces that shape urban identities; it illustrated, he added, "how difficult it is, therefore, to contrive symbols that will unite more than they divide."[84] This becomes especially difficult, and important, at a time when ethnic diversity and pride are on the increase in many American cities.

Increasing interest in public art and public history has intersected with efforts to revive civic culture. As in the progressive era, art and history are important parts of urban self-definition. Recent developments in two northeastern cities, New York and Boston, illustrate these dynamics; they also show the impact of the women's movement and the civil rights movement on ideas about public space and historical memory and commemoration. While revising public art and ideas about history to include more women in their urban pantheons, New York City and Boston have focused on making traditional types of monuments more inclusive.

Until 1992, the only outdoor statue of an actual woman in New York City was an equestrian figure of Joan of Arc, by Anna Hyatt (Huntington) erected in Riverside Park in 1915. Like other statues of the French heroine, this was dedicated to good will between the French and American people.[85] The absence of actual women in civic art and outdoor sculpture was a glaring omission in a city with its fair share of sculpture and where other groups have used public art to assert their place—Irish men, for example with the statue, *Fighting Father Duffy,* the World War I chaplain, in Times Square.

The absence of monuments to women seemed especially egregious considering the amount and quality of written documentation of women's history available in the city, and the major role of New York women in national history. In the 1990s the issue was raised in the press (and elsewhere) and two statues were selected for the city parks. The first, erected in 1992, was a small statue of author Gertrude Stein placed in Bryant Park near the New York Public Library. The second, in 1996, commissioned by the City, was of First Lady and activist Eleanor Roosevelt, and is located in Riverside Park.[86] The Roosevelt statue was unveiled to a crowd that included the then First Lady Hillary Clinton. On that same day, a statue of Ella Fitzgerald—"The First Lady of Jazz"—was dedicated in Yonkers, only a few miles away. Part of an "Art on Main Street" project of that city, the tribute to the African American singer testified to the importance of black women in American culture and to the power of local commemorations to do what larger institutions fail to do.

A statue that also helped nudge New Yorkers to include more women in public sculpture also represents the coming together of local, national and international issues. Again, as at Seneca Falls and Lowell, a national park played a key role. The restoration and reinterpretation in the early 1990s of Ellis Island, in New

York Harbor, included a new recognition of women's distinctive experiences as immigrants. For the centennial of the 1892 opening of the Island's immigration station, the National Park Service dedicated a statue to the first immigrant to enter and pass through the gates.[87] Annie Moore, a fifteen-year-old, who had come from Ireland with her two brothers, now stands in bronze on the second floor of the museum. Mary Robinson, the first woman president of the Irish republic, unveiled the statue in 1993. Another statue of Annie Moore and her brothers, also by sculptor Jeanne Rynhart, is in the port of Cobh, in County Cork, where many Irish migrants' ocean voyage began.

Similar social dynamics have occurred in Boston, but with that city's own distinctive twists. More than perhaps anywhere but Washington, D.C., history and monuments define and reflect physical space and political place in the Massachu-

Figure 2-6. *Annie Moore* at Ellis Island celebrates the first immigrant to pass through the Ellis Island station when it opened in 1892. Jeanne Rynhart, the sculptor, also created a statue of Annie Moore and her brothers in County Cork, Ireland, where the Moores began their journey to the United States. (*Courtesy of the National Park Service.*)

Figure 2-7. *The Lady Doctor* honors Dr. Justina L. Ford, who served northeast Denver from 1902 to 1952, in this statue by Jess E. DuBois. Dedicated in 1998, the statue, which stands at a light rail station, was commissioned by the city of Denver as part of its "Art at the Stations" project. (*Photo by Roger W. Kaufman.*)

setts capital. Efforts of immigrants, ethnic and racial groups to find place in the city have been paralleled by efforts to have their history included in the local and national historical story. The changing lineup of bronze figures on Commonwealth Avenue is one manifestation of these efforts. The *Holocaust Memorial* and *Irish Famine Memorial* are other examples.[88]

In the 1990s activist and academic women organized to bring women and the study of gender into Boston's history. The creation of the Boston Women's Heritage Trail called attention to the lack of monuments honoring women. The effort succeeded in bringing statues of women into the collection in the State House. After considerable political as well as historical consideration, the busts of six women were added to the all male pantheon.[89] After discussion among groups advocating inclusion of particular historical women, three women were selected for the new Boston Women's Memorial: Abigail Adams, first lady famous for her letter urging husband John "to remember the ladies" in constructing a new government; Lucy Stone, a nineteenth-century women's rights activist; and Phillis Wheatley, an eighteenth-century poet and former slave. Sculpted by Meredith Bergmann the monument will be installed on Commonwealth Avenue in 2003.[90]

Debate about which women to honor raised issues about the inclusion of non-white Anglo-Saxon Protestant women. For African Americans in Boston this was an especially strong concern. The city, famous for the "Freedom Trail" and proud of the monuments to white abolitionists, had another history of racism and exclusion. At the same time, the national tendency to focus on male leaders like Dr. Martin Luther King in texts and statues made the role of African American women less visible in the recording of the movement than they had been in the making of it. It was a striking moment then when, in 1999, two monuments were unveiled in Harriet Tubman Square, in Boston's South End.[91] *Step on Board* by sculptor Fern Cunningham shows Tubman, leading a group of men and women, moving forward, to what the viewer knows is freedom. The other statue, *Emancipation* by sculptor Meta Vaux Warrick Fuller, was created in 1913 for the fiftieth anniversary of the Emancipation Proclamation.[92] The statue, not originally cast in bronze, was lost for many years, then restored at the African American History Museum in Boston, and finally, cast and loaned by the museum to be placed in the park with the Tubman statue. The two monuments are a powerful alternative to the traditional emancipation images that emphasized Lincoln's role in freeing the slaves, rather than their own role in taking freedom. Each statue, in different ways, put women firmly into the narrative.

In smaller New England cities as well, women's history is being brought into civic space. In Nashua, New Hampshire, the Franco-American community organized to erect what may be the first monument honoring that ethnic group in New England. Rather than selecting a historical person, they have chosen a symbolic figure: *La Dame de Notre Renaissance Française*. In keeping with the area's history as a mill town, the statue shows a woman in nineteenth-century working-class dress with a boy with a book.[93] In Northampton, Massachusetts, organizers have raised funds for a statue of Sojourner Truth, who lived there from 1843–1857 in a utopian community. The search for a sculptor raised another issue. The first five finalists were all men and the committee decided to add five women finalists.[94] The importance of the role of the sculptor and the opportunities that these statues may offer for women add to the question of who makes history.

When completed, that statue of Sojourner Truth will join with another in Battle Creek, Michigan, the statues of Barbara Jordan in Texas, statues of Harriet Tubman in Boston and at Brenau College in Georgia, an indoor statue of Rosa Parks in Montgomery, Alabama, and others of female civil rights activists, in creating a new kind of historical canon and set of landmarks. Compared to the many statues of male generals, presidents, businessmen, and masculine icons like Paul Bunyan, the one hundred or so statues of real women in public places is still a relatively small number. However, the efforts they reflect and the vibrancy of their designs can tell us much about the changes in our society and our views of history.

In addition to viewing the statues and analyzing the process by which they come to exist, it is important to read the inscriptions that accompany them. In Washington, D.C., in Lincoln Park, a twelve-foot statue honors Mary McLeod Bethune.[95] She was an organizer, educator, and perhaps the first African American woman to hold a significant job in the federal executive branch, in the National Youth Administration under Franklin Roosevelt. The National Council of Negro Women, a group Bethune founded, began plans for the memorial in the late 1950s. Various obstacles interfered with the plan but the group persisted and the statue was dedicated in 1974. It shows Bethune handing a scroll—meant as her legacy—to two children (a boy and a girl). Her words are inscribed on the monument's pedestal: "I leave you love. I leave you hope, I leave you the challenge of developing confidence in one another. I leave you a thirst for education. I leave you a respect for power. I leave you faith. I leave you racial dignity. I leave you also a desire to live harmoniously with your fellow man. I leave you, finally, a responsibility to our young people." That certainly speaks quite differently, and perhaps more loudly, than all the men on Mount Rushmore.

Figure 2-8. *The Mary McLeod Bethune Memorial* in Lincoln Park, Washington, D.C., by Robert Berks shows her handing her legacy to two African American children. Bethune was the founder of the National Council of Negro Women whose members dedicated the memorial in 1974. (*Courtesy of the National Park Service. Photo by Bill Clark.*)

INTERPRETING STATUES OF WOMEN

What we learn from looking at women's place in public sculpture and historical memory will depend on the questions we ask, as well as our own angle of vision. Many of the organizations involved in establishing women's monuments also have been involved in using them in education in local schools. Boston women's groups, for example, worked with teachers to incorporate the sites into lessons in the Boston schools. Another approach is to focus on the public history of a particular place and develop curriculum units the way a group has done using monuments in Washington, D.C.[96]

Another way to go about it would be to consider the following questions and use some of the following kinds of sources.

QUESTIONS

Looking at the history of women's representation in statues can tell us about both art and history. Who is included? Who isn't? Who funds or promotes the statue? Who is the sculptor?

What does the form tell us about the design, the material, the inscription? Is the woman portrayed alone? Who is with her? Where is the statue placed? Has it been moved? How well is it taken care of? Who pays attention to it? Has its meaning changed over time? Who takes care of it? Who interprets it?

What is the historical basis for the monument? What part is myth, what verifiable history? Why is the story important and to whom? What kind of form is really appropriate for statues commemorating women's history?

How do statues compare by region? What about statues of women in other countries? How does commemoration of women change over time?

What kind of ceremony was there at its dedication? Did it evoke controversy? Who is it important to? Who makes money from it? Is it part of tourism? How does it compare to statues of men?

Is the woman included in *Notable American Women*? In local histories? On history trails? How long did it take to complete the project? Has the statue been moved from its original location?

SOURCES

Archives: the sculptor's papers or papers of the organizations that promoted the statue and the programs for the unveiling or dedication ceremonies.

Government documents—federal, local or state laws authorizing statues

Interviews, newspaper accounts

Specific government agencies that deal with statues, e.g., National Park Service Web sites

Art history sources, in particular the Smithsonian's Art Inventories on line at <www.siris.si.edu>

Existing study and curriculum guides, e.g., D.C. and Boston.
"Save Outdoor Sculpture" groups have done reports on individual states.

NOTES

1. Polly Welts Kaufman, *National Parks and the Woman's Voice: A History* (Albuquerque: University of New Mexico Press, 1996), 54.
2. James M. Goode, *The Outdoor Sculpture of Washington, D.C.* (Washington, DC: Smithsonian Press, 1974), 87–88.
3. In this chapter I focus on statues of actual women rather than symbolic figures although I briefly discuss the latter. The statues are those in a permanent material, full-sized, outdoors, and accessible to the public even if on private property. This study does not include statues in cemeteries. In general I concentrate on public sculpture in the United States. I intend this approach to be useful in public interpretation and in classrooms. Teachers can use these ideas to have students look within their own communities for examples of women's representation in public art. A list (necessarily incomplete) of statues follows.
4. For a study of women's representation in public space in Chicago, see Patricia Mooney-Melvin, "The Landscape of Urban Memory: Women in Chicago," a paper delivered at the National Council on Public History Conference, April 2001, Ottawa, Canada. This is part of her larger study on women and historical representation in Chicago.
5. On college campuses specific types of buildings are likely to be named for women. For example, in 1910 the University of Minnesota named its first residence hall for women for Maria Sanford, a professor of elocution and rhetoric and a staunch suffragist. The state later chose Sanford for one of its statues in the U.S. Capitol. Lynn Sherr and Jurate Kazickas, *Susan B. Anthony Slept Here: A Guide to American Women's Landmarks* (New York: Times Books, 1994), 232.
6. This may have been especially true for Dr. Gertrude Kelly, a dedicated activist who opposed the holding of a fund-raising banquet because she thought it inappropriate "to feast" while Irish citizens were being attacked by British soldiers. Joe Doyle, "Striking for Ireland on the New York Docks" in *The New York Irish,* Ronald H. Bayor and Timothy J. Meagher, eds. (Baltimore: Johns Hopkins University Press, 1996), 664. In 2000 the City of Chicago created a "Hillary Rodham Clinton Women's Park and Garden" to honor the then first lady and area native and to commemorate the historic work of hundreds of Chicago women. *Chicago Tribune,* January 18, 2001, 3.
7. Works Progress Administration (WPA) murals of the 1930s generally included representative women, rather than historical figures. See note 54 for a discussion of the portrayal of women in New Deal art. The New Orleans mural depicts former slaves who have broken their own shackles; they look

up to Harriet Tubman, who is portrayed floating in the air on a large book as she reaches down to them. The mural was done by teenagers in 1988 as part of an Urban Arts Training Program sponsored by the New Orleans Arts Council. It is quite different from images in American sculpture of grateful slaves being freed by the white messiah, Abraham Lincoln; it also contrasts with the style of more conventional heroic monuments and paintings. Pam Louwagie, "Mural Instills Pride, Work Ethic," *Times-Picayune*, August 13, 1998, sec. OTA.

8. For a historical discussion of this symbolism, see Marina Warner, *Monuments & Maidens: The Allegory of the Female Form* (London: Vintage, 1985). These were not intended to represent actual women or to be signs of their role in society. In fact, women were excluded from participation in most of the civic institutions that such statues celebrated.

9. Joy S. Kasson, *Marble Queens and Captives: Women in Nineteenth-Century American Sculpture* (New Haven, CT: Yale University Press, 1990), 1.

10. Sculptor Maria Louisa Lander's 1859 portrayal of Virginia Dare, represented as the first English child born America, is now in the Elizabethan Garden of the Garden Club in Manteo, North Carolina. Sherr and Kazickas, 342–43.

11. James M. Goode, 511–12; and "Madonna of the Trail," <http://www.culturalcenter.org/culture/madonna.htm>; and "The Pioneer Woman," <http://marlandmansion.com/pages/pw.html>.

12. *Picture Guide to Historic Plymouth* (Plymouth, MA: Pilgrim Society, 1990), 9, 14, 17, 25.

13. For a critical discussion of European Americans' use of statues to portray "good Indians" see James W. Loewen, *Lies Across America* (New York: New Press, 1999), 438–442.

14. Fairmount Park Art Association, *Sculpture of a City* (New York: Walker, 1974), 110–117; Loredo Taft, *The History of American Sculpture* (New York: Macmillan, 1903), 408–09. For discussion of the Hannah Dustin statue see note 33.

15. Caroline Glassic, "Ashland Mother's Memorial Remains a Sacred Site for All," Shamokin (NC) *News-Item,* May 13–14, 2000; and William F. Gustafson, Historian, Museum of Anthracite History, "The Ashland Boys Association: 'Sentiment, Not 'Commercialism'," unpublished manuscript (c. 2000).

16. Harry Eiss, "Our Lady of the Rockies," *Journal of Popular Culture* 30 (Spring 1997): 33. For discussion of its changing meaning, see note 17.

17. Mark Massa, *Catholics and American Culture: Fulton Sheen, Dorothy Day, and the Notre Dame Football Team* (New York: Crossroad, 1999), 199. On the meaning of the shrines to "Our Lady of Lourdes" and the importance of religious iconography in general see Colleen McDannell, *Material Christianity: Religion and Popular Culture in America* (New Haven, CT: Yale University Press, 1995), 137–162.

18. John M. Holman, "The N.H. Marine Memorial at Hampton Beach," *Lane Memorial Library.* <http://www.hampton.lib.nh.us/hampton> The papers of

sculptor Alice Cosgrove are in the Milne Special Collections and Archives at the Library at the University of New Hampshire. Another kind of marine memorial is the statue erected in August 2001 in Gloucester, Massachusetts. Sculpted by Morgan Faulds Pike, it shows a woman with two children looking out to sea and honors fishermen's wives. *Portland Press Herald,* August 6, 2001.

19. Sherr and Kazickas, 469.

20. *Portland Press Herald* , August 6, 2001, 1.

21. *Homage to Women,* also known as *The Mill Girls,* by sculptor Mico Kaufman is administered by the Lowell Historic Preservation Commission. "Inventories of American Painting and Sculpture" (hereafter "Inventory"), Smithsonian Institution Research Information System (SIRIS), <www.siris.si.edu>.

22. Gaines M. Foster, *Ghosts of the Confederacy: Defeat, the Lost Cause, and the Emergence of the New South* (New York: Oxford University Press, 1987).

23. Two examples in Maine are statues of runner Joan Benoit (Samuelson) and Samantha Smith, a young girl who worked for peace between the United States and the Soviet Union and died in a plane crash.

24. Foster, *Ghosts of the Confederacy.*

25. For discussion of the various images of women presented see Melissa A. Durbin, "Thematic Study of Sculptural Representations of American Women on Civil War monuments," (M.A. Thesis, Bowling Green State University, 1994).

26. Foster, 175–79. For the role of women in shaping the creation and design of a Confederate monument in St. Louis in the early twentieth century see Eileen Eagan, "Whose History Is This Anyway? Urban Parks and Historical Consciousness in Philadelphia and St. Louis, 1870–1914," paper presented to Organization of American Historians Conference, April 1989, and Katharine T. Corbett, *In Her Place: A Guide to St. Louis Women's History* (St. Louis: Missouri Historical Society Press, 1999), 211–12.

27. The women of the St. Louis, Missouri, Ladies' Union Aid Society, did attempt to have three women—Clara Barton, Mother Bickerdyke and Dorothea Dix—included in a proposed "Freedom's Memorial to Abraham Lincoln." The idea was rejected for an allegorical figure of a woman nursing a soldier. The monument itself was never built. See Kirk Savage, *Standing Soldiers, Kneeling Slaves: Race, War, and Monument in Nineteenth-Century America* (Princeton, NJ: Princeton University Press, 1997), 111–12; Ladies' Union Aid Society, *Minute Book 1865–1868,* 91–92, Missouri Historical Society. Those efforts were discussed in Paula Coalier, "Beyond Sympathy: The St. Louis Ladies' Union Aid Society and the Civil War," *Gateway Heritage* 11 (Summer, 1990): 38–51.

28. *Army Nurses Memorial* by sculptor Bela Lyon Pratt, 1911, dedicated in 1914. "Inventory," SIRIS.

29. Savage, *Standing Soldiers.*

30. Ibid., 87. See also "Negro Shrines," *Ebony* 10 (July 1966): 42–45; "Monu-

ments and Landmarks," *Ebony* 18 (1963): 109. For Harriet Beecher Stowe's identification of two other statues with Sojourner Truth, see Savage, 15, 59. On the development of Sojourner Truth as an iconic figure and later efforts to create monuments in her honor see note 74.

31. Charlotte Streifer Rubinstein, *American Women Sculptors: A History of Women Working in Three Dimensions* (Boston: G. K. Hall, 1990), xiii–xiv, 104.

32. Ibid.,104. Kitson also sculpted *The Hiker* a much-reproduced Spanish-American War memorial. See Kaufman, 25–26.

33. Sherr and Kazickas, 207, 276. The statue shows Dustin carrying an axe and holding Indian scalps. For comments on this image in relation to stereotypes about Indian violence, see Diane E. Foulds, "Historians suggest Indians were as much Victims as Perpetrators," *Boston Globe,* December 31, 2000. Historian Laurel Thatcher Ulrich notes that in 1698 Hannah Dustin was "the most famous woman in New England." Laurel Thatcher Ulrich, *Good Wives: Image and Reality in the Lives of Women in Northern New England, 1650–1750* (New York: Oxford University Press, 1983), 167–172.

34. Marion Tinling, *Women Remembered* (New York: Greenwood Press, 1986), 78; Edward J. Cocke, *Monumental New Orleans* (New Orleans, LA: La Fayette, 1968), 7.

35. See Brooklyn Museum, *American Renaissance, 1876–1917* (Brooklyn, 1979) and Michele H. Bogart, *Public Sculpture and the Civic Ideal in New York City 1890–1930* (Chicago: University of Chicago Press, 1989).

36. The women also gained the support of the mayor of New York, John Hylan, who was able to use the controversy for his own purposes. Bogart, 259–270.

37. "Lewanee County Michigan Monument #11/ Dedicated to Laura Smith Haviland," a lengthy engraving describes her life. <http://members.aol.com/ Coslund/LewaneeMI> (08/02/00).

38. Sherr and Kazickas, 85.

39. Women in the Hall of Fame in the Bronx are Mary Lyons (elected 1905); bust installed 1927; Maria Mitchell (1905); Emma Willard (1905) 1927; Harriet Beecher Stowe (1910) 1925; Frances Willard (1910) 1923 (bust by Loredo Taft); Charlotte Cushman (1915) 1925; Alice Freeman Palmer (1924) 1924; Susan B. Anthony (1950) 1952; Jane Addams (1965) 1968; and Lillian Wald (1970) 1971.

    For a list of all those in the hall and a discussion of its history see Elena Kemelman, "The Honorees and Sculptors of the Hall of Fame for great Americans" and "Notes on a Neglected American Renaissance Monument," *Part: The Journal of the CUNY PhD Program in Art History,* 6 (2000); <http:// dsc.gc.cuny.edu/part/ practice/ememel-list.html>.

40. Kimberly Swanson, "Eva Emery Dye and the Romance of Oregon History," *Pacific History* 29 (Autumn 1998): 59–68.

41. Sherr and Kaziackas, 379. The statue, by sculptor Alice Cooper Hubbard, is in Washington Park in Portland, Oregon.

42. Donna J. Kessler, *The Making of Sakagawea: A Euro-American Legend* (Tuscaloosa: University of Alabama Press, 1996), 90–95. Kessler argues that the Progressive Era commemoration of Sakajawea (alternative spelling of Sacajawea) was linked more to celebration of "Manifest Destiny" than to feminist or suffragist interests. She also cites Dye's description of Sakajawea as "the Madonna of her race."

43. Sherr and Kaziackas, 381.

44. Tinling, 371.

45. Ann Uhry Abrams, *The Pilgrims and Pocahontas: Rival Myths Of American Origin* (Boulder, CO: Westview Press, 1999), 261–285.

46. Abrams, 270.

47. Sherr and Kaziackas, 461.

48. Abrams, 270.

49. Walter Muir Whitehill and Katharine Knowles, *Boston Statues* (Barre, MA: Barre Publishers, 1970), 97.

50. Rubinstein, 137–38.

51. The statue provoked controversy again in the 1990s when feminists campaigned to have it brought out of the basement. Critics attacked the statue for omitting the contributions of African American women to the suffrage movement. The statue was also questioned on aesthetic terms and has been referred to as "three ladies in a bathtub"—a kind of insult not likely to be directed at statues, however aesthetically questionable, of the Founding Fathers. Sherr and Kaziackas, 84.

52. Goode, 102. The sculptor was Jerome Connor.

53. Rubinstein, 259. For a discussion of the Federal Arts Program and women sculptors see Rubinstein, 260–312.

54. Barbara Melosh, *Engendering Culture: Manhood and Womanhood in New Deal Public Art and Theater* (Washington, DC: Smithsonian Institution Press, 1991), 203–210.

55. "Inventory," SIRIS. For public sculpture in Los Angeles, see <http://www. usc.edu/isd/archives/la/pubart/sculptures/>. A painting of Jane Addams by Mitchell Siporin was part of the Illinois Arts Project in 1936. Fine Arts Collection, Public Buildings Service, General Services Administration, National Archives and Records Administration.

56. *Emma Willard Memorial,* T. A. Campbell, sculptor, 1941. "Inventory," SIRIS; Sherr and Kaziackas, 452–54. The memorial was part of Vermont's sesquicentennial celebration. Such events have provided important occasions for defining or redefining history, and for efforts to include women in local commemoration.

57. Tinling, 184; Mary Tutweiler, "Voices of St. Martinsville: Stories under the Oaks," *Times-Picayune,* November 9, 1997, sec. D, p1.

58. Sculptural representations of theatrical representations of women occur elsewhere. Outside a library in Weatherford, Texas, is a statue erected in 1976 of

actress Mary Martin in her role as Peter Pan. Carol Morris Little, *A Comprehensive Guide to Outdoor Sculpture in Texas* (Austin: University of Texas Press), 449. Like the statue *Alice in Wonderland* in New York's Central Park—perhaps the most popular female figure in public art—these statues suggest an alternative to the monumental and staple heroic model of historic presentation. They also remind us that nothing in stone is real (except the stone). The statue erected in Minneapolis of Mary Richards/ Mary Tyler Moore from the television show also fits in this category.

59. See <http://parkscanada>, "Grand Pres National Historic Site."

60. Edward J. Cocke, *Monumental New Orleans* (New Orleans: La Fayette, 1968), 34–35. Both Mother Cabrini statues are listed in "Inventory," SIRIS.

61. Sherr and Kaziackes, 85, 476–77, 479; "Inventory," SIRIS for individual statues.

62. Harry Eiss, "Our Lady of the Rockies," *Journal of Popular Culture* 30 (Spring, 1997): 33–50. For an interesting feminist view of the statue see Evelyn Boswell, "The Tie that Binds: Our Lady and the Berkeley Pit," *Montana State University Communication Services*, 2/24/01, <http://www.montana.edu/wwwpb/univ/ourlady.html>.

63. Sherr and Kaziackas, 355. There are many web sites devoted to military women and their experiences in recent wars. There seem to be no statues of individual women from World War II.

64. Glenna Goodacre also created statues of individual notable women including Barbara Jordan and designed the image of Sacajawea on the U.S. silver dollar.

65. The memorial building, whose grounds include grass, glass walls and fountains, also includes a theater and gallery. The use of new technology—the Internet—allows the incorporation on computers of the names, biographies and photographs of the servicewomen registered with the monument. In addition, a "Hall of Honor" recognized women of particular distinction. The memorial thus combines the general and specific in commemorating women in the military.

For a different approach, see the 1925 monument in Pennsylvania dedicated to "the services and sacrifices of the women of Harrisburg in the World War." The bronze bas-relief (43 inches by 50 inches) on stone in Riverfront Park shows seven women in different roles supporting the war. One is portrayed in a military uniform—pants, belted jacket and cap. Another is shown in a nurse's uniform. Others are shown engaged in civilian efforts—farming, knitting, and another perhaps at work in a war-related occupation. *Sacrifices of Women Warriors,* ca. 1925. J. C. Handy, sculptor, "Inventory," SIRIS.

66. See <http://www.wimsa.org>. For the ways in which speeches at dedications can make a monument more specific in terms of individual women, see President Bill Clinton, "Remarks at a Groundbreaking Ceremony for the *Women in the Military Service Memorial,* June 22, 1995," *Weekly Compilation of Presidential Documents,* vol. 35 (June 26, 1995), 1096.

67. "Inventory," SIRIS.

68. "Inventory", SIRIS; Sherr and Kaziackas, 169–170; "The Women Marine Webring: Molly Marine Page," <http://geocities.com/wmarinering>. In *Monumental New Orleans,* Cocke notes the dedication of "Molly Marine" on November 10, 1940. He also describes a monument near "Molly" dedicated in 1962 to all women who had served in the U.S. armed forces. It was the result of efforts of the New Orleans Chapter of the WAC Veteran's Association. Cocke, 23.

69. See <www.nps.gov/wori/visitors.html>, Kaufman, 222–224. The Women's Rights National Park's visitor center features sculptor Lloyd Lillie's statues of nineteen of the women and men who attended the Seneca Falls Convention.

70. Mary LeClair, "Part of the celebration," *Pultney St. Survey* (Fall 1998), Hobart and William Smith Colleges, <http:// www.Hws.NEW/pss/feature_998–4. html>. Ted Aube, the sculptor of both *When Anthony Met Stanton* and *Elizabeth Blackwell* is a faculty member at Hobart and William Smith. For individual statues see "Inventory," SIRIS.

71. Lisa Singhania, "Battle Creek Honors Sojourner Truth," *Detroit News,* September 26, 1999.

72. Nancy Vendrely, "Lasting Legacies mark Celebrate 2,000 Event," Fort Wayne *Journal-Gazette,* October 14, 2000.

73. See <www.aoc.gov/art/suffrage.html>; Janice K. Bryant, "Unfinished Business," *On The Issues* 6 (Fall 1997), web page 11–7-97, OTL Online: <http:// www.echonyc.com/~onissues/f97bry>.

74. See historian Nell Painter's discussion of the changing historical portrayal of Sojourner Truth in *Sojourner Truth: A Life, A Symbol* (New York: W.W. Norton, 1997).

75. Barbara Crow, "The Humanity of Heroes," *Alberta Views Magazine* (Fall 1999): on-line.

76. Maria Bohuslawsky, " 'Famous Five' Sculpture Design Chosen," *Ottawa Citizen,* October 17, 1997.

77. Crow, "The Humanity of Heroes"; Joe Woodard, "But She Was a Feminist Racist," *Western Report, Alberta Report* 25, May 18, 1998, 38.

78. For a bas relief of comedian and actress Gracie Allen see *George Burns and Gracie Allen* (1991) at the Academy of Television Arts and Sciences, see "Inventory," SIRIS. For public sculpture in Los Angeles see <http://www.usc. edu/isd/archives/la/pubart/sculptures/>. See also Celia Alvarez Munoz, *If Walls Could Speak* (Arlington, Texas: Enlightenment Press, 1991) on Los Angeles.

79. *Empire State Carousel,* Islip, New York, sculptors Gerry Holzman, Jim Beatty, Bruno Speiser. "Inventory," SIRIS.

80. Barbara Brotman, "Must memorials to heroic females hit rock bottom?" *Chicago Tribune,* November 20, 1994, sec. 6, p. 1; Betty DeRamus, "Here's the right idea: Oversize statue of a bigger than life woman," *Detroit News,* Sep-

tember 16, 1999: sec. C, col.1, 1. See also Patricia Mooney-Melvin's work on representation of women's history in Chicago.

81. "Inventory," SIRIS, *Ella Grasso*, Hartford, Connecticut-State House, 1987, sculptor Frank Chalfont Gaylord ll; *Millicent Fenwick*, Bernardsville, NJ, 1995, sculptor Dana Toomy; *Kate Smith*, Philadelphia, dedicated 8 October 1987, sculptor Marc Mellon.

82. The Barbara Jordan and Katharine Anne Porter statues are by Glenna Goodacre, the sculptor of the *Vietnam Women's Memorial*. Carol Morris Little, *A Comprehensive Guide to Outdoor Sculpture in Texas* (Austin: University of Texas Press, 1996), 403–408.

83. Little, *Outdoor Sculpture in Texas,* 372.

84. Alan Lessoff, "Public Sculpture in Corpus Christi: A Tangled Struggle to Define the Character and Shape the Agenda of One Texas City," *Urban History* 26 (January 2000): 218.

85. Among other statues of Joan of Arc are those in Philadelphia, by sculptor Emmanuel Fremiet, in 1890 and in Washington, D.C. by sculptor Paul DuBois in 1922. For discussion of Anna Hyatt Huntington's work on the New York Joan of Arc statue see Rubinstein, 164–65. For the Philadelphia statue see Fairmount Park Association, *Philadelphia's Treasures in Bronze and Stone* (New York: Walker, 1974), 82–82. For D.C. see Goode, 418. The Washington statue was specifically given as a gift from the women of France to the women of the United States.

86. David Dunlap "For New York Parks, First Statues of Famous American Women," *New York Times,* July 16, 1992: sec. B, col. 3, 3; Douglas Martin, "One First Lady Salutes Another at Statue's Unveiling," *New York Times,* October 6, 1996.

87. "Statues, With Limitations," editorial, *New York Times,* May 23, 1993. The statue of Moore with her two brothers is in a way a more accurate representation of her and many other young Irish women's, and children's, experience. See <www.cobheritage.com/emigration.html> and <www.americanparknetwork. com/parkinfo/si/history/annie.html>. The National Park Service site has little on Annie Moore but provides information on the history of immigration and on the museum. See <www.nps.gov/stli/serv02.htm>.

88. For outdoor sculpture in Boston and neighboring areas see Marty Carlock, *A Guide to Public Art in Greater Boston* (Boston: Harvard Common Press, 1993). More statues of women have been dedicated since this book was published. On the *Irish Famine Memorial,* see Michael P. Quinlin, "In Honor of our Ancestors," *Boston Globe,* March 16, 1999. The portrayal of women in that sculpture is worth consideration too.

89. Eileen McNamera, "Finally. A Wall of their Own," *Boston Globe,* October, 20, 1999; Nick Capasso, "New Women's Memorials in Boston," *Sculpture* (June 2000): 46–51.

90. "Bringing the Women's Memorial Alive in the Classroom," *Proclaim Her: Newsletter of the Boston Women's Heritage Trail* (Winter 2001): 1.

91. "Tubman Statue Unveiled," *Boston Globe,* June 21, 1999; "Commemorative Program for the Unveiling of *Emancipation* by Meta Vaux Warrick Fuller and *Step On Board* by Fern Cunningham," June 20, 1999.
92. Rubinstein, *American Women Sculptors,* 202; "Commemorative program . . . ".
93. This was unveiled at a ceremony in May 2001. Stacy Milbouer, "Statue, Park to honor Franco Americans," *Boston Globe,* January 14, 2001; Marilyn Solomon, "Three Centuries of Nashua's Families," *Nashua (NH) Telegraph,* July 28, 2001.
94. "Women Added to Finalists for Abolitionist's Statue," *New York Times,* February 20, 2000. Thomas Jay Warren has been selected to be the sculptor. As of this writing, the committee expects the statue to be completed in 2002.
95. Goode, 87–88.
96. "Bringing The Women's Memorial Alive in the Classroom," *Proclaim Her: Newsletter of the Boston Women's Heritage Trail;* Susan Hill Gross and Mary Rojas, *But Women Had No History: Images of Women in the Public History of Washington, D.C.* (St. Louis Park, MN: Greenhurst Publications, 1987).

SUGGESTED READINGS

Michele Bogart, *Public Sculpture and the Civil Ideal in New York City 1890–1930.* Chicago: University of Chicago Press, 1989. Few of the statues in New York in this period were of women. Bogart, however, does discuss the controversy over the portrayal of symbolic female figures. Her work also presents an analysis of the meaning of civic art and its role in defining history.

Jacci Duncan and Lynn Page Whittaker, *The Women's History Guide to Washington.* Alexandria, Virginia: Charles River Press, 1998. In addition to providing information on statues and monuments relating to women, this guide offers a women-centered view of national museums and outdoor historic sites.

Carol Morris Little, *A Comprehensive Guide to Outdoor Scuplture in Texas.* Austin: University of Texas Press, 1996. Organized by area and well illustrated, this survey joins others such as those for New Jersey and Wisconsin that were encouraged by the national Save Outdoor Sculpture Project.

Barbara Melosh, *Engendering Culture: Manhood and Womanhood in New Deal Public Art and Theater.* Washington, D.C.: Smithsonian Press, 1991. Melosh examines the ways in which ideology about gender shaped 1930s art, including sculpture, funded by the New Deal.

Charlotte Streifer Rubinstein, *American Women Sculptors.* Boston: G. K. Hall, 1990. The author provides useful information about sculptors, many of whom had female subjects, and gives a feminist analysis of the relationship between women's political consciousness and the work of women sculptors.

STATUES OF WOMEN IN THE UNITED STATES

Alabama: Mary Cahalan (Birmingham, sculptor Giuseppe Morretti, 1908); Emma Sansom (Gadsden, sculptor unknown, 1906)

Alaska: Mollie Walsh (Skagway, sculptor unknown, 1930)

Arkansas: Belle Starr (Fort Smith, wall sculpture titled *Ft. Smith: The Early Years,* sculptor Ralph Irwin, 1983); Martha Mitchell (Pine Bluff, sculptor Lawrence Ludtke, 1981)

California: Amelia Earhart (North Hollywood, sculptor Ernest Shelton, 1971); Joan of Arc (Title: *Jeanne d'Arc,* Los Angeles, unknown sculptor, date unknown); Mother Elizabeth Seton (San Diego, University of San Diego, sculptor James Hubbell, 1973); Florence Nightingale (San Francisco, sculptor David Edstrom, 1937/1939); Florence Nightingale (Los Angeles, sculptor David Edstrom, 1937); Kate Sessions (San Diego, sculptor Ruth Hayward, 1998)

Colorado: Florence Sabin (Denver, sculptor Joy Buba, 1960); Hazie Werner (Title: *Hazie Werner-Grand Lady of the Valley,* Steamboat Springs, sculptor Jack Finney, 1994); Dr. Justina Ford (Denver, sculptor Jess E. DuBois, 1998)

Connecticut: Ella Grasso (Hartford, sculptor Frank Chalfont Gaylord II, 1987); Alice Cogswell (Hartford, sculptor Frances Laughlin Wadsworth, 1983)

District of Columbia: Indoors in Capitol Statuary Hall: Frances Willard, (Illinois, sculptor Helen Farnsworth Mears, 1905); Maria L. Sanford (Minnesota-sculptor Leone Evelyn Raymond, 1958); Florence Sabin (Colorado-sculptor Joy Buba, 1959); Esther Morris (Wyoming-sculptor Avard Fairbanks, 1958); Mother Joseph (Washington-sculptor Felix W. de Weldon, 1980); Jeannette Rankin (Montana-sculptor Terry Minmaugh, 1985); Elizabeth Cady Stanton, Lucretia Mott, and Susan B.Anthony (sculptor Adelaide Johnson, 1920)

Outdoors: Mary McLeod Bethune (sculptor Robert Berks, 1974); Joan of Arc (sculptor Paul Du Bois, 1922); Alice Cogswell (part of Thomas Hopkins Gallaudet statue at Gallaudet University, sculptor Daniel Chester French, 1889); Olive Riseley Seward (sculptor John Cavenaugh, 1971); Eleanor Roosevelt (at FDR Memorial, sculptor Neil Estern, 1997); Jane Delano (American Red Cross Headquarters, sculptor Robert Tait McKenzie, 1933)

Florida: Kimberly Bergalis (Title: *Kimberly,* Fort Pierce, sculptor Florence P. Hansen, 1992)

Georgia: Harriet Tubman (Brenau College, sculptor Jane DeDecker, 1997)

Hawaii: Queen Liliuokalani (Title: *The Spirit of Lili'uokalani,* Honolulu, sculptor Marianna Pineda, 1982)

Idaho: Marie Darian (Parma, sculptors Art Yoder and Paul Yeadon, 1976); Sacajawea (Lewiston, sculptor J. Shirley Bothum, 1990)

Illinois: Mary Ann Bickerdyke (Galesburg, sculptor Theo Kitson, 1906). Joan of Arc (Chicago, sculptor unknown, date unknown); Annie Louise Keller (White Hall, sculptor Lorado Taft, 1927)

Indiana: Mary Dyer (Richmond, Earlham College, sculptor Sylvia Shaw Judson, 1962); Agnes, Alice and Edith Hamilton (Ft. Wayne, sculptor Anthony Frudakis, 2000); Mishawaka (Mishawaka, sculptor Sufi Ahmad, 1987)

Iowa: Pocahontas (City of Pocahontas, designer W. C. Ballard, 1956)

Kansas: Amelia Earhart (Atchison, sculptor David Jones, 1980–81); Elizabeth Polly (Hayes, sculptor Pete Felton, 1982); Joan of Arc (Wichita, sculptor unknown, stone, 1970, bronze cast 1996)

Kentucky: Capt. Mary Greene (Covington, sculptor Michael Price, 1988)

Louisiana: Margaret Haughery (New Orleans, sculptor Alexander Daigle, 1884); Joan of Arc (New Orleans, cast made from original by sculptor Emmanuel Fremiet, 1964); Emmeline Labiche, *Evangeline*/Dolores Del Rio (Martinsville, sculptor Marcel Rebecchini, 1931); Sophie B.Wright (New Orleans, sculptor Enrique Alferez, 1988); Mother Cabrini (New Orleans, sculptor unknown, 1949); Eunice Pharr Dusan (Eunice, sculptor Jerry Gorum, 1994)

Maine: Samantha Smith (Augusta, sculptor Glen Hines, 1986); Joan Benoit Samuelson (Cape Elizabeth Public Library, sculptor Edward Materson, 1986); Edna St. Vincent Millay (Camden, sculptor Robert G. Willis, 1989); St. Marguerite D'Youville (Lewiston, one, sculptor unknown, date unknown; another, sculptor Carol Hanson, 1999).

Maryland: Queen Anne (Centreville, sculptor Elizabeth Gordon Chandler, 1977)

Massachusetts: Annie Sullivan and Helen Keller (Agawam, sculptor unknown, 1992); Keller and Sullivan (Title: *Water,* Tewksbury, sculptor Mico Kaufman, 1985); Mary Dyer (Boston, sculptor Sylvia Shaw Johnson, 1959); Anne Hutchinson (Boston State House, sculptor Cyrus E. Dallin, 1922); Katherine Lee Bates (Falmouth, sculptor Lloyd Lillie, 1986–88); Harriet Tubman (Boston, sculptor Fern Cunningham, 1999); pending: Abigail Adams, Phillis Wheatley, Lucy Stone (Boston, sculptor Meredith Bergmann); Hannah Dustin (Haverhill, sculptor Calvin H. Weeks,

1879); Mary Baker Eddy (Brookline, sculptor Cyrus E. Dallin, cast 1922, installed 1966); St. Cecilia and Mary (outside St. Cecelia Roman Catholic church in Boston, sculptor unknown, date unknown); Joan of Arc (Gloucester, Anna Hyatt Huntington, 1910); Deborah Sampson Gannett (Sharon, sculptor Lu Stubbs, 1989); Abigail Adams (Quincy, Lloyd Lillie sculptor, 1997); Sojourner Truth (Northampton/Florence, sculptor Thomas Jay Warren, 2002)

Michigan: Laura Haviland (Adrian, designer H. Barnicot, 1909); Sojourner Truth (Battle Creek, sculptor Tina Allen, 1999); Anna Howard Shaw (Big Rapids, sculptor Lloyd Radell, designer, Renee Redell, 1988)

Minnesota: Edith Graham Mayo (Rochester, sculptor Mayo Kooiman, 1953); Wenonoah (Winonah, sculptor Isabel Moore Kimball, 1902); Mary Tyler Moore/Mary Richards (Minneapolis, sculptor Gwendolyn Gillen, 2002)

Montana: Sacagewea (Fort Benton, with Lewis and Clark, sculptor Robert MacFie Scriver, 1976); Sacajawea (Bozeman, sculptor Pat Mathiesen, 1995)

New Hampshire: Hannah Dustin (Boscawen, sculptor William Andrews, 1874), St. Marguerite D'Youville (Manchester, St. Peter's Home, sculptor Bernardi et Nieri, 1984)

New Jersey: Millicent Fenwick (Bernardsville, sculptor Dana Toomy, 1995); Mother Cabrini (Newark, sculptor Francesco Miozzo, 1958)

New York: Sybil Ludington (Carmel, sculptor Anna Hyatt Huntington, 1961); Mary Jemison (Castile/Letchworth State Park, sculptor Henry Kirke Brown, 1910); Gertrude Stein (NYC, sculptor Jo Davidson, 1992); Ella Fitzgerald (Yonkers, sculptor Vinnie Bagwell, 1996); Eleanor Roosevelt (NYC, sculptor Penelope Jencks, 1996); Joan of Arc (NYC, sculptor Anna Hyatt Huntington, 1915); Emma Willard (Troy, a relief by sculptor T. A. Campbell, 1941); Elizabeth Cady Stanton, Amelia Bloomer and Susan B. Anthony (Title: *When Anthony Met Stanton,* sculptor Ted Aube, Seneca Falls 1999); Elizabeth Blackwell (William Smith College, Geneva, sculptor Ted Aube, 1994); Annie Moore (Ellis Island, sculptor Jeanne Rynhart, 1993)

North Carolina: Virginia Dare (Elizabethan Gardens, Manteo, sculptor Louisa Lander, 1859); Queen Charlotte (Charlotte Airport, sculptor Raymond Kaskey, 1990)

North Dakota: Sacajawea, also Sakakawea (Bismarck, sculptor Leonard Crunelle, 1910)

Ohio: Sharon Lane (Canton, sculptor John M. Worthington, 1973); Betty Zane (Martin's Ferry, sculptor unknown, erected 1903, dedicated 1928), Annie Oakley

(Greenville, sculptor Terry Mimnaugh, 1988); Helen Keller (Cleveland, sculptor Allan Scher, 1965)

Oregon: Sacajewea (Portland, sculptor Alice Cooper, 1905)

Pennsylvania: Mary Dyer (Philadelphia, sculptor Sylvia Shaw Judson, cast 1959–60, installed 1975); Joan of Arc (Philadelphia, sculptor Emmanuel Fremiet, 1890); Kate Smith (Philadelphia, sculptor Marc Mellon, 1986); Amelia Earhart (Greenville, Thiel College, 1938); Mother Elizabeth Ann Seton (Greensburg, Seton Hill College, sculptor unknown, 1959)

Texas: Joanna Troutman (Texas State Cemetery, Austin, sculptor unknown, ca.1915); Margaret Harper (portrait bust, Canyon, sculptor Jack Hill, 1981); Barbara Jordan (Austin-Bergstrom International Airport, sculptor Bruce Wolfe, 2002); Barbara Jordan, (San Antonio, sculptor Glenna Goodacre, 1988); Selena (Corpus Christi, sculptor Buddy Tatum, 1997); Elizabeth Crockett (Acton, sculptor unknown, 1913); Angelina (Lufkin, sculptor Jim Knox, 1986); Mary Martin as Peter Pan (Weatherford, sculptor Ronald Thomason, 1976); Mildred "Babe" Didrikson Zaharias, (San Antonio, sculptor Lawrence Ludke,1988); Katharine Anne Porter, (San Antonio, sculptor Glenna Goodacre, 1988).

Vermont: Emma Willard (relief on marble) (Middlebury, sculptor T. A. Campbell, designer Piere Zwick, 1941)

Virginia: Jane Delano (Arlington National Cemetery, sculptor Francis Rich, 1938); Pocahontas (Jamestown, sculptor William Ordway Partridge, 1922); Pocahontas (Gloucester, sculptor Adolph Sehring, 1994)

Washington: Mother Joseph (Vancouver, sculptors Felix de Weldon and George Weihs, 1987), Mother Joseph (Title: *The Call and the Challenge,* Spokane, sculptors Ken Spiering and Howard Belazs, 1986); Ilchee (Vancouver, sculptor Eric Jensen, 1995)

Wisconsin: *Virgen de Guadalupe* (Milwaukee, sculptor Alejandro Romero, 2000)

Wyoming: Esther Morris (Cheyenne, sculptor Avard Fairbanks, 1958, installed 1963); Sacajawea (Cody, sculptor Harry Andrew Jackson, 1980); Sacajawea (Central Wyoming College, Riverton, sculptor Harry Andrew Jackson, 1981)

Chapter 3

SPIDER WOMAN'S GRAND DESIGN: MAKING NATIVE AMERICAN WOMEN VISIBLE IN TWO SOUTHWESTERN HISTORY SITES

Tara Travis

Navajo trading posts are small, single-story, rectangular buildings made of stone or wood. Inside they are dark, cramped spaces—the smooth and notched counters hug you, the paraphernalia of ranching life crowds shelves filled with cans and jars, and the wood stove and cold pop machine vie for the rest of the space. But when visitors follow the trader to the back, suddenly they are confronted with color, pattern, and beauty. They have entered the rug room. Their eyes are filled with a kind of controlled splendor. Like voices over voices, the colors and designs of the Navajo weavings are at the same moment individual and collective. Stretching back over time, masterpieces of Navajo weaving reflect generations of mothers, daughters, and grandmothers who are descendants of Spider Woman's grand design.

The American Southwest is a beautiful and complex landscape shaped through time by the cultural practices of Native American women and richly reflected in their artistic visions. Growing up on the Colorado Plateau and traveling to the Navajo reservation and Hopi mesas impressed upon me the central place of women in Native American life. How different some of those experiences are when compared to the static dioramas and displays of the "prehistoric past" in park museums at that time—where tucked to one side of a plaza sat a woman grinding corn. Yet it was corn, the Corn Mother and the giver of life, that made possible the large communities of the past. Not only did women contribute to the vital nourishment of the people, they also participated in the maintenance of fields, the collection and administration of healing plants, the construction and arrangement of buildings, and the manufacture of an enormous material culture that included pottery, basketry, and cloth weaving.

Today an array of new voices, methods, materials, and gender-related questions have reawakened an appreciation of woman/the mother/the grandmother in Native American life. In 1986 Paula Gunn Allen defined her Be-ing as the Sacred

Figure 3-1. A Navajo woman wearing traditional clothing looks after her daughter in the 1950s. (*Courtesy of the National Park Service. Photo by David de Harport.*)

Hoop. "She is the Old Woman Spider who weaves us together in a fabric of interconnection."[1] If our task is to find ways to make Native American women visible in Southwestern history sites, then perhaps we should begin by entering the sacred hoop. Remind ourselves that she is always there and we have simply to stand up and acknowledge her presence. Once inside, so many trails open before us—innovation in the arts, biography, oral tradition, and intergenerational knowledge. However, the method of this chapter will be landscape analysis as a way of discovering the influence of Native American women on a broad scale. What was the role of Native American women in the formation of the Southwestern landscape? What clues exist in the landscape to illuminate her presence? How do we chart that influence over hundreds of years? What means did Native American women use to create, maintain, and alter their physical space? What other materials can we consult to add context to our observations?

Although this chapter will explore the role of Native American women in the formation and maintenance of a complex Southwestern landscape over hundreds of years, it will be necessary to narrow our examination, given the vast number of Native American communities inhabiting the Southwest and the immense time frame in question.[2] The focus will be on Navajo women and two National Park Service (NPS) units located in Arizona in the center of the Navajo Nation— Canyon de Chelly National Monument and Hubbell Trading Post National Historic Site. Navajo women in these two sites are critical to creating and maintaining a sense of continuity in space despite significant alterations to the physical landscape over time. The phrase "continuity in space" is defined as the creation and maintenance of the core settlement area or "homestead" comprised of hogan, ramada, corrals, and fields.

Both Canyon de Chelly National Monument and Hubbell Trading Post National Historic Site interpret Navajo culture and history. Although they are not generally considered women's history sites, they are linked, in fact, through Native American Women's history. Canyon de Chelly National Monument, established in 1931 with the prior approval by the Navajo Tribal Council, was set aside for the preservation of the prehistoric ruins nestled within the magnificent red-walled canyon. Explicit in the legislation, however, was the mandate that the National Park Service would not impair the right, title, and interest of the Navajo tribe. This decision, which broke from the nineteenth-century precedent of removing Native Americans from park areas, resulted in a vital partnership that continues today.[3] There was never any question that Canyon de Chelly was and would remain a Native American homeland. As early as 1933 the "life and culture of the Navajo" was considered one of the four interpretive themes.[4]

Hubbell Trading Post National Historic Site entered the Park Service in 1965 with the creative distinction of a "living trading post" and *not* a historical museum. John Lorenzo Hubbell started trading in Ganado in 1876 and the family business has survived as the oldest continually functioning trading post on the reservation. While Canyon de Chelly and Hubbell Trading Post are very different expressions of the Native American past, they both share in interpreting contemporary Navajo life. Both these parks are exceptional in terms of the broader National Park System for exhibiting an initial awareness (although incomplete) of the Navajo communities residing within or adjacent to the park's physical boundaries and the necessity for interpreting contemporary Native American life.

In many ways the task of making Native American women visible in these two places is an easy one because these sites are sister parks linked through the roles, responsibilities, and artistic vigor of Native American women. As visitors adjust their eyes to the dim light of the Hubbell rug room, they take in the vibrant, pulsating life of the neatly stacked Navajo rugs. The fragrant odor, the brilliant colors, and the artistic magnitude hail the visibility and centrality of Navajo women's experience. From that room we might visualize a piece of colored thread winding its way some thirty miles north through Beautiful Valley to Canyon de Chelly. There the canyon landscape reveals the beginning of one of the rugs: the grassy bottom lands where sheep herds graze tended by women, the shearing and carding pens under a cottonwood tree, the riparian glens where plants are collected to make dye, and the half finished loom tied to the bough of a pinon tree. If Hubbell Trading Post represents the product of Navajo women's talent and creativity, then Canyon de Chelly represents the process—the idealized landscape where core values are instilled that will bring forth the patience and skill necessary to produce the woven rug.

However, this idealized landscape has been threatened and altered during the last several hundred years. And yet looking from the rim into the canyon, the extent of Navajo history and cultural continuity is astounding. To what or whom do we owe this continuity? Why do Navajos continue to consider this place sacred? What spaces are women's spaces? And in turn how did their activities, decisions, and values help create the landscape we see today? First let us consider the place of Navajo women within Navajo society and identify those spaces that are traditionally associated with Navajo women.

Anthropologists have long considered Navajo women as holding a place of power in Navajo society. Part of that analysis is based on the organization of traditional society that is described as matrilineal (meaning the family line is traced on the mother's side) and matrilocal (meaning that after marriage the man goes to live with the wife's family). In matters of kinship, clans provide the foundation of association and proper conduct throughout one's life. At birth and when introducing oneself, Navajos are born "into" their mother's clan and "born for" their father's clan.[5] Yet within this formal introduction are also clues to the gender parity that exists in the symbolic structure of Navajo religion and in the formalized behavior of everyday life.

In addition to kinship, reciprocity is a prominent aspect of the Navajo social structure; indeed, kinship and reciprocity are core Navajo values.[6] Mary Shepardson in her analysis of the gender status of Navajo women writes, "sharing," not "dominating," is the theme of daily life, and men's roles are also valued.[7] Gary Witherspoon identified the ideal sharing relationship as that between a mother and child. Reciprocity begins with the mother and child and from there moves out into the broader domain of human interactions. It is the example that one is to follow through life. Navajo educator and community leader Ruth Roessel defines the role of Navajo women this way:

> If Navajo women were anything in traditional society they were independent and hard working. They were not abrasively independent in the sense of "I'm the best and I'm the most important," but rather in the sense of quiet confidence in their own ability, along with a belief in the help and presence of the Holy People—two factors, which when combined, could care for the needs not only of themselves and their families but also of their clans and communities.[8]

The status and centrality of Navajo women is also expressed symbolically in the landscape with the basic configuration of homesteads. For much of Navajo history, families organized themselves around a head mother. This arrangement of hogans (traditional Navajo dwellings) and traditional use areas comprised the basic residence group or homestead, sometimes called a compound or simply, "camp." Historically, individual households moved around in order to utilize seasonal pasturage. Generally, Navajo families moved at least twice a year to summer and winter pastures. At Canyon de Chelly families moved herds of sheep and cattle into the canyon during the summer months and up to the rims during the winter. These types of actions resulted in considerable fluidity in the number and duration of certain homestead configurations, but at the center of these movements was the head mother and her extended kin.

Witherspoon emphasizes the significance of the homestead by calling it, "the fundamental unit of Navajo social organization." "The homestead," he explains, "is organized around a head mother, a sheep herd, a customary land-use area, and sometimes agricultural fields, all of which are called mother." Witherspoon calls the homestead, "both a social and an economic unit, structured, and integrated by the symbols of motherhood."[9]

If the homestead space represents "motherhood" then it is by its very nature a woman's space, and it is the hogan that forms the symbolic center of that space. The Navajo meaning of hogan is home place, a dwelling of one room that may take many shapes from circular, to polygonal to conical.[10] In the past hogans were

Figure 3-2. A young Navajo woman herds her sheep with her two dogs in Canyon del Muerto at Canyon de Chelly National Monument in the 1960s. (*Courtesy of the National Park Service. Photo by Fred Mang, Jr.*)

constructed of forked sticks and mud; today they are most often made of corbeled logs although newer materials are also employed, including prefabricated kits. The hogan serves both domestic and ceremonial purposes and is a sacred dwelling. It is the only place where the space is divided into sex-specific activity areas. Generally, the head male uses the southeastern portion and the women and children use the northern half of the hogan. Meals are consumed in the southwest. Susan Kent explains that the division of space within a hogan is "not a result of the Navajos' division of labor or sex roles, but of the hogan's symbolism of the cosmos, which is similarly divided."[11] Outside the hogan, spaces and tools are used equally by men and women and there is a marked lack of sex-specific areas. But in terms of who is responsible for the space and how it is maintained, hogans represent women's spaces.

There are several sources that support the central role of women in the maintenance of the hogan and overall homestead space. One recent source is the newly published autobiography of Tall Woman, also known as Rose Mitchell (c. 1874–1977), whose life history was carefully recorded with the editorial assistance of Charlotte Frisbie. Her homestead was located in the Chinle area just west of Canyon de Chelly. She described in some detail the marriage advice of her parents. She remembered her mother saying, "You should just stay home and take good care of your children, your home, and your sheep." Mitchell continued, "She said over and over my job was to stay home and take care of all the things there—the children, the sheep, the home, and the fields."[12] From these words it is clear that the homestead—including the family, hogan, sheep, and fields—was the specific responsibility of Mitchell as wife and future mother. A mother's role and a mother's space brought esteem and power to Navajo women within the broader context of the overall society. For example, flocks of sheep represented wealth and property and were passed down from mother to daughter. Sheep were also eminently practical, providing wool for the weaver and food for the family. The gardens and fields provided families with their other primary food source up to the industrial era. And once again, we must consider the significance of the hogan as both the primary dwelling in the winter months and as a ceremonial space.

Having identified the homestead as a woman's space through her various roles and responsibilities, and having considered the significance of the place as a symbol for "motherhood," let us trace the evolution of this space through time at Canyon de Chelly. By doing so we can ascertain how women's decisions, activities, and values impacted the landscape. How did the homestead survive and change? How did various components within the homestead survive and change? How did the preservation and alteration of some spaces reflect changes going on in Navajo life? What does the landscape "say" about women and how might we use these methods at other locations throughout the Southwest?

Landscapes are both natural and cultural constructs exhibiting stability and evolution at different times and at different rates. At Canyon de Chelly strong forces altered many characteristics of the natural landscape and the Navajo cultural landscape represents responses and/or resistance to these physical changes.

Some of the more significant changes included the alteration of the watercourse and the introduction of non-native species (both typical twentieth-century phenomena in the West). During this time the cultural landscape evolved as well. The evolution represents three thematic time periods: the Landscape of Memory, the Landscape of Uncertainty, and the Landscape of Instruction. In each thematic landscape we will look for evidence of women in the physical landscape and in the cultural traditions described in oral and written sources. By locating "spaces" considered the responsibility and purview of women we can then seek to characterize those spaces and trace their preservation or alteration through time. I will suggest that the Navajo women's role in preserving the homestead greatly contributed to cultural continuity through time.[13]

The Landscape of Memory began with the actions of Spider Woman. Her presence demonstrates the many ways Canyon de Chelly encompasses a sacred space.[14] As the canyon Navajo built agricultural communities noted for extensive fields and orchards, conflicts with outsiders increased.[15] When the nineteenth century opened to a landscape increasingly fortified, the Landscape of Uncertainty began. In the winter of 1863 the U.S. military embarked upon a brutal campaign designed to remove the Navajos to a reservation in New Mexico and eradicate their presence from Canyon de Chelly. A journey of hardships and heartache known as the "Long Walk" awaited those captured Navajos who would make the forced march to Fort Sumner, New Mexico, near Bosque Redondo. Community dislocation and environmental stress followed the Navajos return from their prison known as "Hweeldi" and their return to Canyon de Chelly ushered in the Landscape of Instruction. This is a landscape altered by the goods and cash economy of the Railroad Era. It is a time when Navajo women wove fewer blankets and more rugs, and the influence of local traders was at its zenith. The uncertainty of the years preceding the Treaty of 1868 passed into an era of instruction during the early reservation years. Missionaries, teachers, traders, and government officials came to the Navajo reservation with a range of motives from goodwill to exploitation. The Landscape of Instruction particularly characterizes Canyon de Chelly in the 1930s, when canyon Navajos faced livestock reduction, the scientific experiments of the Soil Conservation Service, and the presence of the National Park Service.

LANDSCAPE OF MEMORY

The term, Landscape of Memory, is meant to infer more than reflections upon the past, but rather a kind of perceptual document regarding the canyon landscape. In other words, it is a "cognitive map" based on observations, familial associations, and traditional histories. These memories served as a point of departure against which present and future decisions could be weighed; it is how the canyon people managed to preserve their canyon in times of stress. Peter Iverson has noted in his writings on the significance of place to Native Americans that the stories may be sacred or secular, but, he wrote, " In either instance they instruct an individual from example and attest to values and priorities."[16] Two stories fall into this category and suggest the significance of women in creating the Landscape of Memory at Canyon de Chelly. The first recounts the actions of Spider Woman who inhabits an 800-foot spire that rises from the junction of the de Chelly, Bat, and Monument canyons.

A simple version of this story appears in Gladys Reichard's 1934 work, *Spider Woman: A Story of Weavers and Chanters:*

> Spider Woman instructed the Navajo women how to weave on a loom which Spider Man told them how to make. The crosspoles were made of sky and earth cords, the warp sticks of sun rays, the healds of rock crystal and sheet lightning. The batten was a sun halo, white shell made the comb. There were four spindles: one a stick of zigzag lightning with a whorl of cannel coal; one a stick of flash lightning with a whorl of turquoise; a third had a stick of sheet lightning with a whorl of abalone; a rain streamer formed the stick of the fourth, and its whorl was white shell.[17]

Figure 3-3. Two Navajo women weave one large rug together as part of a demonstration at Hubbell Trading Post National Historic Site in the 1960s. (*Courtesy of the National Park Service. Photo by Fred Mang, Jr.*)

The story of Spider Woman and her association with the most prominent geologic feature in the canyon reminds us of the scale of women's place within this complex landscape. Here Canyon de Chelly serves as a site for one of the significant Holy People. With her skill at commanding the elements of the earth, Spider Woman taught Navajo women how to weave. The landscape of the Holy People is immense and the scale of Spider Rock reinforces the cosmological significance of women's place in Navajo society.

Robert Roessel Jr. in *Navajo Arts and Crafts* adds to our understanding of this story. He reminds us that some versions specify that Spider Woman taught Changing Woman to weave and to care for the weaving tools. From this point forward, Navajo women would be able to clothe and care for their families. Navajo Gods would always be able to recognize Navajo women by their weaving because it was a gift of the Holy People.[18]

A second story explains how the canyon Navajo acquired their famous peaches. According to an account by Little Man from Canyon del Muerto and told to W. W. Hill in the early 1930s, a Hopi woman gave peaches to Canyon de Chelly in reciprocity for taking care of her and her baby when they were starving. The account follows.

> One day a strange woman came into camp with a baby on her back. She was a Hopi woman who had left her village because of starvation. . . . . The child grew up and married a Navajo. . . . Besides the corn that was raised, seeds and berries were gathered in the Canyons, especially the sumac berries. This Hopi woman told where she was from, and from time to time the Navajo visited the Hopi, bringing back the peach seeds. She told them of this fruit being raised among the Hopi. The first peaches were planted in Canyon de Chelly at the White House. After a time more sites were cleared in de Chelly as far down as its junction with del Muerto. Del Muerto was so full of mountain lions, wolves, and bears that it was impossible to go up it. From the White House in de Chelly there was found a trail which led to the Antelope Ruin in del Muerto, where a man discovered an open place in the brush. . . . The first peaches in del Muerto were planted at the Antelope Ruin.[19]

In many ways these accounts complement each other. On the one hand the Holy People bestowed a gift to Navajo women that helped them care for their families and to be recognized by the Holy People. In return Navajo women honored Spider Woman through their commitment to the weaving tradition. In the second account, a woman sought compassion from her Navajo neighbors. In return, she gave them a lasting gift of peaches. Again, Navajos accepted the gift and reciprocated, growing large orchards and committing to their renewal even after their destruction during the Carson campaign.

Early Spanish accounts of Navajos describe their abundant fields. They are kings of the soil occupying a canyon of wheat. As sedentary agriculturists, early Navajo settlement in the canyons consisted of multiple homesteads grouped together near agricultural fields. Homesteads were situated in high open terraces.

Alcoves were used selectively along trails that led to the rim. Households occupied the canyon floor during the planting season and along the rims in colder months. The homesteads (comprised of five or so hogans, firepits, brush structures, and corrals) were situated along high terraces in order to avoid the periodic flooding of the canyon floor. Navajos observed the flow of water and strategically positioned their fields in the rich alluvium of the canyon floor.

This configuration of the landscape was not to last. During the mid-to late eighteenth century Spanish soldiers received permission from the governor of New Mexico to start arming Zuni, Commanche, and Mexican Indian auxiliary troops. Utes acquired horses and guns. Feeling the need for protection, the canyon Navajo began to move their homesteads to more easily guarded talus slopes. Homesteads now contained fewer hogans (perhaps two or three) positioned farther away from fields. The agricultural surplus was hauled to high alcoves and stored in rough masonry granaries imperceptible from the canyon floor.[20]

LANDSCAPE OF UNCERTAINTY

Navajo rock art paintings record the escalating conflict as the Landscape of Uncertainty unfolded. The Antonio Narbona expedition in Canyon de Chelly on January 17, 1805 and the Ute Raid that occurred sometime in the 1830s and 1840s are both depicted in substantial pictorials on the canyon wall. Although they differ in terms of artistic expression, both images stress the importance of horses. In the Ute Raid Panel, women wearing clothes made from woven blankets appear to the side of armed Navajo warriors who bravely face Ute riders with shields. Perhaps the women are heading toward the corrals or perhaps they intend to aid smaller figures (perhaps children?) that appear to be moving in a similar direction.[21]

In the winter of 1863, Colonel Christopher "Kit" Carson implemented a scorched earth military campaign designed to remove Navajos to a remote reservation and eradicate their presence from the canyons. Although Colonel Carson and Captain A. W. Pheiffer did not adequately understand the scale of Canyon de Chelly (which includes three main canyons and numerous side canyons), they wreaked havoc on the canyon floor. They burned homesteads, chopped down trees, and slaughtered livestock to impress upon Navajos the intent of their mission. Although Navajo warriors fought the troops, and others tried to defend themselves, the harshness and bitter cold of the 1863 winter had left many Navajos undernourished and less able to fend off the surprise assault. Carson records shooting one brave Navajo woman from the canyon, "who obstinately persisted in hurling rocks and pieces of wood at the soldiers."[22]

Marching over 300 miles across desert and mountain terrain, all struggled to survive—with the children, the pregnant women, and the elderly facing the greatest hardship. By the summer of 1864, approximately 4000 Navajos had arrived at "Hweeldi" Fort Sumner.[23] In August, Captain Thompson returned to Canyon de Chelly intent on eradicating the evidence of canyon Navajo prosperity. Writing in his official campaign report, General Carson noted that the fighting had not permitted him to destroy, "a large orchard of peach trees." So Thompson returned to the canyons and for several days he perfected the cruel art of destruction. He cut down hundreds of peach trees full of fruit—laying waste to the gift of the Hopi woman.[24]

The decision to incarcerate the Navajo failed. The land around the fort the Navajos attempted to farm was alkaline. The Pecos River water caused dysentery. The cost in human and economic terms could not be justified. Gary Henry credits the decision to abandon the effort to the persistence of the Navajo leadership and their ability to communicate to those in power the desire of the Navajos to return home. His family remembers the leader's words. "We need to return to Canyon de Chelly. This is where our medicine is. This is where our food is. This is where we can grow again, as a people."[25] The final Treaty of 1868 was signed at Fort Sumner and the Navajos began the long walk home. One can only imagine the range of emotions upon return. But the feelings of uncertainty regarding their future remained. Many turned to their traditions as Sonlatsa Jim-James explained:

> My great-grandmother told me of the time the Dine [Navajo] were forced to go on the Long Walk. She was only a child, but she said that when they returned home, all the people started to settle down in hogans. Clans joined together to survive and so there were many marriages.[26]

As mentioned before, Rose Mitchell's mother encouraged her to stay home and take care of the hogan and family during this post-Long Walk period. This strategy seemed to work overall and the reservation population nearly doubled between the years 1870 and 1900. In 1910, the U.S. Census Bureau made a special effort to include the Indians of the United States. In Navajo Country the enumeration resulted in an uneven survey—New Mexico counts appear consistent while the Arizona counts appear low due to "deficient coverage" in the northern and western regions of the state. However, despite these inaccuracies, the figures provide a glimpse into the work Navajo women performed at home. Navajos ranked first in the nation in the number of Native American women "gainfully employed" (4,564 women out of 7,368) and of those, 4,005 were identified as weavers.[27] Navajo women wove their tribe into the twentieth century.

As Navajos adjusted to the reservation years, they found a market for their wool, rugs, and hides, at the local trading post.[28] The expansion of the railroad and its attendant access to off-reservation markets enabled the trader to engineer a central economic position within many Navajo communities. As cultural brokers, traders worked with Navajo women to produce a product marketable throughout the United States. John Lorenzo Hubbell's business ventures expanded and contracted over the years, but the center of his trading realm and his homestead was Ganado, Arizona—where the Hubbell Trading Post still operates today. Into this time of uncertainty, traders such as J. L. Hubbell assisted Navajo weavers in their shift from blankets to rugs, from a subsistence to a cash economy, and from a Landscape of Uncertainty to a Landscape of Instruction at Canyon de Chelly.

Martha Blue observes that the bullpen arrangement of such trading posts as Hubbell Trading Post mimicked the spatial organization of the hogan, "[T]he post's womblike central area, called the bullpen, was warm, snug, and close like a hogan." Perhaps the architectural similarity made it a little easier for the weaver to part with her creation, one that had evolved over several months, and to focus this accomplishment on the sustenance it would provide the family. Blue writes:

> To the Navajos J. L. [Hubbell] provided the economic underpinnings of the weaving trade. Weaving was, after all, a way for homebound women to contribute to the economic well-being of their families; the weaving process itself was also considered a nurturing one.[29]

LANDSCAPE OF INSTRUCTION

Back in the canyons, the sheep that supplied the wool for the rugs had not been kind to the landscape. The destruction of the trees and sheep herds of the canyon took years to rebuild. Meager distributions of farming implements could not meet the immediate demands of a hungry and dislocated people. Returning the canyons to agricultural productivity took time, so many families concentrated on building up their herds. This in turn made the canyons less hospitable to agriculture. Until you've actually watched a lamb wander aimlessly out on a thin, narrow ledge several hundred feet off the canyon floor, it's hard to appreciate the number of high alcoves filled with several feet of historic sheep dung. But the evidence is there. Along with sheep came drought and the continuance of a long cycle of regional erosion. The Landscape of Instruction refers to the time in the early years of the twentieth century when canyon Navajos made decisions to allow more government administration and assistance in pursuing their agenda of canyon restoration. This mirrors the slow reorganization of the entire reservation along more systematic lines.

During the Landscape of Instruction, Canyon de Chelly became an experimental model farm for scientists working for the Soil Conservation Service. Analyzing data from soils and aerial reconnaissance photographs, the scientists determined that a stable channel of water would improve agricultural productivity. To force the main Chinle Wash from a meander to a stream they embarked upon a construction program of check dams, irrigation canals, and head gates. They employed canyon Navajos to complete the installation of wire gabions and wood spider jetties around Antelope House. They also planted thousands of such invasive exotic species as the Russian Olive and Tamarsik. They enclosed uniform field areas behind fences, and tied land tenure to a fixed boundary. The Soil Conservation Service worked with the National Park Service and widened the canyon road in order to accommodate more visitors to the new "National Monument" and to ease access to the town of Chinle for the canyon residents.

What was the legacy of the Landscape of Instruction? First, the results of the Soil Conservation Service effort produced an ecological transformation of the

Figure 3-4. A Navajo man and woman lift a large "spider jenny" to help stabilize the Chinle Wash in Canyon del Muerto, Canyon de Chelly National Monument in 1964. (*Courtesy of the National Park Service. Photo by Bureau of Indian Affairs Branch of Land Operations.*)

canyon bottom, with channelization of the wash altering the canyon's riparian ecology. Thereafter, more and more vegetation filled the canyon bottomlands. In a characteristic response to the external environment, Navajos again altered the position of the homesteads. They built their hogans, ramadas, corrals, and fields along the first alluvial terraces or canyon floor in relative access to the canyon road. They built fewer hogans and more ramadas, as more and more activities began to take place after work or on the weekends. Left without the option of floodwater farming, many adopted the techniques and mechanized tools of western farming. In addition, perhaps most ephemerally, the canyon community became more fragmented, as families became cattle ranchers, cash crop farmers, homesteaders, and tour guides.

What are we to make of all these broad scale changes through time? And to what extent have we made Native American women visible in the landscape? First, there is considerable evidence to suggest that the location of the homestead changed through time in response to social, economic, and physical pressures. During the Landscape of Memory, Navajos arranged homesteads in groups. During the Landscape of Uncertainty, Navajos positioned discrete, dispersed settlements in talus slopes, and during the Landscape of Instruction, they located open homesteads along the canyon floor.

What remained constant in the landscape were the components of the homestead: hogans, ramadas, corrals, and fields. In the face of change, Navajos built,

Figure 3-5. Contemporary Navajo women as Youth Conservation Corps workers maintain the White House Trail at Canyon de Chelly National Monument. (*Courtesy of the National Park Service.*)

renewed, and retained central elements of daily life. Depending on economic circumstances, canyon Navajo owned more or less amounts of sheep, cows and corn—but the basic symbolic components of "motherhood" remained present. Perhaps this accounts for the appearance of continuity from the canyon's rim. Despite differences in settlement patterns over time, visitors can still identify the hogans, ramadas, and green fields—components of a traditional Navajo life. It is these components that speak to the roles and responsibility of Navajo women.

In undertaking landscape analysis as a method for making Native American women visible in Southwestern history sites we have encountered and overcome many problems. To apply this methodology to other Native American sites, researchers might begin by asking, "What spaces are women's spaces?" Finding the answer to this question often requires stepping back from one's own cultural perspective in order to appreciate the roles and responsibilities of Native American women within their tribal context. The much more lengthy and difficult process involves identifying and describing the activities, decisions, and values that helped shape the landscape. In this instance, "weaving and taking care of the hogan" spun out into the wider community—taking care of the hogan provided stability, even if the placement of the homestead changed. Weaving, an activity performed primarily by women in an isolated hogan, produced a rug and a trade that led to new economic opportunities in the face of the uncertainty of the post-Long Walk reservation years. This analysis has used as evidence ethnographic studies, stories of Navajo deities, and the words and remembrances of Navajo women as well as gross changes in the landscape and rock art panels.

If there is any reluctance to apply landscape analysis to questions of gender, perhaps it is because we are less unaccustomed to considering women's actions on both the broad and small scale. The symbolic landscape of Canyon de Chelly—including towering Spider Rock—is home to a powerful and generous female god. The roles, responsibilities, and artistic vigor that connect Canyon de Chelly and Hubbell Trading Post came about through Spider Woman's gift of weaving, but it was individual Navajo women who sustained the weaving tradition.

Teddy Henry, a silversmith, and canyon Navajo holds open the book, *Ansel Adams: The National Park Service Photographs* and draws our eye to a picture of his mother taken in 1942 near White House Ruin, reproduced in this chapter. She faces the photographer directly with a soft smile. In her arms is a cradleboard

Figure 3-6. Rose Chee Henry, mother of Navajo silversmith Teddy Henry, holds Teddy's brother in a cradleboard in a 1942 photograph taken near White House ruin in Canyon de Chelly. (*Courtesy of the National Archives. Photo by Ansel Adams.*)

and the baby is one of his brothers. Teddy has just completed a series of neck-laces in her honor. They are two-sided pendants, the kind for which he is known. On one side is a stylized depiction of his mother and brother executed in silver overlay. On the reverse he has copied one of her rug designs, because she was a weaver. The next piece also has the stylized image of his mother and brother, but the reverse is executed in multicolored inlaid stones depicting the cosmological world of mother earth. Her face floats in a black twilight filled with stars. Canyon de Chelly and Hubbell Trading Post represent a long series of changes in the lives of Navajo women, but through it all Spider Woman continues to weave a web of social cooperation and interconnectedness—it is Spider Woman's grand design.[30]

NOTES

1. Paula Gunn Allen, *The Sacred Hoop: Recovering the Feminine in American Indian Traditions* (Boston: Beacon Press, 1986; reprint, 1992), 11.
2. For an overview of North American Native American Women's connection with landscape see Rebecca Bales, "Native American Women: Living With Landscape," *OAH Magazine of History* 12, no. 1 (Fall 1997): 13–15.
3. David M. Brugge and Raymond Wilson, *Administrative History Canyon de Chelly National Monument Arizona* (Washington DC: US Government Printing Office, 1976), 7–8.
4. Verne E. Chatelain, "A Report dealing with Canyon de Chelly National Monument," 10 March 1933, Canyon de Chelly National Monument Archives, Chinle, Arizona. Chatelain indicates John C. Merriam classified the four interpretive themes as 1) geologic processes and history, 2) archae-ological history, 3) exceptional scenic elements, and 4) life and culture of the Navajo.
5. Mary Shepardson, "The Gender Status of Navajo Women," in Laura F. Klein and Lillian A. Ackerman, eds., *Women and Power in Native North America* (Norman: University of Oklahoma Press, 1995), 160.
6. Gary Witherspoon, "Navajo Social Organization" in Alfonso Ortiz, ed., *Handbook of North American Indians,* vol. 10, (Washington, D.C.: Smith-sonian Institution, 1983), 525.
7. Shepardson, "The Gender Status of Navajo Women," 174.
8. Ruth Roessel, *Women in Navajo Society* (Rough Rock, AZ: Navajo Resource Center, Rough Rock Demonstration School, 1981), 62–3.
9. Gary Witherspoon, "Navajo Social Organization," 525.
10. Stephen C. Jett and Virgina E. Spencer, *Navajo Architecture: Forms, History and Distributions* (Tucson: University of Arizona Press, 1981), 14.
11. Susan Kent, *Analyzing Activity Areas: An Ethnoarchaeological Study of the Use of Space* (Albuquerque: University of New Mexico Press, 1984), 201.
12. Rose Mitchell, *Tall Woman: The Life Story of Rose Mitchell, a Navajo Woman, c. 1974–1977,* Charlotte J. Frisbie, ed. (Albuquerque: University of New Mexico Press, 2001), 84.
13. Tara Sidles Travis, "The Cultural Landscape of Canyon de Chelly," paper

presented at the conference, Interpreting Historic Places: Images, Myths and Identity, University of York, UK, 4–7 September 1997. The landscape analysis is based on my field research at Canyon de Chelly National Monument 1990–1998.

14. Klara Kelley and Harris Francis, *Navajo Sacred Places* (Bloomington: Indiana University Press, 1994), 164.

15. Archaeological reconstructions generally place the Navajo arrival in Canyon de Chelly sometime in the mid-eighteenth century. See Wesley R. Hurt, "Eighteenth Century Navaho Hogans From Canyon de Chelly National Monument," *American Antiquity,* 8, no. 1 (1942).

16. Peter Iverson and Linda MacCannell, *Riders of the West: Portraits from Indian Rodeo* (Seattle: University of Washington Press, 1999), 32.

17. Gladys A. Reichard, *Spider Woman: A Story of Weavers and Chanters* (New York: Macmillan, 1934).

18. Robert A. Roessel, Jr., *Navajo Arts and Crafts* (Rough Rock, AZ: Navajo Curriculum Center, Rough Rock Demonstration School, 1983), 13.

19. W. W. Hill, *The Agricultural and Hunting Methods of the Navajo Indians,* Yale University Publications in Anthropology no. 18 (New Haven, CT: Yale University Press, 1938), 48–49.

20. Scott Travis, "18th and early 19th c. Navajo Tactical Landscapes, Canyon del Muerto," paper presented at the Tactical Sites Conference, Arizona Archaeological Society, Flagstaff, October 1998.

21. In the summer of 1991 I spent a week camped at Ute Raid Panel helping to document the rock art for conservation purposes. I base the observation that the figures appear to be women on their triangular shape dresses that look like mantas.

22. Clifford T. Trafzer, *The Kit Carson Campaign* (Norman: University of Oklahoma Press, 1982) and historical files on Col. Kit Carson at Canyon de Chelly National Monument.

23. Gerald Thompson, *The Army and Navajo: The Bosque Redondo Reservation Experiment, 1863–1868* (Tucson: University of Arizona Press, 1976), 46, 54, 66, 67, 80, 100, 130.

24. Campbell Grant, *Canyon de Chelly: Its People and Rock Art* (Tucson: University of Arizona Press, 1978; reprint 1987), 114–117. Howard W. Gorman in Albert L. Hurtado and Peter Iverson, eds., *Major Problems in American Indian History* (Lexington, MA: D. C. Heath, 1994), 328.

25. Gary Henry, personal communication.

26. Sonlasta Jim-James in Joy Harjo and Gloria Bird, eds., *Reinventing the Enemy's Language: Contemporary Native Women's Writings of North America* (New York: Norton, 1997), 490.

27. Denis Foster Johnson, *An Analysis of Sources of Information on the Population of the Navaho,* (Washington, DC: U.S. Government Printing Office, 1966), 36, 103.

28. Peter Iverson, *The Navajo Nation* (Albuquerque: University of New Mexico Press, 1981), 11–12.

29. Martha Blue, *Indian Trader: the Life and Times of J. L. Hubbell* (Walnut, CA: Kiva Press, 2000), 43, 225.

30. Alice Gray, *Ansel Adams: The National Park Service Photographs* (New York: Abbeyville Press, 1995), 46.

SUGGESTED READINGS

Paula Gunn Allen, *The Sacred Hoop: Recovering the Feminine in American Indian Traditions.* Boston: Beacon Press, 1986; reprint, 1992. A landmark work in the exploration of voices and perspectives by and about Native American women.

Martha Blue, *Indian Trader: the Life and Times of J. L. Hubbell,* Walnut, CA: Kiva Press, 2000. Blue brings an ethnohistorical approach to the study of this prominent trader and reveals that J. L. Hubbell was a complicated power broker on the Navajo Reservation.

Klara Kelley and Harris Francis, *Navajo Sacred Places.* Bloomington: Indiana University Press, 1994. Kelley and Francis undertake the difficult task of identifying and defining Navajo sacred places through the use of oral interviews and traditional knowledge. One of the few books to define a Native American view of historic preservation.

Rose Mitchell, *Tall Woman: The Life Story of Rose Mitchell, a Navajo Woman, c. 1974–1977,* Charlotte J. Frisbie, ed., Albuquerque: University of New Mexico Press, 2001. Here is the life story of a traditional Navajo weaver in her own words, carefully edited by a well-known anthropologist.

Chapter 4

WOMEN'S VOICES: REINTERPRETING HISTORIC HOUSE MUSEUMS

Bonnie Hurd Smith

The lives of the women who came before us can be frustratingly difficult to understand. Only a privileged few were able to write letters or keep diaries. Fewer still were memorialized in biographies. Students of women's history have always had to look for documentation in other kinds of places, and historic house museums are one such resource. We can walk through the rooms where women ate, slept, prayed, gave birth, raised children, read, wrote, discussed issues of the day, and planned action. We see the tools they handled, the gardens they maintained, the proximity of their home to neighbors, the town center, or their outside workplaces. In describing the interpretive policies for the Society for the Preservation of New England Antiquities (SPNEA), Jane C. Nylander wrote, "in our buildings, landscapes, and furnishings, we see the particulars that define the actual texture of people's existence. Places and objects can also tell us about more intangible issues, like beliefs and aspirations or economic and societal change."[1]

The material culture that still exists in the form of historic house museums can make the lives of women compellingly real and accessible. But in today's museums, how often are women's stories told? In what way? Who decides?

As a movement, the idea of historic house museums really began in the middle of the nineteenth century with the establishment of Mount Vernon as a museum — "an innovation" on the cultural landscape, according to Patricia West. While there were such precedents as when women displayed romanticized versions of colonial kitchens at Sanitary Fairs designed to raise money for the Union Army, the patriotic fervor behind saving Mount Vernon defined the movement. The Mount Vernon Ladies' Association considered it essential to preserve the home of America's first president and they inspired similar efforts to save the homes of other great (white, male) political and literary figures. These houses were preserved as "shrines," writes West. The directors purposefully included only selected information about the historic house inhabitants.[2]

The lives of women in these houses were of peripheral importance at best, along with those of servants and slaves. As Page Putnam Miller asserted, "If Americans

Figure 4-1. Alice Mary Longfellow sits in her study at Longfellow House in a photograph taken about 1891. Her chair and the belongings around her remain just as she left them. (*Courtesy of the National Park Service, Longfellow National Historic Site.*)

had to rely on existing historic sites for their understanding of women's history, a very limited and distorted picture would emerge."[3] What is especially ironic about omitting women from historic house interpretation is that they often lived in the home longer than the men for whom the houses are named—either because the men were traveling, perhaps serving in a legislature, or because the men died earlier.[4]

Often the homes of prominent men were maintained by their descendants—usually well-off, culturally engaged people whose desire to honor their ancestors led to the preservation of many of the historic homes we enjoy today. These family boards of directors also determined what was said about their ancestors, how, and to whom. Needless to say, the information about these houses disseminated by such caretakers could be subjective and incomplete.

A second motivation behind establishing historic house museums came to a head in the late nineteenth century when the number of immigrants to America increased dramatically. Founders of historic house museums often justified their work as necessary for Americanizing immigrants. When the Daughters of the American Revolution (DAR) was founded in 1890, for example, they actively set about acquiring historic properties specifically "to carry the gospel of Americanism to every American home" and to "safeguard the land against the ravages of ignorance and sedition." The DAR, and other like-minded groups and individuals, wanted to preserve upper class, white American heritage by using house museums as living testimonials.[5]

When the Colonial Revival Movement came along in the early 1900s, historic house museums were a perfect vehicle to enshrine an idealized remembrance of the past—celebrating women's domestic sphere, or the home- and family-centered activities in which women were expected to engage exclusively. Not surprisingly, what fueled this portrayal of women's domesticity was a reaction to the pivotal social and political changes affecting women at the time. The women's suffrage movement had grown in size and power, seeing its ultimate victory in 1920 when women achieved the right to vote. Women's educational opportunities had been improving steadily, including at the college level. Women were working outside the home in growing numbers, and the kind of work open to them was expanding. They were politically and economically active.

The response to women's new roles from the historic house museums that celebrated the colonial or Victorian past often reflected the founders' isolation from the changing social landscape. Many of them were conservative women and men who saw women's work in historic preservation as an extension of their domestic duties. As a group, they were elite women who were generally not suffragists, social reformers, or even historians. The houses they maintained were seen in their surrounding communities as private spaces focusing on the past. Their actions were, however, highly political. Even though Orchard House, Louisa May Alcott's home in Concord, Massachusetts, was preserved to honor her, Alcott's politics were ignored in the early interpretive tours. Instead, guides described domestic life at Orchard House in romanticized fictional terms to echo the stories Alcott had detailed in *Little Women*. Her ideas on suffrage, antislavery, and women's work were ignored. Orchard House became part of what James Loewen has called a "landscape of denial."[6]

But over the past three decades, thanks at least in part to the civil rights and women's movements, new scholarship has transformed how public historians present history. Researchers have uncovered and published voluminous records on the lives of women, African Americans, Native Americans, and early immigrant experiences not documented before. The information is available, and the research methods used for documentation can be learned and replicated. Today public historians are more open to telling a more complex American story because they understand the interrelationships among different groups of people. The public expects the stories told about historic events and sites to be honest—and the public expects them to include women.

Public historians are also much more attuned to the concept of the public trust.

The statues and memorials in the nation's capital that honor the nation's early leaders, for example, belong to everyone. The monuments the nation has erected to commemorate important battles, the historic markers that designate significant sites—they belong to everyone. So, too, in the same sense, do the homes of the women and men who helped shape America. Public tax dollars pay to maintain historic sites either directly through the National Park Service and state humanities councils, or indirectly through the tax exempt status conferred on nonprofit historic house museums. Visitors have a right to expect a fair treatment of American history in these places—and to expect women's history.[7]

How have historic house museums responded to this expectation? As an industry, they are trying. Individually, each historic house has its own set of challenges in terms of available and applicable research materials, funding, and volunteer and staff time to develop new tours and programs. But the desire is there, as well as the ingenuity and, increasingly, caretakers of historic houses understand that telling women's stories goes beyond the kitchen and the crib.

At Longfellow National Historic Site in Cambridge, Massachusetts, the staff wanted to "say more" about what is popularly known as "Longfellow House"—the home of the popular nineteenth century poet Henry Wadsworth Longfellow. The National Park Service was fortunate in two key ways: first, that the site manager and superintendent were committed to reinterpretation efforts including allocating staff time and resources, and second, that the lives of the residents were extremely well documented—and the materials were still in the house.

One woman the staff wanted to include on the tour, Alice Longfellow, Henry and Fanny Appleton Longfellow's oldest daughter, was responsible for the thorough documentation. Alice dedicated her life to historic preservation work, and served as vice-regent of the Mount Vernon Ladies' Association from 1880–1918. Her work served her well when she decided to turn her family home into a museum that would pay tribute to her famous father and the house's earlier prominent resident, George Washington. According to Kelly Fellner, the site's education manager, Alice wanted the house to serve as "a source of education and inspiration for the public, whether they were students from Radcliffe (which she helped found) or a group of working women from Boston."[8]

The house continued to be cared for by the Longfellow Family Trust after Alice's death in 1918, until the trust transferred the house to the supervision of the National Park Service in 1972. It is largely because of Alice's tireless caretaking of the building, collection, and papers, that staff and volunteers have been able to begin piecing together information about who else lived in the house. As the site's curator, Janice Hodson, explained, when they began the process of reinterpreting the house and changing the tour, they were only interested in conveying information if it was grounded in fact. In 1991, they began an intensive effort to catalog their archives and collection, knowing how unusual it was to have such extensive primary source documentation tied directly to the collection. Not only are there letters and diaries but the collection includes sales receipts for items of furniture, old photographs of interiors, mementos, building and garden plans. The cataloging will take many years to complete and will include a historic furnishings plan listing the provenance of each piece, its location in the house, and any supporting material that exists. Already their work has revealed important details about the lesser-known female residents of the Longfellow House.

Along with Alice, the role of her mother Fanny Appleton Longfellow is included in the tour. Before her tragic death in 1861, Fanny not only served as an inspiration and sometimes as editor for her husband, she also made their home an inviting salon for writers and artists from around the world, many of whom visited the Longfellows in Cambridge and brought exotic gifts or wrote letters describing their experiences. Other former women residents included in the tour are Elizabeth Craigie, who created some of the first greenhouses in Cambridge in the early nineteenth century, and Martha Washington, who lived in the house with her husband from 1775 to 1776 when it was the headquarters of the Continental Army

Figure 4-2. Longfellow National Historic Site in Cambridge, MA, is an example of a successful reinterpretation effort that includes the lives of women connected with the building. (*Courtesy of the National Park Service, Longfellow National Historic Site.*)

during the siege of Boston. According to eyewitness accounts (documented in letters owned by Longfellow NHS), the crowds gathered around when Martha's carriage first pulled into sight were jubilant in their welcoming cries, and she was very much a regal presence in Cambridge during her stay.[9]

Adding the stories of lesser known women to the interpretation of homes of prominent men was the same challenge faced by the House of the Seven Gables in Salem, Massachusetts. Long associated with nineteenth-century author Nathaniel Hawthorne whose book of the same name put the house on the map historically, "The Gables," as it is popularly known, had always drawn visitors through its doors. They came first, because of Hawthorne's reputation, and, second, to hear about the lives of such prosperous sea merchants as Captain John Turner. Like Alice Longfellow, the founder of The Gables as an historic house was a woman—Caroline Emmerton—and she is today as much a part of the Gables' story as Alice Longfellow is part of the Longfellow House story.

Like Alice, Caroline Emmerton was the daughter of a prominent family. Their philanthropic initiatives in Salem were numerous. Caroline was particularly concerned with meeting the health care and educational needs of the growing number of families immigrating to Salem from Europe, and as a young woman at the turn of the twentieth century she founded a settlement house named for The Gables. She also devised a plan to pay for the settlement house by saving the House of the Seven Gables from demolition, restoring it, and opening it as a museum to the public. Two other historic properties were later added to the museum's property, as well as a shop. Today The Gables remains the successful venture it was when "Miss Emmerton" first created it—and admission fees continue to help pay for programs at the settlement house.[10]

Because Caroline's life is well documented, including information about her founding of the Salem Fraternity (which became the local Boys' and Girls' Club) and her early activities as a member of SPNEA, it was relatively easy for The Gables' staff to weave the story of their founder into the tour. What has not been as easy is finding documentation for the lives of two earlier women residents—Susannah Ingersoll and Mary Turner Sargent. As did the Longfellow NHS, The Gables' management decided in the early 1990s that it was time to join the reinterpretation movement. They hired a new museum director, David Olson, to oversee the process.

The Gables' staff started with what they knew and began digging. Although they did not have the kind of on-site archives that Longfellow NHS has, they did have ready access to the Essex Institute (now the Phillips Library at the Peabody Essex Museum) just blocks away. They looked first for primary documents and found useful letters, reminiscences, organizational records, and newspaper clippings. Now visitors to The Gables learn that Susannah Ingersoll, Nathaniel Hawthorne's older cousin, entertained him for hours with stories about their family and Salem history—serving, it is believed, as an inspiration for much of his writing. Susannah was also active with the Salem Female Anti-Slavery Society and might have been part of Underground Railroad activities. She kept a farm in nearby Danvers and was quite a successful business woman overseeing many details herself.

Figure 4-3. The House of Seven Gables in Salem, MA, preserved for the public by philanthropist Caroline Emmerton, now includes stories of the lives of women in its interpretive tour. (*Courtesy of the House of Seven Gables.*)

Mary Turner Sargent has proven more difficult to document. Family history relates that she was born at The Gables in 1743 and presumably grew up there. She was the wife of a prominent merchant, Daniel Sargent, who helped build Long Wharf in Boston, and the mother of renowned painter Henry Sargent and author Lucius Manlius Sargent, but to date her beautiful portrait by John Singleton Copley is the only artifact connected to her that The Gables staff has found. She was, however, a regular correspondent with her niece, Judith Sargent Murray, whose letter books, did survive. Some of the letters to Mary Sargent that Judith copied into her book provide insight into Mary's character and activities.

Similarly, the museum is piecing together the lives of the various servants who lived at The Gables, one of whom was indentured and others who may have been slaves. It is still unclear who they were, and even where in the house they lived, but The Gables is making every effort to find the answers. "We keep raising the standards," David Olson explained. "As an organization, we have to be as accurate as we can be."[11]

That is a sentiment echoed by Carolyn Wahto, site manager of the Otis House in Boston, one of the SPNEA properties open to the public. Verbal legend has no place at SPNEA, and Wahto, working closely with the manager of research, Susan Porter, is part of an organization-wide reinterpretation of their twenty-five historic house museums.[12]

Something as simple as changing the name of a house raises awareness and implies new thinking about interpretation. Instead of referring to the Harrison Gray

Otis House by its traditional name, SPNEA now calls it, simply, the Otis House out of respect for Sally Otis, Harrison's wife, and the couple's numerous children. In fact, it is Sally whose many activities filled their fashionable home on Bowdoin Square while her husband, an attorney, was away serving in the U.S. Congress during the early Federal period. At home, Sally took care of his business dealings, ran a large household of children and servants, gave birth to several children whom she also educated, and received guests as dictated by Boston society. The hundreds of letters she wrote to her husband did not survive, but thousands of his are carefully preserved in the Massachusetts Historical Society. "An interesting problem we have here," Carolyn Wahto relates, "is that we have to interpret Sally's voice through her husband's letters. That's really tricky. We have to work harder on her story to make her come alive."[13]

As at other historic sites, SPNEA started with bills of sale documenting the transfer of the Otis House in 1801 to its next occupants, Catharine and John Osborne, to determine how rooms were used. That led to staff discussions about differences between male and female and formal and informal uses of space before they could agree on how to interpret the Otis House rooms. They conducted paint and wallpaper analyses throughout the house and replicated what existed in the late 1700s. They perused federal period inventories of similar homes in the Boston area, pulled from their collection what was appropriate, and then went shopping for key pieces that were missing. They were also able to rely on two paintings by Henry Sargent, both owned by the Museum of Fine Arts, Boston, that depict the high style interior of Sargent's town house, Franklin Place, designed by Charles Bulfinch, and located just blocks away from the Otises. These paintings, *The Dinner Party* and *The Tea Party,* include rich detail about color, fabric, floor coverings, wall and window treatments, decorative and displayed items, modes of dress, and choices and presentation of food.

Today two rooms on the first floor of the Otis House, clearly inspired by Sargent's paintings, include reproductions of his work on easels so visitors can appreciate the interpretive process. The drawing room is set up as if Sally were entertaining—complete with piano forte for the children's lessons and her sewing table. Judith Sargent Murray's letter books have been helpful to SPNEA as well. They know from one of her letters written after she moved to Boston, that "morning visits [were] all the rage" during those years. Still, it is a challenge to balance general information about upper class Boston with information specific to the Otis House and make it historically responsible. As Wahto points out, "I try not to assume too much. I try to stay away from the average woman and really talk about Sally with accuracy, but this isn't always possible. But being honest about not knowing is an education in and of itself. How little we know about the lives of women when they inhabited these rooms makes a bold statement."[14]

Because the Otises only occupied the house for four years, the staff at the Otis House is also looking at the lives of other residents. In addition to researching the lives of the Osbornes, they are looking for sources to tell them about the Williams sisters, who ran a boarding house at the site from 1854 to 1868, and Mrs. Mott, who offered "Champoo Baths" to discerning customers in some part of the house for a year in the mid-1830s. In the 1970s, the Otis House was on the "cutting edge" of historic houses in terms of paint analysis and interior design, Carolyn Whato explained, "and we want it to be again today in the area of interpretation."[15]

Like SPNEA, the Peabody Essex Museum (PEM) seeks to achieve this same high standard of interpretation and also strike a balance between specific and general information about its twenty-six historic house properties. Their staff is also rethinking the titles of the houses themselves—each one named for a prominent white man. "Invariably," explained Deputy Director of Special Projects John R. Grimes, "there are socioeconomic factors involved in these decisions that need to be looked at. We want to dismantle decades of assumptions, and do it in terms of what is fair historically and what will make the visitor experience meaningful."[16]

The person heading this daunting task is Kimberly Alexander, PEM's curator of architecture who is herself an architectural historian. Each property presents its own set of issues: the seventeenth-century houses come with very little documentation, while the eighteenth-and nineteenth-century houses, many lived in by generations of the same family, often contain artifacts and documents that are original to the house. But in general, compared to other organizations, the museum has a wealth of documentation. As PEM acquired each property, the staff made extensive studies; now staff and volunteers are revisiting these documents with fresh eyes. Alexander explained, "These details [about social history] that people weren't interested in years ago are exactly what we want to know now."[17]

Like other organizations, PEM believes that the use of space is a good starting point for discussing people's lives. In its houses the Peabody Essex Museum has the unique ability to show the progression from essentially one large universal room (John Ward House), to multiple rooms and prescribed uses of space (Pierce-Nichols House), to what appears to be vast areas of "wasted space" in the homes of the early nineteenth century wealthy merchant class (Gardner-Pingree House). These architectural changes had a profound impact on women's lives. The evolution of spaces for women that were separate from the main functioning of the household—particularly kitchen and garden areas—isolated women from more public activities and strengthened the idea that separate spheres for women and men were natural. The museum can also illustrate the impact of the role of technology as the houses moved from the simple wood-burning fireplace in the common room to kitchen fireplaces with such installed apparatus as reflector ovens and roasting spits, to Franklin stoves in individual rooms, and to central heating with coal.

Probate inventories are especially helpful when trying to reconstruct seventeenth-century daily life. Inventories from the John Ward House listed between twenty-three to thirty-five chairs in the front room. "Why all these chairs?" Kimberly Alexander asked. "Obviously, this was a very social place and meetings took place here. And since this was before women were banished to a separate kitchen, they would have been listening to, and perhaps participating in, whatever was being discussed."[18]

Figure 4-4. Before separate kitchens kept women isolated, they might be included in public discussions held in the family's universal room. Pictured here is the interior of the seventeenth-century John Ward House in Salem, MA, which was located across from the jail used during the Salem Witchcraft Trials in 1692. (*Courtesy of the Peabody Essex Museum. Negative/Catalog #: 137966.*)

Another central element of the 1684 John Ward House story is that many years ago it was moved about a mile from its original location opposite the jail used during the Salem witchcraft trials of 1692. Using this evidence, one can easily imagine the subject matter of the gatherings that took place in the house. House moving in New England was not uncommon, especially during the Colonial Revival period of the early 1900s and during the urban renewal efforts of the 1970s. While it is critical to ground visitors in the context of the house and its environment to fully understand what its residents' lives were like, it is not always easy to separate out nearby buildings, highways, and parking lots that often appear to suffocate them. Finding out the original proximity of the John Ward House to the Salem Jail speaks volumes.[19]

The context of Salem itself plays a role, Alexander pointed out. She explained that Salem was a fluid society, "part city, part rural area, and part international port." These characteristics made Salem very self-sufficient and engendered a lot of bartering. "Who was doing the bartering?" Alexander asked. "It was the women, because they tended to have control over the family's resources. The men were often away at sea, and it was the women who dealt with issues of purchasing, land, and managing family wealth."[20]

Specialized tours are one goal the Peabody Essex Museum has set as reinterpretation begins, particularly ones that focus on women and servants, and ones that relate to museum exhibits. For a recent exhibition, *Painted with Thread: The Art of American Embroidery,* Alexander developed tours focusing on textiles. She has also designed a tour highlighting women residents through three museum properties—the John Ward House (1684), the Crowninshield-Bentley House (ca. 1727), and the Gardner-Pingree House (1804). She is presently developing what she calls a "backwards tour" of the Gardner-Pingree House, in which the tour begins in the winter kitchen and the servants' work area, and may involve assigning such tasks to visitors as carrying wood to the third floor and preparing meals and serving them on the second floor. The tour will have special appeal to young people, Alexander believes: "They will appreciate how vastly different the experiences in this house were, even though geographically close—making the 'downstairs' experience as interesting as that of the 'upstairs.'" What has the response from the public been to the new interpretive strategies? "Huge," replied Kimberly. "Every one of these thematic or 'different' tours we do is packed. It's what people want."[21]

Each interview conducted for this chapter showed the determination of modern caretakers of historic houses to bring change. Visitors want social history, and they expect women's history. For some historic house museums, reinterpretation will involve a whole new way of thinking. While our understanding of history has changed, its presentation has not always kept up with new insights. The resources and methodology needed to effect change are available. Change requires resources—research time, tour guide training, and generally an updated publication. Although the solution for each site depends in part on funding limitations, reinterpretation can be done—and it should be an ongoing, enjoyable process of discovery.

Where does one begin? Each of the organizations discussed here started with what they knew and continued from there. The important men who lived in historic houses had wives, mothers, daughters, and, in many cases, servants. There are generally letters, diaries, other family papers, published genealogies, obituaries, and old newspaper articles about residents that can shed light on their lives. Researchers should tap the expertise of local librarians, archivists, and historical societies as well as those in state historic preservation commissions and archives. Volunteer organizations like the Daughters of the American Revolution also can be helpful. You never know what you will find once you start asking questions and look at existing information with fresh eyes. The process of asking both specialists and community boards of directors new questions will engage them all in rethinking the interpretation of historic sites in their communities.

Legal documents reveal unexpected kinds of information: probate court records list the contents of a house at its sale and wills detail possessions, financial arrangements, and beneficiaries. Organizational records that include catalogues of collections and minutes of early meetings can be mined for information about acquisitions and family history.

Many houses still contain such artifacts that belonged to its residents as portraits, collections of books, a writing desk, and collectables from a journey. At the Sargent-Murray-Gilman-Hough House in Gloucester, Massachusetts, where Ju-

Figure 4-5. Personal artifacts like this book of moral lessons and dictionary owned by Judith Sargent Murray offer house museums an opportunity to connect ideas with material culture. (*Photo by Westin Boer.*)

dith Sargent Murray lived from 1792–1794, the curator, who had to catalog from scratch, combed through the minutes of early meetings to begin the process. Along the way, she was able to determine what belonged to whom—and the extent to which verbal legend had driven the guided tour. Tours that weave the material culture into personal stories are much more compelling; using cataloging as part of the interpretation process leads to new insights.

If the researcher finds that the details specific to the women she or he is investigating are few or vague, there is a wealth of secondary sources which will help achieve a balance of specific and general information. Local and state histories, especially old ones, can establish a historical context and offer insight into daily life. Histories of African Americans in a particular town or accounts of the arrival and treatment of different immigrant groups can shed light on the experiences of less documented residents. Books describing details of domestic life over time are valuable resources.[22]

Bringing the interpretation of historic houses up to today's standards of inclusiveness and historical accuracy must be done—and it can be done—but the central question remains: who decides that change is needed? The best of volunteer and staff intentions will never see the light of day unless there is a commitment to change at the leadership level. Too often boards of directors cling to the "great white male" and "artifact" approach. They do this to the detriment of their organizations and to the peril of the houses they so earnestly want to preserve. They are violating the public's trust. They will drive people away, become irrelevant, and lose the support of their broader community, just when the house should be loved and supported.

Historic houses are wonderful educational tools. They connect us with our past in a way that effectively, and even emotionally, brings the past to life. Women were part of the story each one should be telling—and the public must insist upon it.

NOTES

I am grateful to the following individuals for generously sharing with me their experience in interpreting women's lives in historical settings: Kimberly Alexander, Peabody Essex Museum (Salem, MA); Irene Axelrod, The House of the Seven Gables (Salem, MA); Kelly Fellner, Longfellow National Historic Site (Cambridge, MA); John Grimes, Peabody Essex Museum; Janice Hodson, Longfellow National Historic Site; Caroline Keineth, Adams National Historic Site (Quincy, MA); David Olson, The House of the Seven Gables; Susan Porter, Society for the Preservation of New England Antiquities (Boston, MA); Cynthia Robinson, Bay State Historical League (Waltham, MA); James Shea, Longfellow National Historic Site; Carolyn Wahto, Society for the Preservation of New England Antiquities; and to William La Moy, Peabody Essex Museum, for additional assistance.

1. Jane C. Nylander, "A View from Our Windows," *SPNEA* (Society for the Preservation of New England Antiquities) *Newsletter* (Boston,1999), 1.
2. Patricia West, *Domesticating History: The Political Origins of America's House Museums* (Washington, D.C.: Smithsonian Institution, 1999), 1.
3. Page Putnam Miller, *Reclaiming the Past: Landmarks of Women's History* (Bloomington: Indiana University Press, 1992), 3.
4. Perhaps the most famous example is that of Abigail Adams, who ran the Adams homestead in Quincy, Massachusetts, now Adams National Historic Site, while her husband John served in Europe and in the Continental Congress in Philadelphia.
5. West, *Domesticating History,* 44. For another example, see the story of the Americanization projects run by the women founders of the Theodore Roosevelt Birthplace in Polly Welts Kaufman, *National Parks and the Woman's Voice: A History* (Albuquerque: University of New Mexico Press, 1996), 49.
6. Cynthia Robinson and Gretchen S. Storin, *Going Public: Community Program and Project Ideas for Historical Organizations* (Waltham, MA: Bay State Historical League, 1999), 2; West, *Domesticating History,* 84. 91; James W. Loewen, *Lies Across America: What Our Historic Sites Get Wrong* (New York: New Press, 1999), 19.
7. Sherry Butcher-Younghans, *Historic House Museums* (New York: Oxford University Press, 1993); Walter Muir Whitehill, *Independent Historical Societies: An Enquiry into their Research and Publication Functions and Their Financial Future* (Boston: Boston Athenaeum, 1962). For a discussion of the necessity of including women's historic sites that provides many examples,

see Miller, *Reclaiming the Past* and "Placing Women in the Past," National
Park Service, *Cultural Resource Management Bulletin* 20 (No. 3, 1997).

8. Kelly Fellner interview, 5 November 1999.
9. Janice Hodson interview, 5 November 1999. Fanny Longfellow died when
    her dress accidentally caught on fire from a burning match or hot sealing wax.
10. David K. Goss, Richard B. Trask, Bryant F. Tolles, Jr., Joseph Fibbert, and
    Jim McAlister, *Salem: Cornerstones of a Historic City* (Beverly, MA: Com-
    monwealth Editions, 1999); Salem Maritime National Historic Site, Peabody
    Museum, Essex Institute, *Salem: Maritime Salem in the Age of Sail* (Wash-
    ington, DC: National Park Service, U.S. Department of the Interior, 1987).
11. David Olson interview, 19 August 2001.
12. SPNEA owns ten "study houses" that are for architectural study only.
13. Carolyn Whato interview, 24 August 2001.
14. Ibid.
15. Ibid.
16. John R. Grimes interview, 10 October 2001.
17. Kimberly Alexander interview, 22 August 2001.
18. Ibid.
19. At the homestead of Abigail and John Adams in Quincy, Massachusetts (Adams
    NHS), the National Park Service has been able to preserve the continuing rela-
    tionship between the house and grounds to illustrate how the surrounding farm-
    land impacted the lives of the Adamses—particularly Abigail's.
20. Kimberly Alexander interview, 22 August 2001.
21. Ibid.
22. See especially, Jane C. Nylander, *Our Own Snug Fireplace* (New York:
    Knopf, 1994) and Jane C. Nylander, *Windows on the Past: Four Centuries of
    New England Homes* (Boston: Bulfinch Press, 1999).

SUGGESTED READINGS

Elisabeth Donaghy Garrett, *At Home: The American Family 1750–1870.* New York:
Harry N. Abrams, 1990. This thorough, scholarly, and well-illustrated presentation
of its subject makes this book a key resource for researchers and interpreters.

James W. Loewen, *Lies Across America: What Our Historic Sites Get Wrong.*
New York: New Press, 1999. A delightful and well-documented dismantling of
dozens of historic sites in the United States that should make everyone in the history business sit up and take notice. It validates the efforts of interpreters to rethink their own sites.

Page Putnam Miller, *Reclaiming the Past: Landmarks of Women's History.*
Bloomington: Indiana University Press, 1992. Women active in public history
present essays on how women used space in the fields of architecture, the arts, education, politics, religion, and work.

Jane C. Nylander, *Our Own Snug Fireside*. New York: Alfred A. Knopf, 1994. This essential, highly detailed resource for researchers and interpreters was written by the president of the Society for the Preservation of New England Antiquities (SPNEA).

Jane C. Nylander, *Windows on the Past: Four Centuries of New England Homes*. Boston: Bulfinch Press, 1999. SPNEA president takes readers on an illustrated tour through three centuries of SPNEA properties and discusses their interpretations.

Cynthia Robinson and Gretchen S. Sorin, *Going Public: Community Programs and Project Ideas for Historical Organizations*. Waltham, MA: Bay State Historical League, 1999. The authors present a useful guide for connecting history activities to the community.

Bonnie Hurd Smith, *Salem Women's Heritage Trail*. Salem, MA: Salem Chamber of Commerce, 2000. Like its predecessor in Boston, this book details the overlooked contributions of women to Salem history over four centuries, adding depth to existing historic sites and revealing new ones.

Harriet Welchel, ed., *Caring for Your Historic House*. New York: Harry N. Abrams, 1998. A practical, hands-on guide that can become a bible for caretakers of historic houses.

Patricia West, *Domesticating History: The Political Origins of America's House Museums*. Washington, DC: Smithsonian Institution, 1999. This key intellectual and political contribution to reinterpretation efforts in the historic house museum field was written by a National Park Service curator.

Susan Wilson, *Boston Sites and Insights: A Multicultural Guide to Fifty Historic Landmarks In and Around Boston*. Boston: Beacon Press, 1994. This second look at well-known sites in Boston adds the history of women and people of color to the city's story.

Chapter 5

SUNLIGHT AND SHADOW: FREE SPACE/SLAVE SPACE AT WHITE HAVEN

Pamela K. Sanfilippo

Julia Dent Grant, the wife of General and later President Ulysses S. Grant, wrote wistfully of her childhood years on her father's Missouri farm, White Haven. Her earliest recollection was of the front porch, or piazza as she called it, where her father lifted her "high in the air, telling me to look, the very trees were welcoming me, and, sure enough, the tall locust trees were tossing their white plumed branches gleefully." For Julia, "Life seemed one long summer of sunshine, flowers, and smiles to me and to all at that happy home."[1]

In contrast to Julia's memories of sunlight and smiles, the enslaved women of White Haven most likely recalled the darkness of the two kitchens on the property, where they spent a majority of their time. Only a small window, high on the front wall, and a back door break the thick stone walls of the basement winter kitchen, and although the stone summer kitchen is above ground, the one window and door do little to dispel the shadows. For the African American women who lived and worked in these rooms preparing meals for the white owners while caring for their own children, life was not as idyllic as Julia would have her audience believe.

White Haven, now Ulysses S. Grant National Historic Site, provides one example of how the study of the built environment can inform us about race and gender issues at a site primarily established to commemorate a white male. The spaces occupied by the free and enslaved women, where they worked and spent their leisure time, are indicative of social and economic status and provide context for understanding their lives. In particular, the built environment of White Haven provides the setting for exploring the life of First Lady Julia Dent Grant, and contrasting her experiences with those of the enslaved African American women of White Haven.

The methodology used by the research team at White Haven blends documentary sources, archeological investigations, architectural analysis, and oral history. Documentary records include memoirs, correspondence, photographs, census records, books, and newspaper articles. Artifacts unearthed at White Haven have been documented and compared to objects found at other sites to better inform us

Figure 5-1. A Park Service interpreter plays the role of Julia Dent Grant when welcoming visitors to White Haven, her childhood home, now restored at Ulysses S. Grant National Historic Site, St. Louis, MO. (*Courtesy of the National Park Service.*)

about these cultural remains. Architectural analysis provides concepts of space and usage of the structures to understand lifestyles. Oral history, including newspaper interviews, is often considered the weakest evidential link, although it can be extremely useful if the researcher clearly understands that a reporter mediated the source. This multidisciplinary approach provides a more comprehensive basis for understanding the racial and gender issues at White Haven than can be acquired through traditional historical methodology alone. These methods would be useful at other historic sites where public historians want to expand their interpretation to include social and cultural history issues previously ignored.

The site, with its five historic structures, was preserved and is significant because of Ulysses S. Grant's long association with the property. White Haven is where he met, courted, and proposed to Julia Dent, where three of their four children were born, and where he hoped to retire following his second term as president. It is a place where we can understand the personal side of Grant's life and the importance of family and home to him. That story cannot be told, however, without including his wife Julia Dent Grant as a central figure and her experiences and relationships with the other women of White Haven, enslaved and free.

Grant's association with White Haven spanned more than forty years, from 1843 until shortly before his death in 1885. Following his graduation from the U.S. Military Academy, Grant was assigned to Jefferson Barracks, just south of the city of St. Louis. He soon visited the family of his former roommate Fred Dent at their slave plantation, White Haven. He met Fred's younger sister, Julia, in 1844, and they were married in 1848 following his return from the War with Mexico. In the early years of their marriage, the Grants were stationed at posts in Detroit and New York, and Julia made several visits home, including one in May 1850 for the birth of their first child. The army transferred Grant to the Pacific Coast in 1852, but Julia returned to White Haven following the birth of their second son at Grant's family home in Bethel, Ohio. After a two-year separation, Grant resigned from the military, returning to St. Louis and his family to farm his father-in-law's estate with the assistance of the Dent slaves. The reunion was a happy one and the Grants set up housekeeping. They initially lived in a home built by Julia's brother on the White Haven property, then for a brief period in the log cabin the Grants named Hardscrabble. They returned to Julia's childhood home, the main house, following the death of her mother, Ellen Dent. The Grants had two more children during their years at White Haven, then in 1859 lived in the city of St. Louis for a brief period before moving to Galena, Illinois, in 1860.

During the Civil War, Julia often returned to her father's estate with the children, and as Colonel Dent's fortunes dwindled, Grant began purchasing the land from his father-in-law. Although the Grants hoped to retire to the farm following the war, Ulysses' military responsibilities and his election to the presidency kept them in Washington, with only occasional trips to St. Louis. From 1868 until 1875 Grant took an active role in managing the farm from the White House through St.

Figure 5-2. This photograph of White Haven and its surroundings about 1860 supports Julia Dent Grant's description of the peaceful setting of her childhood home. (*Courtesy of the National Park Service.*)

Louis friends, agents, and caretakers. Plans to turn the farm into a profitable horse breeding enterprise were thwarted by caretakers who felt little pressure from an absentee landlord, and by Grant, to whom the property initially represented everything that the terms family and home embodied, but who by 1876 no longer felt such an association with White Haven. He gave up his active involvement in managing the estate, eventually transferring ownership shortly before his death in 1885.

Until recently, the study of famous white males, such as Ulysses S. Grant, and the national events in which they played important roles have been the focus of American history. Not surprisingly, the majority of historic sites throughout America commemorate the political and military lives of these famous men or the events in which they participated. The first Thematic Framework adopted by the National Park Service (NPS) in 1936, guided the establishment and interpretation of sites along these lines. Based on the "stages of American progress," the framework "served to celebrate the achievements of the founding fathers and the inevitable march of democracy."[2] NPS staff evaluated sites under consideration for addition to the NPS system according to the compliance of the site with these ideals.

Beginning in the 1960s, cultural, social, racial, and gender issues forced historians to reexamine the past and recognize the influence of different groups and ordinary people in shaping America's collective past. The new scholarship that resulted from this reexamination has expanded the scope of historical inquiry to include the diversity and complexity of the human experience. As historians explored these new fields, individuals working at historic sites and museums began evaluating their interpretive themes and collections to identify the untold stories at their sites.[3]

The timing of the establishment of Ulysses S. Grant National Historic Site in 1990 coincided with the important social history work that had been done up to that point in the National Park Service. Rather than emphasizing Grant's military and political careers, the site explores Grant's personal life and, therefore, the compelling story and interpretive themes of White Haven include racial and gender issues. Although other parks and historic sites have revisited their themes to address these concerns, this Missouri site is one of the few properties in the NPS system specifically mandated to interpret women associated with a property preserved to commemorate a white male. The 1989 enabling legislation stated that the site was established to

> preserve and interpret for the benefit and inspiration of all Americans a key property associated with the life of General and later President Ulysses S. Grant and **the life of the First Lady Julia Dent Grant,** knowledge of which is essential to understanding, in the context of mid-nineteenth century American history, his rise to greatness, his heroic deeds and public service, and **her partnership** in them.[4] (emphasis added)

Fulfilling the mission to interpret the full story of the site has required going beyond the historical written record. Historical, architectural, and archeological research methods have been used separately and collectively to accomplish the goal of restoring the historic physical landscape for White Haven. The importance of these tangible resources is not just in the objects themselves, however, but in what they reveal about the people associated with them. These same research methods have made it possible to explore the contrasts in the lives of White Haven's free and enslaved women.

The written historical record about the residents of White Haven is extensive. Researchers are fortunate to have primary source documents such as the published memoirs of Julia Dent Grant, Ulysses S. Grant's published papers, census records, Emma Dent Casey's unpublished reminiscences, and countless other articles and books about the White Haven estate and its white and African American inhabitants. Yet this exclusively white perspective is only nominally balanced by one interview of Mary Robinson, a former female slave of the Dent family. Published in the *St. Louis Republican* as part of a tribute edition following Grant's death in 1885, the several anecdotes Mary Robinson recalled revealed aspects of the African American experience at White Haven. This account must be read with the knowledge that Mrs. Robinson was being interviewed by a white reporter immediately following Grant's death, and therefore her remarks might not have been completely candid.[5] The recent scholarship on slavery and African American women in general supplements the scant primary source material available at White Haven.

Architectural investigations of the five historic structures conducted over the course of several years have produced a comprehensive analysis of the physical attributes of the site, necessary research for understanding the spaces occupied by the residents of White Haven. Using historic photographs and sketches, the written record pertaining to the architecture of the buildings, and the structures themselves, the staff has established with a fair degree of accuracy the visual attributes of the exteriors and interior finishes of the buildings, as well as the use of these spaces by the nineteenth-century inhabitants of the property.

The third research method, archeological investigation, enhances understanding of African American culture at White Haven, as well as the lives of the white residents. During several investigations, archeologists employed field research methods to study the structures and uncover buried artifacts to fill in some of the blanks left by the scant written evidence on the enslaved. Literally thousands of items have been excavated from areas primarily identified with slaves, and they are being cleaned, cataloged, and examined.

Site staff members are studying these artifacts, photographs, and documents to record and interpret the experiences of the women of White Haven. The differences in lifestyles between the white women and their enslaved African American counterparts is revealed through these items and in the different spaces of the buildings occupied by these women. The sunlit areas reflect Julia's life as a well-to-do white lady, while the dark rooms of the kitchens suggest the struggles faced by the enslaved women.

An explanation of the physical layout of the main house helps in understanding the dynamics of difference for these two groups of women. Various early sketches of the property and an 1860s photograph of the main house correlate with Julia's description of the grounds and exterior of the house, enhanced with sunlight, trees, and the openness of the front porches. Since no photographs of the interior of the house during this period are extant, some speculation has been necessary in determining how the rooms were used.

From the attic to the basement, residents most likely used the spaces in the following manner. The attic, with its sloped walls that join at the roof peak, was unfinished, but such a large space would not have been left empty for any length of time. The four Dent sons were away from the home by the mid-1840s, so the attic was not needed on a daily basis for sleeping quarters and was probably a storage area for clothing and other family items. Colonel and Mrs. Dent's bedroom was most likely one of the two rooms on the second floor. Their three daughters, Julia, Ellen, and Emma probably shared the other upstairs room.

The four rooms on the first floor include those Julia identified as the parlor, the dining room, the sitting room, and the office without specifying their exact location. It is possible that a bedroom might have been on the first floor, but Julia's memoirs do not seem to support this. She wrote that a nephew of Mrs. Dent came to visit and "he was sleeping in a room on the first floor," suggesting that it was not a bedroom, and that someone sleeping on the first floor was an unusual occurrence.[6] Given other evidence, it is probable that the nephew was sleeping in a detached room, adjacent to the house, which could be used as a spare guestroom in the summer. Emma, Julia's youngest sister, mentioned that Grant frequently stayed overnight on his visits to White Haven during his courtship of Julia, and it is possible that he slept in this room. Julia's story of an unexpected visit from Grant during their courtship provided some clues as to the position of the various rooms. While Julia prepared to take an afternoon siesta, her maid saw Grant approaching the house. She recalled, "As soon as I could arrange my toilet, I repaired to the sitting room and, to my surprise, found Lieutenant Grant in the dining room, not far from my door."[7] Julia was probably in her bedroom upstairs, came downstairs, turned left into the dining room and headed toward the sitting room, when she found Grant already in the house, perhaps looking for her and headed toward the sitting room himself. At this time Grant visited White Haven on an almost daily basis, and would have been received into the informal sitting room, rather than in the more formal front parlor.

A large basement room identified as the winter kitchen was definitely used as such, based on the presence of a large fireplace as well as archeological evidence discovered during the 1995 investigations. The rest of the area below the first floor was a low crawl space, rather than actual rooms, perhaps used as a root cellar.

White Haven was initially a summer retreat for the Dent family—a place to escape the heat, pollution, and disease prevalent in urban St. Louis. Large front and back porches, which Julia called piazzas, helped cool the air and provided a relaxing place to socialize, read, or simply enjoy the peaceful sounds of the country. The interior of the home, while not expansive, was decorated in the style of

Figure 5-3. The recently excavated winter kitchen in the basement of the main house at White Haven is the space where the enslaved women cooked for the Dent family. (*Courtesy of the National Park Service.*)

the day. Colonel Dent had been a merchant in the city with access and means to furnish the house accordingly. A formal parlor and a separate family sitting room allowed the Dents to entertain friends and family, and Julia recalled in her memoirs numerous parties and activities at White Haven.

As the first daughter after four sons born to Colonel Frederick and Ellen Wrenshall Dent, Julia was treated well (some would say spoiled) by her father and brothers. She was educated at a neighborhood school with her male siblings in her early years, and then attended a finishing school for girls in the city of St. Louis. Julia spent most of her childhood summers playing on the grounds of White Haven, collecting flowers, bird nests, and berries. She went fishing, explored the fields, and had become an accomplished horsewoman by the time she met Ulysses S. Grant in early 1844. During their courtship, she and Ulysses fished "along the shady banks" of the Gravois Creek which ran through the property. According to Emma, they went riding in the mornings before breakfast or "through the sunset and twilight after supper."[8]

The front porch of the main house is still bright, airy, and inviting, and was the setting for many positive events in Julia's life. She recalled that her father spent most of his time reading the newspaper as he sat on the porch and her mother "loved to hear us sing her favorite ballads to Emmie's guitar as we sat on the piazza in the summer moonlight."[9] From the front porch Julia, her mother and sister Ellen used to watch the four older boys play games on the front lawn. On Grant's first visit to White Haven, he sat on the porch visiting with Colonel Dent, as Emma sat gazing up into his face, enchanted by his handsome features that she declared made him "as pretty as a doll."[10] It was also on the front piazza that Grant first asked Julia to wear his class ring as an engagement ring. At this time, she told Grant her mother would not approve of her accepting such a gift from a gentleman. When he returned a year later, he again found Julia on the piazza, where neighbors had arrived to say goodbye to her father who was headed east on business. Later, as they sat on the front porch alone, Grant told her he would ride to St. Louis with her father to officially ask for her hand in marriage.[11] She recalled that the two weeks of his visit "were passed in reading, walking, and riding, and full of such pleasant, pleasant memories to me. . . . The forests were more tenderly green, and our seat on the piazza was one bower of eglantine and white jessamine."[12] Several years later, when Grant returned home after two years of being stationed on the Pacific Coast, his own sons were playing on the porch and witnessed the happy reunion of their parents.

Other rooms of the house also reveal Julia's privileged upbringing, and the sunlight aspect of the white residents' experience. The bedrooms on the second floor of the house have large windows facing the southeast and northwest to allow indirect sunlight throughout the day. The rooms on the first floor have numerous windows that let in light and give a sense of openness despite the modest size of the rooms. Whether it was on the front piazza, her brightly lit bedroom, or the other public and private spaces of the main house where Julia spent most of her time, the feeling is one of openness and sunlight. Accompanying these spaces are the happy memories Julia recalled of her years at White Haven. It is evident she was surrounded and nurtured by love there, developing into a self-confident woman prepared to meet the challenges of adulthood.

Although Missouri never left the Union and Grant led Union forces during the Civil War, Julia's life at White Haven had been similar to that experienced by elite slaveholding women in the Confederate South. These women were born and raised into a society that believed that white slaveholding women were ladies whose lives should center on husbands and families, the domestic sphere.[13] Dependent on fathers and husbands, they were equally dependent on slave labor for housework and personal care. The skills needed to handle even basic tasks such as cooking or hairdressing were not part of the training most of these women received in their formative years. Their lack of experience became evident during the Civil War, when many slaves walked away from plantations leaving their former mistresses to handle all domestic tasks. Not only did the white women find themselves unprepared to do the work, doing it destroyed their concept of themselves as ladies who organized, planned and assigned work rather than completed it, an identity that was only restored when someone else resumed those chores.[14]

Julia's upbringing in a slaveholding family in St. Louis taught her to identify more closely with these women rather than with Yankee farmers' wives. Julia was accustomed to having slaves perform the majority of household chores. Whether they cooked, cleaned, or cared for the white children, the enslaved women on the Dent farm were vital to the smooth operation of the home. Julia recalled that her mother "was a generous housekeeper. She trusted her servants . . . she was delicate and often unable to attend personally to such matters. Frequently, Kitty, one of mamma's devoted maids, received her orders and carried them out perfectly."[15] Julia, who became mistress of White Haven in 1857 after her mother died, managed the home much as Ellen Dent had, relying on slaves to do the housekeeping, prepare meals, and attend to her children. When she tried to direct the making of many dishes, she failed and "gradually allowed the cook to have her own way."[16] She once (and only once) churned butter, making it clear to her readers that "my

Figure 5-4. Although Julia Dent Grant no longer lived at White Haven in 1879 when this photograph was taken, her *Memoirs* provide valuable information about the lives of its nineteenth-century residents both white and enslaved African Americans. (*Courtesy of the Library of Congress.*)

dear husband on all occasions furnish[ed] me with the necessary *help* to do my work."[17]

Julia's dependence upon slave labor was evident to her father, who pampered his favorite daughter throughout her childhood and early adult years. When the Grants prepared to move to Galena in 1860, they hired out Julia's four slaves. She recalled that "Papa was not willing they should go with me to Galena, saying the place might not suit us after all, and if I took them they would, of course, be free, 'and you know, sister, you cannot do without servants.' "[18] Julia's reliance on Jule, a slave nurse and maid, was so great that when Julia visited Grant in the south during the Civil War, she took Jule along. Years later, Julia was to regret the loss of her slaves as a result of the Civil War and emancipation, believing they had been well provided for at White Haven.[19] In contrast to her southern white counterparts her husband's rise to fame during and after the war improved her situation, while most upper class Southern women found their fortunes reversed.

It was important for Julia to focus her memories on her life at the main house rather than in the log cabin Grant built for their home, as she clearly recognized that the latter structure did not fit with her perception of herself as a lady. It is evident from her memoirs that she felt her role was to support her husband emotionally and be a proper hostess when in the public eye. In order to achieve those goals, she relied on the services of the slave women of White Haven prior to and during the Civil War, and hired servants after the war.

The enslaved women of White Haven lived on the same estate with the Dents and Grants, but their experiences were vastly different. While Julia provided much information in her reminiscences about the slave women, her perspective is unmistakably that of a slave owner. However, Julia's *Memoirs* still provide some idea of the conditions under which the slave women lived. Slave narratives from other sources, including Harriet Jacobs's *Incidents in the Life of a Slave Girl* and the 1930s Federal Writers Slave Narratives Project, give additional insight into the common experiences of enslaved women.[20]

As slave children on the Dent farm, Susanna, Julia Ann, Eliza, Phyllis, Sisy, Rose, Lucy, Louisa, Ann, and Sue were playmates of Julia and her sisters, Ellen and Emma, but always with a clear distinction in status.[21] Susanna, Julia Ann, and Eliza, would follow *behind* Julia on her forays into the countryside—carrying baskets for the berries she picked, or buckets for the fish she caught on lines baited by the enslaved children. One of Julia's fondest memories was of a bower alongside the creek where she reigned as princess, while her slave playmates decorated the niches with shells taken from her mother's parlor. Emma also recalled the slaves who were given to her at an early age by her father, all of them about her age. They, too, were playmates in those early years, tagging along *behind* her to do her bidding. She remembered them as her "full train of little darkies, with my small self acting as engine and pilot."[22] Although she referred to them as chums with whom she had some good times, she made clear the difference between herself and these darker-skinned children.

When Julia returned home from boarding school in the city of St. Louis, she noted that her childhood slave companions had grown and "attained the dignity of white aprons (not pinafores) and with gay bandannas bound around their heads making picturesque and becoming turbans."[23] These aprons symbolized formal slave servitude, a departure from the less structured days of childhood play. As these young girls grew, they were required to take on responsibilities that left little time for outdoor play or friendly interaction with the white young ladies they now called "mistress."

It was in the dark winter and summer kitchens that the food Julia remembered so well was prepared by Mary Robinson, the woman she called "black Mary"— "loaves of beautiful snowy cake, such plates full of delicious Maryland biscuit, such exquisite custards and puddings, such omelettes, gumbo soup, and fritters."[24] Most of Mary's day was spent preparing delicacies to be served to the Dent family, while "old Aunt Eadie" prepared corn bread cakes for the farmhands. Aunt Eadie also cooked lesser cuts of meat, such as the back, ribs, and feet, for the slaves.[25]

Objects uncovered at the site provide material evidence about the lifestyles of the slaves at White Haven. Chief site archeologist Jim Price believes the winter kitchen provides the best evidence of slave life found in the Midwest. Remains of food such as pork, beef, possum, raccoon, fish, and other small animal bones and fragments of beads, pipes, sewing items, lighting, and other artifacts, reveal what the slaves were eating, how they lived, and some of their beliefs.

Artifacts found in the summer and winter kitchens suggest that slave children played in these two rooms. Many porcelain and clay marbles dating from the 1830s to the 1860s were discovered in both places. Marbles was a popular game for children, and their presence indicates that children spent time in these two kitchens. Although the slave children were often outside attending to the Dent children, they played in these kitchens because their caregivers, the enslaved adult women, spent a majority of their time in these two rooms. Other child-related artifacts include pieces of a complete slate and slate pencils, perhaps used as a writing board by the children. Julia learned to read and write in a small neighborhood school among friends, while her enslaved African American playmates may have learned in seclusion in the winter kitchen, hiding their writing instruments beneath the floorboards because it was illegal in Missouri to teach a slave to read or write. There was a small cache of trinkets discovered in a corner of the winter kitchen, indicating a child may have collected these items and hidden them beneath the floorboards. Enslaved children collected marbles and other miscellaneous pieces of glass and slate to acquire personal possessions, no matter how meager.[26]

Archeologists also identified materials, known as "diviners' bundles," that may have been used by the slaves in "white magic" rituals. Slaves carried this type of religious practice from Africa and adapted it to new circumstances in America. These bundles gave slaves some measure of control over their uncertain lives. They believed glass drawer knobs, buttons, coiled wire, and stones protected those who resided in the room or building. Although it is not clear what each of these objects signified, bundles indicate that slaves who were generations removed from their

Figure 5-5. Park Service archeologists uncovered many artifacts in the winter kitchen of White Haven including marbles, a drawer pull, brass spoon bowl, iron dinner knife, brass door knobs, teapot or sugar bowl lid, and brass wire. (*Courtesy of the National Park Service.*)

African roots continued this practice as a means of coping with the harsh realities of enslavement.[27]

Fear of punishment for breaking something, whether by accident or on purpose, may have induced one or more of the household slaves to hide broken dishes and other items beneath the floorboards in the winter kitchen. All pieces of one dish were found together during a recent archeological dig, as well as other pieces too large to fall between the spaces in the floorboards, leading the principal investigator to conclude that a slave succeeded in concealing evidence of the mishap.[28]

The darker rooms of the main house and other structures were most often spaces occupied by slaves. Based on evidence from other plantation homes, it is logical to assume that the African American women who cared for the Dent girls and their parents would have slept nearby, possibly on mats in the hallway, to be summoned at a moment's notice. There is also evidence that one or more of the slaves lived in the winter kitchen. The slave cabins (none of which are extant) reportedly had wood floors and windows, and stone fireplaces for heating, but any decoration or comfort would have been minimal. Furniture was most likely hand-made, or handed down from the Dents when they replaced worn items with new pieces.

Mary Robinson served as the Dent cook for many years. Her reminiscences following Grant's death on July 23, 1885 reveal another aspect of the lives of the African American women of White Haven. Like many enslaved women, Mary was at times a confidant of the white women, but at other times was an unnoticed observer to many of the events and listener to conversations that took place among the white residents. She recalled that Mrs. Dent "took a great fancy to Grant," despite her husband's opposition to him when he first began courting their daughter Julia. Ellen Dent confided in Mary Robinson, telling her, "I like that young man. There is something noble in him. His air and the expression of his face convince me that he has a noble heart, and that he will be a great man some day." Mary reported several conversations with Grant, including one when he said "he wanted to give his wife's slaves their freedom as soon as he was able."[29]

As often as she was involved in conversations with family members, Mary was more frequently a silent observer of conversations and events that occurred in the Dent household. She overheard relatives speak of Grant's unassuming manner, and listened to their discussions regarding his poor financial condition during their prewar years at White Haven. Mary remembered Julia insisting "'we will not always be in this condition. Wait until Dudie (Grant) becomes president. I dreamed last night he had been elected president.'" Mary also heard Grant and his father-in-law talking through the night during one of Grant's visits to the farm at the beginning of the war. She said, "I heard part of their conversation, and can remember what was said very distinctly to this day. Dent was opposed to Lincoln, and tried to induce Grant not to fight with the Union army. He wanted him to cast his destiny with the South. This Grant refused to do. . . . The interview between the general and his father-in-law was a very long and heated one. It was not very satisfactory to either, I imagined, at the time."[30] In fulfilling her role as slave cook and housekeeper for the Dents, Mary Robinson came out of the shadows when directly addressed by the white residents, but otherwise receded into near invisibility, silently hearing and observing the conversations and actions of her white masters and mistresses.

Julia and her siblings considered the slaves at White Haven to be members of the plantation family. Yet all of these individuals left the estate before they were officially freed by The Missouri Emancipation Ordinance in 1865. These women and men had always understood their subservient status at White Haven, and were anxious to begin new lives as freed individuals. Julia's confusion as to why they would want to leave emphasizes a final ideological contrast between the white and enslaved women that correlates with the physical contrast of the sunlight and shadow spaces at White Haven.

After the slaves were freed under Missouri's new constitution in 1865, the winter kitchen was seldom used. Grant purchased the property from his father-in-law, and hired a caretaker to manage the farm during his long absences. With his permission, a portion of the back porch was enclosed to make a first floor kitchen for the house. The new caretaker, William Elrod, his wife Sarah (a cousin of Grant's), their three daughters, and one son moved into the house. Elrod received a salary, and Grant wrote him at one point that he assumed Sarah and the girls would raise additional income through selling eggs.[31] Their opportunity to earn money for their labor, and the elevation of the kitchen from the basement to the first floor represented a new era in women's lives at White Haven and throughout the country during the post-Civil War years.

Researchers used each of the methods to guide them in restoring the five historic structures on the property to their 1875 appearance. Architectural, historical, and archeological evidence indicates that the icehouse and the barn were both constructed during this period, when Grant actually owned the property. Extensive correspondence from Grant to various individuals in St. Louis reveals his planning, activities, and frustrations with acquisition and absentee management of the estate. Restoring the structures to the period when the Grants actually resided on the property would have limited the opportunities for interpreting these subsequent aspects of Grant's life and the White Haven farm. The stone summer kitchen and the basement winter kitchen, although no longer used as such after the war, however, remain as visible evidence of the years during which the slaves lived and worked there. The decision to use the 1875 restoration date, which left slave-related structures intact, therefore, provides the best opportunity for interpreting the property and its many inhabitants over the course of nearly one hundred years.

Given its name, few first-time visitors to Ulysses S. Grant National Historic Site anticipate that women and slavery are major interpretive themes. As a result of the multidisciplinary research approach, interpreters are able use the built environment to tell a more complete story; one that assists visitors in finding a connection with its nineteenth-century residents, female and male, black and white, enslaved and free, famous and ordinary.

This approach can be used at other historic sites to provide visitors with a more inclusive view of our collective past. Attention to gender and race perspectives that were always there, but seldom emphasized in the past, enhances the visitor experience and brings all historical individuals out of the shadows and into the sunlight.

NOTES

1. Julia Dent Grant, *The Personal Memoirs of Julia Dent Grant (Mrs. Ulysses S. Grant)* John Y. Simon, ed. (Carbondale, IL: Southern Illinois University Press, 1975), hereafter JDG *Memoirs,* 33. For information on Julia Dent Grant and Ulysses S. Grant see also *The Papers of Ulysses S. Grant,* John Y. Simon, ed. (Carbondale, IL: Southern Illinois University Press, 1990) and Ulysses S. Grant, *The Personal Memoirs of U.S. Grant* (New York: Charles Webster, 1886).

2. National Park Service, *Revision of the National Park Service's Thematic Framework, 1996,* 1.

3. Among those responsible for a shift to a more inclusive view at National Park Service sites is Heather Huyck. Initially, Huyck and others began incorpo-

rating new scholarship on racial and gender issues into the interpretive themes at the sites where they worked. They then led the movement within the Park Service to reconsider how potential new sites would be evaluated as well as to expand themes at other parks already in the system. In 1995, the Chief Historian for the NPS, Dwight Pitcaithley, brought together a group of consulting scholars, NPS staff, and others to revise the Thematic Framework for the NPS. The resulting document represents a clear break with the previous framework, emphasizing, "how scholarship is dramatically changing the way we look at the past, reconstructing it as an integrated, diverse, complex, human experience." With this framework in place, NPS staff began the task of integrating the untold stories of women, minorities and all social, cultural, and economic classes into the parks.

In the field of women's history, Marie Rust, Field Director of the Northeast Region of the NPS, brought together key individuals to "develop a vision for the role of the National Park Service in the research, identification, interpretation, and commemoration of the contributions and experiences of American women." From that meeting, *Exploring a Common Past: Interpreting Women's History in the National Park Service* became the first in a series of resource guides designed to assist employees at historic sites (both NPS and non-NPS) in "reviewing and evaluating interpretive programs and media and adjusting them in light of recent scholarship." Additionally, Polly Welts Kaufman listed over one hundred national parks that interpret women in her 1996 book, *National Parks and the Woman's Voice* (Albuquerque: University of New Mexico Press). A 1997 study of all national parks indicated that every single one included a female historical presence, and efforts were underway to interpret the stories of women in these parks.

4. Public Law 101–106, October 2, 1989.

5. "Auntie Robinson's Recollections," *St. Louis Republican,* July 24, 1885. Another newspaper article of an interview with Jennie Rhodes was published in the December 25, 1912 *Globe Democrat.* The article relates only that Rhodes came to White Haven shortly before the Civil War, and remained serving "her white folks" for many years. One interesting feature is that Mrs. Rhodes had several items from the Dent household, including china, silverware, and glassware. "Dent Family Slave to Mark 70th Year," *Globe Democrat,* December 25, 1912.

6. JDG *Memoirs,* 43.

7. *Ibid.,* 50.

8. Emma Dent Casey. "When Grant Went A-Courtin'.", unpublished manuscript, 15.

9. JDG *Memoirs,* 42, 34.

10. *Ibid.,* 35; Casey, 6–7.

11. JDG *Memoirs,* 49, 51.

12. *Ibid.,* 51–52.

13. Drew Gilpin Faust, *Mothers of Invention: Women of the Slaveholding South in the American Civil War* (New York: Vintage Books, 1997).

14. *Ibid.*, 77–8.

15. JDG *Memoirs*, 34.

16. *Ibid.*, 60.

17. *Ibid.*, 78. Julia's reliance on the enslaved was such that when she set up housekeeping as a young bride, she did not know where to start, and remembered that "We had such fine old servants at home [White Haven] that I was under the impression that the house kept itself." JDG *Memoirs*, 60.

18. *Ibid.*, 82–83. The 1857 decision by the Supreme Court in Dred Scott v. John F. A. Sanford left Scott enslaved despite the fact that his owner had taken him to free territory. In addition, even though Scott had been taken to the free state of Illinois, he was restored to slavery when he returned to the slave state of Missouri, according to Justice Taney's ruling. The Court's decision and its interpretation by many to mean that owners were legally entitled to take their slaves, as property, anywhere, led to confusion and debate. Colonel Dent was correct that Julia's slaves would be free in Illinois, but it is difficult to determine if the slaves would have known that or, like Scott, would have stayed with Julia until she returned to Missouri. See Walter Ehrlich's *They Have No Rights: Dred Scott's Struggle for Freedom* (Westport CT: Greenwood Press, 1979) for a detailed account of Scott's case.

19. *Ibid.*, 83, 34.

20. Harriet Jacobs, *Incidents in the Life of a Slave Girl* (Cambridge, MA: Harvard University Press, 1987); George P. Rawick, *The American Slave: A Composite Autobiography* (Westport, CT: Greenwood Press, 1972).

21. The names of the slave children are recorded by Julia in her *Memoirs* and in Emma Dent Casey's unpublished reminiscences.

22. JDG *Memoirs*, 36–37; Casey, 11.

23. JDG *Memoirs*, 39–40.

24. *Ibid.*, 40.

25. *Ibid.*, 44–5.

26. James E. Price and Mary Jane Hastings, "A Report on the 1995 Excavations at Ulysses S. Grant National Historic Site, St. Louis, Missouri," Draft (National Park Service, 1998); David K. Wiggins, "The Play of Slave Children in the Plantation Communities of the Old South, 1820–1860," *Journal of Sport History*, v. 7, n. 2, 27.

27. Bill Broadway, "Digging Up Some Divining Inspiration," *Washington Post*, 16 August 1997; John Noble Wilford, "Slave Artifacts Under the Hearth," *New York Times*, 27 August 1996; Price and Hastings, 19–20.

28. JDG *Memoirs*, 39–40; Price, 19.

29. "Auntie Robinson's Recollections," *St. Louis Republican*, 24 July 1885.

30. *Ibid.*

31. Ulysses S. Grant to William Elrod, 27 May 1868, *The Papers of Ulysses S. Grant*, vol. XVIII, 263.

SUGGESTED READINGS

Drew Gilpin Faust, *Mothers of Invention: Women of the Slaveholding South in the American Civil War*. New York: Vintage Books, 1997, first published by the University of North Carolina Press in 1966. Using hundreds of letters, memoirs and diary excerpts, Faust explores what it meant to be a "lady" in the South, and how those notions were changed by the social upheaval of the Civil War. When visitors use this text in conjunction with visits to Civil War-era homes, their experiences become more relevant.

Elizabeth Fox-Genovese, *Within the Plantation Household: Black and White Women of the Old South*. Chapel Hill: University of North Carolina Press, 1988. This groundbreaking study of slaveholding and enslaved women of the South explores the intricacies of the relationships within Southern households. It is an excellent source for Southern women's history in the antebellum period.

Eugene D. Genovese, *Roll, Jordan, Roll: The World the Slaves Made*. New York: Vintage Books, 1974. This classic work on slavery in America was one of the first to use primary source documents in analyzing the slave experience in the United States.

Julia Dent Grant, *The Personal Memoirs of Julia Dent Grant (Mrs. Ulysses S. Grant)*. John Y. Simon, ed., Carbondale, IL: Southern Illinois University Press, 1975. Mrs. Grant's manuscript, written in the 1890s, remained unpublished until 1975. An intensely personal reminiscence about her loving partnership with her husband, the reader can almost hear Julia tell her story. Recommended reading before a visit to White Haven, now Ulysses S. Grant National Historic Site, Julia's childhood home that Grant later purchased for their retirement.

Wilma King, *Stolen Childhood: Slave Youth in Nineteenth-Century America*. Bloomington: Indiana University Press, 1995. King uses extensive resources to examine the experience of slave children, the difficulties of familial relationships in the slave community, and the ways in which families maintained some degree of control over their lives.

National Park Service, Organization of American Historians, *Exploring a Common Past: Interpreting Women's History in the National Park Service*. Washington, DC: 1996. This resource guide offers a list of themes and questions that can be used by staff at historic sites and museums to assess programs and incorporate women's pasts into preservation and interpretive programs. The bibliography includes a section on "Resources on Women and the Built Environment" that is useful for understanding how the built environment can inform us about gender issues.

Alan W. O'Bright and Kristen R. Marolf, *The Farm on the Gravois: Historic Structures Report*. St. Louis, MO: National Park Service, 1999. The Historic Structures

Report for the five historic buildings on the Ulysses S. Grant National Historic Site property provides photographs, sketches, and architectural drawings to supplement the architectural analysis of the buildings that guided the restoration process.

George P. Rawick, ed., *The American Slave: A Composite Autobiography*. Westport, CT: Greenwood Press, 1972. The nineteen-volume set of the printed transcripts from the Federal Writers' Project Slave Narratives of the Works Progress Administration was completed between 1936 and 1938. These transcripts were long ignored by historians as being inaccurate remembrances of former slaves. They are now used in conjunction with other sources to present the slave perspective long missing from most works on slavery.

John Michael Vlach, *Back of the Big House: The Architecture of Plantation Slavery*. Chapel Hill: University of North Carolina Press, 1993. This is an excellent book that documents and describes the structures and spaces in which plantation slaves lived.

Charles G. Waugh and Martin H. Greenberg, eds., *The Women's War in the South: Recollections and Reflections of the American Civil War*. Nashville, TN: Cumberland House, 1999. Written from a white perspective, the collection of letters, diaries, and postwar writings provide insight into the daily activities of white, mostly slaveholding, women, as well as their perspectives on war, slavery, and women's roles and responsibilities during the Civil War era.

Chapter 6

THE SERVANT SLANT: IRISH IMMIGRANT WOMEN DOMESTIC SERVANTS AND HISTORIC HOUSE MUSEUMS

Margaret Lynch-Brennan

> . . . from every house, sooner or later, they went away.
> —Mary Carbery, *The Farm by Lough Gur*[1]

The young people of Ireland emigrated, many to America where they clustered in the urban Northeast. There Irish women commonly worked as live-in domestic servants (cooks, waitresses, chambermaids, child nurses [nannies], laundresses and maids-of-all-work) in private homes. Some of those homes stand today as historic house museums. For example, Irish women worked as servants in such New York State historic house museums as Lindenwald, the Kinderhook home of President Martin Van Buren and Olana, the Hudson River home of the artist Frederic Church. Interpretations at most nineteenth-century American historic house museums, however, tend to focus only on one class of the women who resided in historic houses—they celebrate primarily the Protestant elite.[2]

The purpose of this chapter is to serve as a guide to the incorporation of Irish-born domestics into historic house museum interpretations. Methods will be suggested on how this can be accomplished, and an interpretive context will be set by providing information on why Irish women immigrated to, and became domestic servants in, America circa 1845–1900. In addition, information will be provided on the class, cultural, ethnic, and religious conflicts that helped define their experience. The suggested methods can be adapted to incorporate other women who worked as servants in nineteenth-century America, such as Scandinavian and German immigrants and African Americans, into the interpretations of historic house museums.

The Irish usually came to the United States in a chain migration, in which their passage was paid by a relative already established here. Once settled in America the immigrant was expected to do the same for another family member. In this system, by the end of the nineteenth century, more Irish daughters than Irish sons

Figure 6-1. Annie Walsh McMaster, born in 1853 in County Roscommon, Ireland, immigrated to the U.S. in 1872 and worked as a domestic servant until her marriage in 1883 to James McMaster from County Tyrone, Ireland. (*Courtesy Daureen Aulenbach, Annie's great-granddaughter.*)

left Ireland for the United States. These Irish daughters, the Irish Biddy or Bridget (the general name given to Irish-born female domestic servants during the nineteenth century), appeared to dominate American domestic service. In 1850, for example, more than 70 percent of Boston's domestic servants were Irish-born, and in 1900, more than 50 percent of all the working women in America who were born in Ireland worked as domestic servants. And, Irish domestics captured the American imagination, if popular literature is any indication. After 1850, Biddy, the stereotypical servant, was ubiquitous in nineteenth-century popular American literature.[3]

Irish women servants, however, are often the "ghosts" of historic house mu-

seum interpretations. Given the importance of the Irish as nineteenth-century immigrants to America, this lack of attention to Irish domestics is surprising. Although the Irish immigration to the United States was unusual in the high number
of women included in the immigrant stream, historians, tend to focus more on
Irish men, particularly Irish men in politics, than they do on Irish women. But, in
the nineteenth century, the most familiar frontier of contact between Irish immigrants and middle-class Protestant Americans was the private home, wherein the
mistress and her Irish servant confronted each other across a gulf of class, cultural,
ethnic, and religious differences.[4]

The first task in developing an interpretation of Irish immigrant servants is to
determine whether or not they lived and worked in a particular historic house museum. This information can be obtained by checking federal census records —
they provide the country of birth and names and ages of live-in servants; the 1870
federal census was the first to include information on the employment of all women.
State census records may also prove helpful. Employer account books may also
be a source of information on the servants who inhabited the historic house —
employers sometimes listed the names of their servants, as well as the wages paid
them, in these account books. If the account books do not precisely indicate the
ethnicity of the servants, the servants' surnames will certainly provide clues that
can be cross-checked with census records. Account books may contain other clues
that the servants were immigrant Irish women, such as notations that the employer
posted letters to Ireland for particular servants. The letters and diaries of the owners of the house are also good sources for information as to whether they employed Irish servants. Elizabeth Cady Stanton's correspondence, for example,
shows that she employed Irish domestics. She apparently shared the negative view
of Irish servants that was pervasive in the nineteenth century. Stanton was afraid
that she might one day be called to account for " 'breaking the pate' of some stu-
pid Hibernian for burning my meat or pudding on some company occasion."[5] In
addition, local histories, old newspaper articles, and Roman Catholic Church
records may shed light on whether Irish domestic servants worked in the historic
house.

In considering how to interpret Irish servants in historic house museums, a cau-
tion is in order — interpretations must be based on accurate historical research material and must not perpetuate nineteenth-century stereotypes of Irish domestics.
And, in considering how the experience of Irish servants might be interpreted, it
is important to note that some historians of women have found that there was no
"universal sisterhood" of women in nineteenth-century America.[6] The mistress
represented but one of the classes of women resident in the historic house; even
in the best of situations, within the intimate sphere of the home, their differences
probably separated the Irish domestic from the mistress.

While museums can, on their own, develop an interpretation featuring servants,
interpretations can also be developed through collaborative efforts with members
of the Irish-American community. Oral history interviews might be conducted
with former servants, for example, or their children, or those knowledgeable about

Irish servants, to learn details of what these women were like as people, as well as workers. Interpretations can also be developed in collaboration with educators. The study of Irish immigrant women working in domestic service connects to college courses in women's studies, nineteenth-century American history, and public history. Such a study also relates to the elementary and secondary social studies curricula in many states. New York State, for example, includes immigration and the Great Irish Famine in its social studies curricula.

Once it has been determined that Irish domestics worked in the historic house museum, and the period in which they lived and worked has been identified, museum professionals might collaborate with other interested parties to develop a first-person tour of the house. This tour would be conducted by a guide (or guides) in the guise of an Irish servant(s) who actually lived in the house. Using primary source material, including quotations from actual servants, this Irish domestic-led tour would interpret the house from the servant's point of view. The sample tour delineated below emphasizes three themes.

Theme One explains that most Irish immigrant women came to the United States from poor, rural Ireland for economic and social reasons, and most were young and single. *Theme Two* focuses on the contrast between the cultural and material world in Ireland from which the servant came, and the American cultural and material world in which she lived and worked. *Theme Three* centers on demonstrating that the historic house museum was a work site for domestic servants, and that for Irish immigrant women, there were both positive and negative aspects to the occupation of domestic service.

THEME ONE

Irish women immigrated to America primarily for economic and social reasons that remained consistent over the second half of the nineteenth century: to improve their material circumstances and to marry. Irish immigration to the United States began long before the massive migration of the Great Irish Famine of 1845–52, in which the potato, the staple of the Irish diet, was destroyed by the potato blight. The Famine, however, served to greatly accelerate Irish immigration to the United States as did the changes in Irish land inheritance patterns and family life that were attendant on the Famine. In the post-Famine period the custom of "strong" (i.e., big or successful) Irish farmers of giving land to only one son, rather than dividing it among the children, became widespread throughout Ireland. It also became a widespread practice for marriages to be arranged affairs, and a dowry became necessary to make a match. With their "long" (i.e., large) families, the Irish usually could provide only one daughter with a dowry. Without the necessary dowry, an Irish woman could not marry. For the surplus children for whom no provision for land or dowry could be made, there were few options; emigration to America was one of those options.[7]

Irish women came to America for adventure, too, longing for something beyond what has been characterized as the dull social life of post-Famine, rural Ireland. They evidently aspired to a higher standard of living than Irish men did and this desire for an improved material life has been linked to emigration. Marriage was an important goal for Irish women because traditionally in Irish culture, marriage conferred adult status. Irish women acquired authority through motherhood, as the heart at the center of the family. In America, where a dowry was unnecessary, marriage was a more attainable goal for an Irish woman than it was in Ireland.[8]

Many Irish servants were really just young girls. Helen Chapman wrote to her mother in October 1848 that Ann Mitchell, her "little Irish girl," was "not yet thirteen."[9] For such transplanted young girls, domestic service could have been a lonely experience, at least initially. Irish servant Mary Malone, for example, wrote that she was " 'verry lonseom [*sic*] and down hearted' and 'wish[ed] my Sister Margaret was here.' "[10]

THEME TWO

The cultural and material world of the immigrant's home in Ireland contrasted greatly with her new life as a servant girl in America. The American world emphasized refinement; it was a world in which good taste was associated with Christian morality, and the parlor, books, and the piano, were seen as tokens of a family's respectability. In this middle-class world table manners emerged as the ultimate test of gentility and breeding. Etiquette books, those "social bibles" of the American middle class, failed to even address immigrants; etiquette itself was used to distinguish the middle class from the lower classes.[11]

It is likely that Irish servants were nurtured on a potato-based diet in rural Ireland that contrasted greatly with the meals they were expected to cook and serve in urban America. Certainly, the potato was the staple of the pre-Famine Irish diet. Data from 1839 indicate that the typical mature male Irish worker ate nearly thirteen pounds of boiled potatoes, and drank nearly three pints of buttermilk, per day. The Irish diet also included cabbage and traditionally oats, commonly in the form of porridge (oatmeal). The blandness of this diet was offset by salt, water, or milk, or by relishes of strong butter or salt herrings called "kitchen."[12]

Housing of the poorer rural Irish would have stood in dramatic contrast with the middle-class homes in which Irish women worked in America. The 1841 Irish census showed that 85 percent of the population lived in rural areas, and some 50 percent of rural families lived in mud cabins consisting of a single room, the lowest class of housing. Furniture would have been minimal in many rural Irish homes, where life revolved around the kitchen and the hearth with its turf fire. Little housework of the kind that was expected in middle-class American homes would have been required in the cabins of rural Ireland. And certainly the kind of elaborate cooking that became more common among middle-class Americans from 1845–1900 would have been unheard of in rural Irish homes. Housework in rural Ireland increased over time, however, especially from 1890 on, as an Irish form of domesticity came into existence.[13]

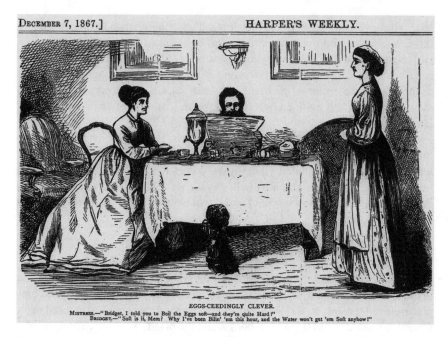

EGGS-CEEDINGLY CLEVER.

Mistress.—"Bridget, I told you to Boil the Eggs soft—and they're quite Hard!"
Bridget.—"Soft is it, Mem? Why I've been Bilin' 'em this hour, and the Water won't get 'em Soft anyhow!"

Figure 6-2. A typical cartoon makes fun of "Bridget," the Irish servant, for her limited knowledge of cooking. It was published in *Harper's Weekly* (7 December 1867), 781. This cartoon was also printed in Susan Williams, *Savory Suppers and Fashionable Feasts* (1985).

The clothing of rural Irish women differed from that of middle-class American women, too. While such American magazines as *Godey's Lady's Book* featured the latest fashions for middle-class women, Mr. and Mrs. S. C. Hall, touring Ireland in the pre-Famine period, described Irish girls as wearing the long, blue, hooded cloak traditional for Irish women. Such clothing continued to be worn by some Irish women into the twentieth century, according to Padraic Colum, who commented on old women in Cork City attired in old-fashioned long cloaks and on women who wore shawls on their heads. Over the course of the nineteenth century, observers remarked on the red clothing worn by Irish women; an American woman was told that it was worn to keep away the fairies. They also declared that Irish women went barefoot. Irish women, however, knew they should change from their Irish clothing when going out to America, and once here apparently were fond of fashion.[14]

The behavior and habits deemed permissible for women in Ireland often differed from those deemed appropriate for middle-class American women. For, although it was not uncommon for some rural Irish women to smoke a pipe, this was just not done by middle-class women in urban America. Women from rural Ireland also were known to drink alcohol, in marked contrast with those middle-class American women who enthusiastically embraced temperance. And Irish servants did not seem to accept their social inequality, much to the annoyance of middle-class Americans.[15]

Irish women in America have been characterized as assertive; Peig Sayers used an Irish expression, "a woman's tongue is a thing that doesn't rust," that is indicative of female assertiveness.[16] Such assertiveness diverged from the submissiveness valued in women in the American cult of domesticity. The *Boston Pilot,* termed a bible for the Irish in America, ran a piece about a servant girl who displayed such assertive behavior. The servant girl filed suit against her employer because the number of people in her employer's family was greater than the number for which she had contracted — nine people rather than five. She won her suit, recovering an additional monthly allowance.[17]

Their ethnicity and religion also distinguished Irish servants, most of whom were Roman Catholics, from their Protestant employers. Frequently, the terms Irish and Catholic were deemed synonymous. That servants were discriminated against on the basis of ethnicity and/or religion is borne out by contemporary accounts. And, warnings of such discrimination wended their way back to Ireland.[18]

Prior to the arrival of the Irish in America, being American was seen as synonymous with being Protestant. Many Protestant Americans felt their way of life threatened by Irish Catholic immigrants; the Know-Nothing Movement of the 1850s exemplified such nativism. Some Protestant employers of domestics did not consider Catholics to be Christians. And, the inconvenience caused them by servants taking time off to go to Mass on Sundays and Holy Days of Obligation also annoyed some employers. Hence, advertisements for domestic servants might specify that applications would not be accepted from Catholics or the Irish.[19]

On the other hand, their Catholicism was important to Irish domestics. The Catholic Church served as a contact point for servants to keep in touch with the Irish community, and they derived solace from Catholic devotions. Contemporary observers believed that Catholicism was a great source of consolation for displaced Irish servants. Harriet Spofford thought that within a Catholic Church building Irish servants felt "at home once more; it is the atmosphere of the sweet old land that breathes about them; . . . strangers in a strange land, the church is father and mother, home and country, too!"[20] And, in 1888, Irish domestic Mary Ann Rowe attested to the importance of her Catholicism. Indicating that she was pleased to work near a Catholic Church, she wrote, "I am within two or three minutes walk from the church. There is a splendid church here . . . and three priests. I can go to mass every Sunday and to confession whenever I want to."[21]

Mistress and Irish servant may have viewed each other across a gulf of class, cultural, ethnic, and religious differences, but not all employer-servant relations were fraught with problems. The situation was dependent on the specific domestic circumstances in which a servant worked. Irish servants worked for good as well as bad employers. Certainly some mistresses were sympathetic to their plight. Catharine Beecher and Harriet Beecher Stowe reminded employers that their Irish servants were young girls, on their own, far from home, without their parents, struggling to save money to send home to Ireland. The authors asked, "If our daughters did as much for us, should we not be proud of their energy and heroism?"[22]

And, while Clarence Cook blamed the "carelessness" and "slovenliness" of "the invasion of the Biddy tribe from the bogs of Ireland" for the loss of pleasant American ways of living, the affability, good humor, and wittiness of the Irish were also recognized. Irish servants were described as "cheerful" and of "vivacious nature," and of "a glad gay race, fond of talking and laughing, fond of their quips and jokes, eager for pleasure."[23]

THEME THREE

Many historic house museums were once work sites for Irish immigrant women. Domestic service was the most significant waged occupation for women in both nineteenth-century Ireland and nineteenth-century America. With industrialization, urbanization, the rise of the urban middle class, and the spread of gentility in America, standards of cleanliness rose. As the size of the middle class in urban America increased, the demand for servants also increased as women sought help with the physically taxing toil of housework. Hiring servants meant more free time for leisure pursuits. It also advertised class standing; servants were status symbols for the family. Consequently, there were plenty of domestic service jobs available to Irish immigrant women in middle-class American homes. If a servant did not like her position, she could quit and usually find a new one. The inconvenience caused by the frequent turnover of servants drove some mistresses wild.[24]

Domestic service met the immediate needs of young, single Irish immigrants of this era. Girls from rural Ireland became domestic servants in urban America because jobs were available, and they met the basic criteria established for servants: they were female and most spoke English. Over the course of the nineteenth century, Irish-speaking parents came to see speaking the Irish language (as the Irish call Gaelic) as a detriment for the children they expected to emigrate to America, where they would need to speak English. Female Irish emigrants were also increasingly literate in English over the course of the nineteenth century.[25]

In both Ireland and America, domestic service was a low-status occupation. But, because the wages paid to servants in America were higher than those in Ireland, there was no loss in status for an Irish girl to go into service in America. Regarding wages, Patrick McKeown wrote home in 1883 from Philadelphia, "Single women can get along here better than men as they can get employment more readily than men. For instance liveing [sic] out girls or as the[y] are called at home servant girls gets from eight to twelve shillings per week and keep, that is from two to three dollars of American money. . . ."[26]

Live-in domestic service provided Irish girls with a room—a place to live—and board—meals. It furnished the appearance, but not necessarily the reality, of a home. For the house in which a domestic worked was not a home or refuge; it was a work site. As one employer told her servant, "If you take a servant's place, you

Figure 6-3. One of the work spaces of an Irish domestic servant was the basement kitchen. This example at Lindenwald is open to the public. (*Courtesy of the U.S. Department of the Interior, National Park Service, Martin Van Buren National Historic Site.*)

can't expect to be one of the family."[27] The main advantage that domestic service presented was that since it included room and board, wages could be saved to remit to the family at home in Ireland. Servants could send home "American money" in their "American letters."[28]

Domestic service was hard, physical work, and both the work day and the work week were long. For live-in servants, the work day was longer than that of other working women. Servants were often on-call to employers all day. Most servants worked more than ten hours a day; the average work day was between eleven and twelve hours. Servants also worked seven days a week. Time off was usually limited to one afternoon and an evening per week, usually Thursday and Sunday. If a servant wanted additional time off, the special permission of the employer was required.[29]

Domestic service provided neither occupational advancement nor security. Illness and/or advancing age could preclude a woman from continuing to support herself in service work. One voluntary way to leave service was to marry because live-in service required remaining single. Some Irish domestics used their earnings for the dowry or fortune necessary for marriage, and went back to Ireland to find husbands. Others married in America, and thereby ended their work in service. Because of the cultural value the Irish placed on the central role of the wife and mother, in America married Irish women traditionally did not work outside the home for wages. In fact, Irish mothers were the least likely of all married European immigrant women to be involved in manufacturing work or home "sweatshop" work.[30]

For those Irish domestics who never married, but instead spent their life in serv-ice in other people's houses, the future could be dim. There was no guarantee that, in her old age, the servant's employer would take care of her. Instead, a servant faced possibly ending up in a poorhouse. Such was the fate of Margrett Baggs, a domestic from County Tipperary, Ireland. In September 1880, at age sixty-six, af-ter thirty-three years in America, she entered the Rensselaer County Poor House in New York State. The notation on her record states the reason for her depend-ence as "old age & no home."[31]

WHO WAS BIDDY?
THE IRISH SERVANT GIRL TOUR

The three themes outlined above are reflected in the sample first-person tour of a hypothetical historic house museum detailed below. The tour is to be conducted by an interpreter in the guise of an Irish servant who actually lived in the house. Although the period for this interpretation is circa 1867, it can be adapted to the interpretative date of specific historic house museums. Using primary source ma-terial, this Irish domestic-led tour (the guide's accent must be credible) features the house from the servant's viewpoint.

The tour begins at the front door of the historic house museum. Visitors ap-proach the door. Wearing clothing akin to that of the Irish servant in the *Harper's* cartoon shown in the illustration accompanying this chapter, the interpreter/tour guide portraying the Irish servant girl greets them at the door. She asks the visi-tors if they have come for the *Who Was Biddy? The Irish Servant Girl Tour,* to

Figure 6-4. The stark third-floor servant quarters at Lindenwald are a contrast to the ele-gant family rooms below. (*Courtesy of the U.S. Department of the Interior, National Park Service, Martin Van Buren National Historic Site.*)

learn about life as a domestic servant in the house. As they respond affirmatively, the guide tells them to be quiet so that the mistress will not know that they are in the house. She leads the visitors into the front hall. A service bell can be heard ringing in the background. She whispers, "Quiet, now, it's the mistress's bell I must be answering. I do try to please her because she's a good mistress, and is very careful of me.[32] She's not like my dear friend Nora's mistress. Sure Nora says at her place the mistress thinks she's no better than a machine—the mistress is up there in her sitting room, while Nora's trying to clean the dining room and parlor, and she'll ring for Nora twenty times a day to do little things for her! And she wants Nora up late, too, 'til eleven o'clock!"[33] She sniffs indignantly. "Well, let me take ye down to the kitchen—wait for me there while I'm after seeing what the mistress wants. I'll be there later." The Irish servant girl then leads them down the stairs to the basement kitchen area (a basement kitchen area is shown in the illustrations) and exits.

In the hall, at the base of the staircase, before the kitchen entrance, visitors gather. Exhibits on moveable panels can be set up around the perimeter of the hall. They can include, among other items, facts about domestic service, an advertisement for a maid, a cartoon satirizing an Irish domestic, and photographs of Irish domestic workers, including, if possible, photos of servants who worked in the historic house museum.

After the visitors have had time to look at the exhibit, the Irish servant gives a signal to them to come back upstairs. They go up to the first-floor dining room where the servant, feather duster in hand, is cleaning. She explains that since her mistress has gone out, she is now free to speak with them. She begins by saying, "My name is Mary Collins, it's **not** Biddy. They call all the Irish girls here 'Biddy.'"

"Well, what do ye want to know about me? I come from County Cork, near Leap, in Ireland. I left home because there was no work for me there. And there was no dowry for me, either. A marriage match could be made for only the one, and that would be my sister Kate. Sure now a fortune isn't needed to marry here, though. I wrote that to my people at home. I told them that, 'Over in Ireland people marry for riches, but here in America we marry for love and work for riches.'"[34]

"My sister Annie, oh yes, we've a long family, four sisters and three brothers. 'Twas my sister Annie that sent me the ticket for my passage. I come out last year when I was eighteen. I'm one year in this country now. [Mary looks at the visitors.] Is it that you've ever gone away from home? Were you not then lonely? Sometimes I get so lonesome that I have to cry, thinking of all the good old times with my friends and relations at home. 'The ways of this place is so different from home,' don't you know?"[35]

Mary looks at the visitors' feet, and then at her own, and points out that they are all wearing shoes. She tells them that she often went barefoot at home in Ireland, where she was teased about her big feet. She confides, "Now, though, I wear shoes every day, which makes my feet smaller."[36] She looks at the visitors' clothing and remarks, "Here in America, there is no end to fashion. I do love fashion. I don't care if some people do be thinking my dress too fine for a servant girl."[37]

Mary looks around the dining room. "In this place," she says, "there are two girls—Ellie Driscoll, the cook, and me. Now while Ellie cooks, it's the housework I do, and it's purty hard work. I care for the silver, crystal, and china in here. On Fridays, I clean the carpets and dust here. What day do you be cleaning your dining room? See that table? It's my job to set it, and to serve as a waitress when the family eats. And it's quiet I'm to be while I serve them." Mary questions the visitors about who cooks for them and who waitresses for them in their houses. She informs the visitors that her other jobs include answering the door, sweeping the front steps, cleaning the upstairs bedrooms, and cleaning the parlor. Since the mistress is still out, she volunteers to show them the parlor.[38]

Mary leads them into the parlor and asks them to look around. She asks, "Is it that you've such a parlor at home? Lovely, is it not? So different from home. We had no such lovely furniture there, nor such a parlor. We did have the one fine bit of furniture, though, the kitchen dresser holding the 'delph'; it was like a hutch don't you know. Oh the dresser, wasn't it the mother's pride and joy! 'Twas not such a parlor as this that was the center of life at home. No, indeed, instead 'twas the kitchen and the hearth, with its turf fire, on which our home life centered. And my mother had no servant to help her, but [Mary laughs], she did have the 'countrywife's maid-of-all-work.' That would be the three-legged pot she used for cooking![39]

"Now this room is a lovely place, but och, 'tis not lovely to clean. I have to move the rugs out 'and shake them, and clean the jambs, hearth, and fire-furniture.' Then I have to 'sweep the room, moving every article.' After that, I 'dust the furniture with a dust-brush and a piece of old silk.' I use a' painter's brush . . . to remove dust from ledges and crevices'. I also use a feather brush to dust the books, decorations and such."[40] Mary looks at the visitors and wonders aloud who cleans their parlors and how often they remove their rugs and shake them. She then suggests that they go upstairs to see the family bedrooms.

She leads them upstairs and lets them admire the family bedrooms. She then tells them that after breakfast every morning she comes up here and makes the beds, empties the slops, and empties the pitcher and basin. Mary points out each item as she mentions it. She inquires who takes out the slops and who empties the pitchers and basins in their homes, and then asks them what they think of these chores.[41]

She quizzes the visitors on what time they get up in the morning, and what time they go to sleep in the evening. She announces that she starts work at six in the morning and often has to work until ten or eleven at night.[42] Mary complains, " 'I work all the time.' " and " 'I am so tired and almost dead.' " She tells them, "I work every day and feel so tired. I don't have them idle times like I use to at home in Ireland. This place is work, not home."[43]

Mary inquires where the visitors sleep, that is, what are their bedrooms like? She informs them that she sleeps right here in the house where she works. She laments that her room is in the attic where it's cold in the winter and hot in the summer. Mary observes sadly that her bedroom does not look like the family bedrooms; it is very stark and bare. She tells them that the only decoration her bedroom has is the one picture of the Blessed Virgin Mary she put up on the wall, and the couple of palm branches she got at Mass on Palm Sunday. And, she tells them, there is no running water up there in the attic, so to wash up she must go all the way down to the kitchen. She then reveals that she cannot, however, take them up to the attic to see her room themselves. Instead, she suggests that they go back down to the kitchen to meet the cook.[44]

Mary leads the visitors into the kitchen, but Ellie Driscoll, the cook, is not there when they arrive. Mary observes that this kitchen is nice and clean and tells them that this is most unusual—kitchens are usually dark and dank, unventilated and smelly. She questions whether the visitors are hungry, and proclaims, "Oh, Ellie, the cook, she makes beautiful meals. Not like what we had at home. (She picks up an uncooked potato in its jacket.) We boiled and ate the potatoes, lovely potatoes they were, too. The 'praty,' that's what we called the potato. We ate it from the hand, don't you know—and with our fingers or thumbnails peeled the skin. Cabbage, too, we had, and we ate the porridge and drank lovely buttermilk. Yes, Ellie makes the beautiful meals, and we get to eat them, too. Now it's altogether different at my dear friend Nora's place, she has a hard place. The food her mistress gives her is not nearly so nice as what the family eats."[45]

Mary announces that the kitchen is where she entertains her friends. She remarks that she is lucky that her mistress lets her sister, Annie, and some of her friends visit her here, because many mistresses forbid such gatherings in their homes. Her sister and friends come some Thursday afternoons or Sunday evenings—which is all the time off Mary gets, except for Sunday mornings. She informs them that she insists on being able to go to Mass, and comments that her Protestant mistress doesn't like it, because it inconveniences her. Mary confides, "I wish I could go to church every Sunday. I do be seeing my sister Annie there and friends from home. But, Ellie, the cook, and I have to take turns going—she goes the one Sunday, and I the next." Mary picks up a pair of rosary beads from the table. She shows them to the visitors and inquires whether anyone can tell her what they are. She sighs, "Ah, well, at least I have Ellie to say my beads with at night. We get down on our knees and say them together." She indicates that Ellie must have been in a rush to have dropped her rosary beads here, noting that she and Ellie usually hang them from the bedposts in their rooms, so that they are within easy reach to say their prayers at bedtime.[46]

Mary then points to a plant growing in a small pot on the kitchen windowsill and questions whether anyone can name the plant. (It is a shamrock plant.) She inquires whether they have ever seen shamrocks before, and if so, if there is a particular day in the year in which shamrocks are widely displayed in America? (She expects the visitors to know that she is referring to March 17, St. Patrick's Day.) She wistfully confides that the shamrock plant reminds her of home.[47]

Mary sighs and laments that her work is very hard, her work day long, and she has little time off. Says she, "I do be getting my room and board here, but this ain't my home." She asks them if they know what the term "room and board" means. "Sure, I'm after saving the money I make," she tells them. "I send some to my family at home in Ireland. They call the letters I send the American letters, and the money I send in them American money. And why is it, you might be asking, that I send the money home? Why, indeed? Because they're my family and they need the money, of course. The only reason they haven't been evicted from the farm is that they use the money I send to pay the rent! Well, I'm just after writing a letter to my dear parents. I have it here. She pulls a letter out of her pocket and begins to read a formulaic beginning to the American letter. "Dear father and mother, I take the pleasure of writing these few lines to ye hoping to find ye in good health as this leaves me at present, thanks be to God for his mercy. As Christmas is now coming, I thought I would send ye two pounds for a present, so ye would have a good Christmas of it."[48] Mary smiles, pleased with herself, looks up and wonders aloud whether the young people among the visitors help their parents in any way, and when they might provide such help.

She cocks her ear and asks whether they hear a noise. She looks out the window. "Oh," says Mary, "'tis nothing." She smiles sheepishly and says, "I thought it might be I heard Mr. Fitzgerald, he that delivers the groceries here, coming along. He's an Irishman, from Limerick, so he is." She announces proudly that, "We're going to be married one day, soon, but not now. It takes money to be married, and I must be sending some money home to my dear parents once in awhile, and if I get married, I won't be able to send them any. But marry we will, and when we do, I will not be doing housework at any place but my own. And, if ever I have a daughter, she won't be doing housework in a place like this, no matter how nice the mistress be."[49]

The service bell is then heard ringing in the background. Mary exclaims that the mistress must have returned and urges the visitors to leave quickly and quietly. She first tells them to exit from the back, from the servants' entrance, and then decides that it would be better if they left as they came, through the front door. They leave; the tour ends.

VARIATIONS ON THE SUGGESTED INTERPRETATION

If it proves impossible to develop a first-person Irish domestic-led tour of a historic house museum, there are other possible variations on this interpretation. One possibility is to feature a "from the bottom up" tour of the house. That is, consider having a visit to the historic house museum commence from the servant spaces and conclude in the family quarters, with visitors leaving through the front door. In such a "from the bottom up" interpretation, the guide can comment on the actual Irish domestics who worked in the house, noting their names, ages and any personal details known about them. During the tour, the guide can identify the location of the servants' rooms. He or she can also indicate whether servants in the house had a place in which to entertain company. If they did, the guide can ask visitors to compare this space with the family company rooms, and to indicate what such comparison tells about the respective positions of servant and family in the house. If the servants had no place in which to entertain guests, the guide could ask visitors to consider what that might have meant for young girls living far from home.

Proceeding through the house, the guide could ask visitors to try to see the family's rooms from the servant's viewpoint. For example, how might the parlor have appeared to her, the person required to clean it? For the mistress the parlor was a place of relaxation, the center of her home and family life. For the servant, however, the parlor was more likely to be seen solely as a work space. In the kitchen, the guide could identify and discuss the actual technology that was used in the historic house museum kitchen. For example, the type of cooking range servants used in the house can be identified. If period clothing is on display in the museum, the guide could comment on what it cost the servant in time and labor to do the washing and ironing required for the mistress to be properly attired. Visitors could be shown where clothes were laundered, informed of the method of laundering used in the period, and could be asked to handle the irons used to press clothing. The guide could point out how domestics differed from the family for whom they worked in terms of ethnicity and religion, and suggest what such differences meant to both the servants and the family.[50]

* * *

Irish women learned American ways in domestic service despite the difficulties it presented to them. According to Irish cook Ann McNabb, her sister's mistress, "laid out to teach her. She larned [sic] her to cook and bake and to wash and do up shirts—all American fashion."[51] Consequently, historians view domestic service as an acculturating occupation for Irish immigrant women. Within the confines of the middle-class American home, Irish servants are seen as having learned the manners and mores of the genteel middle class. Scholars consider the acculturation of Irish women as a positive by-product of their experience in service in America. They contend that Irish women aspired to join the American middle class. That Irish women read literature intended for the middle class is indicative of such aspirations. Historians speculate that when Irish women had their own homes and raised their own families, it is likely that they modeled their home and family life on that of the middle-class American homes in which they previously worked. Because in America Irish immigrant women tended to marry Irish men, their acculturation in domestic service, therefore, is likely to have affected positively the social and economic progress of Irish immigrants.[52]

A question then remains whether or not the cultural exchange between Irish servants and the families for whom they worked was a one- or a two-way street. Can culture be transmitted from the bottom up as well as from the top down? Did middle- and upper-class Protestant women see the relative freedom, independence, and assertiveness of Irish domestics as contrasting favorably with their own lives that were constricted by notions of appropriate female behavior? Could daily interaction with women whom they considered their social inferiors, who were yet "freer," have unconsciously increased the longing of these elite women for more personal autonomy?[53]

Questions remaining or not, the use of historic house museums to interpret the experience of Irish domestics can make museums "more real" to visitors, because such houses were not only lovely homes, they were work sites, as well. These historic houses/work sites were the familiar frontier of contact between middle-class Protestant and Irish Catholic immigrant women. Study of Irish domestics illuminates the divisions of class, culture, ethnicity, and religion that separated American women from each other in the nineteenth century. The study also reveals how American women began to bridge these differences within the confines of the domestic frontier. In addition, study of this one group of nineteenth-century working women illustrates unfamiliar aspects of ethnic, immigrant, and working-class life, and highlights the influence of gender on immigrant life. Such study provides a fuller, richer picture of the diversity of women's lives and work in nineteenth-century America.[54]

NOTES

1. Mary Carbery, *The Farm by Lough Gur: The Story of Mary Fogarty (Sissy O'Brien)* (Longmans, Green, 1937; reprint, Dublin: Mercier Press, 1973), 38.
2. P. J. Drudy, "Editorial introduction," in *Irish Studies 4, The Irish in America: Emigration, Assimilation and Impact,* P. J. Drudy, ed, (London: Cambridge University Press, 1985), 2; Blaine Edward McKinley, *"The Stranger in the Gate: Employer Reactions Toward Domestic Servants in America 1825–1875"* (Ph. D. diss., Michigan State University, 1969), 153, 156; Hasia Diner, *Erin's Daughters in America: Irish Immigrant Women in the Nineteenth Century* (Baltimore: Johns Hopkins University Press, 1983), 89; David Katzman, *Seven Days a Week: Women and Domestic Service in Industrializing America* (New York: Oxford University Press, 1978), 44; Mrs. J. Sadlier (Mary Sadlier), *Bessy Conway: or, The Irish Girl in America* (New York: D & J Sadlier, 1861; reprint, New York: D & J Sadlier, 1863), iii, iv; in this chapter, the terms mistress and employer will be deemed synonymous.
3. Arnold Schrier, *Ireland and the American Emigration 1850–1900* (Minneapolis: University of Minnesota Press, 1958), 16, 111; Patrick J. Blessing, "Irish emigration to the United States, 1800–1920: An overview," in *Irish Studies 4,* P. J. Drudy, ed., 19; "Servants in America," *All the Year Round,* 3 October 1874, 584; McKinley, 149; Faye E. Dudden, *Serving Women: Household Service in Nineteenth-Century America* (Middletown, CT: Wesleyan University Press, 1983), 60, 65. For this chapter, the terms domestic servant, domestic, and servant will be deemed synonymous. Oscar Handlin, *Boston's Immigrants: A Study in Acculturation.* Revised and Enlarged Edition (1941, 1959; reprint, New York: Atheneum, 1972), 253, and McKinley, 152, are the sources for the 1850 statistics, while Katzman, 67, is the source for the 1900 statistics.
4. Diner, xiv, 30–31; 159–160; Robert E. Kennedy, Jr., *The Irish: Emigration, Marriage and Fertility* (Berkeley: University of California Press, 1973), 84; Kerby A. Miller with David N. Doyle and Patricia Kelleher, " 'For love and liberty': Irish women, migration and domesticity in Ireland and America,

1815–1920" in *The Irish World Wide: History, Heritage, Identity, vol. 4, Irish Women and Irish Migration,* Patrick O'Sullivan, ed. (London: Leicester University Press, 1995), 43; Kerby Miller and Paul Wagner, *Out of Ireland: The Story of Irish Emigration to America* (Washington, DC: Elliott & Clark, 1994), 70; Rita M. Rhodes, *Women and the Family in Post-Famine Ireland: Status and Opportunity in a Patriarchal Society* (New York: Garland, 1992), 248–49; Janet Nolan, *Ourselves Alone: Women's Emigration from Ireland 1885–1920* (Lexington: University of Kentucky Press, 1989), 2; and Schrier, 4.

5. Dudden, 121.

6. Nancy A. Hewitt, "Beyond the Search for Sisterhood: American Women's History in the 1980s," in *Unequal Sisters: A Multi-cultural Reader in U.S. Women's History,* 2d ed., Vicki L. Ruiz and Ellen Carol DuBois, eds. (New York: Routledge, 1994), 11.

7. Diner, xvi, 5–7, 9–12; 50; Nolan, 20, 32–35, 67, 73–74; Blessing, 17; K. H. Connell, *Irish Peasant Society* (Oxford University Press, 1968; reprint, Portland, Oregon: Irish Academic Press, 1996), 116–118; David Fitzpatrick, "The Modernisation of the Irish Female," in *Rural Ireland 1600–1900: Modernisation and Change,* Patrick O"Flanagan, Paul Ferguson and Kevin Whelan, eds. (Cork: Cork University Press, 1987), 163,164,168,169, 174–175; idem, "'A Share of the honeycomb': education, emigration and Irishwomen" in *The Origins of Popular Literacy in Ireland: Language Change and Educational Development 1700–1920,* Mary Daly and David Dickson eds. (Dublin: Department of Modern History, Trinity College Dublin and Department of Modern Irish History, University College, Dublin, 1990), 167; Pauline Jackson, "Women in 19th Century Irish Emigration" *International Migration Review* xviii, no. 4 (1984): 1009–1010, 1017–1018; Kennedy, 208; Miller, Doyle, Kelleher, "'For love and liberty,'" 41–42, 51–52; Schrier, 15.

8. Sadlier, 7; Nolan, 73; Padraic Colum, *The Road Round Ireland* (1926; reprint, New York: Macmillan, 1937), 39, 43–44, 243–244; J. M. Synge, *In Wicklow, West Kerry and Connemara* (Dublin: Maunsel and Co., 1910; reprint, with essays by George Gmelch and Ann Saddlemyer, Totowa, NJ: Rowan and Littlefield, 1980), 154; and Rhodes, 185–16, 190. On marriage conferring adult status, see S. J. Connolly, "Marriage in pre-famine Ireland," in *Marriage in Ireland,* Art Cosgrove, ed. (Dublin: College Press, 1985), 92; Kevin Danaher, *In Ireland Long Ago* (Dublin: Mercier Press, 1964), 131; and Caoimhin O Danachair, "Marriage in Irish folk tradition," in *Marriage in Ireland,* 99–100.

9. The quotes are from Caleb Coker, ed., *The News from Brownsville: Helen Chapman's Letters from the Texas Military Frontier, 1848–1852* (Published for the Barker Texas History Center by the Texas State Historical Association in cooperation with the Center for Studies in Texas History at the University of Texas at Austin, 1992), 82. See also Schrier, 4; Dudden, 234–235; Katzman, 52.

10. Kerby A. Miller, "Assimilation and alienation: Irish emigrants' responses to industrial America, 1871–1921," in *Irish Studies 4,* P.J. Drudy, ed., 101.

11. Susan Williams, *Savory Suppers and Fashionable Feasts* (1985; reprint, Knoxville: University of Tennessee Press, 1996), 17, on the "social bible," see also 21–22; Richard L. Bushman, *The Refinement of America* (New York: Knopf, 1992), xv, xvi, xvii, 208, 227–228, 251–252; John F. Kasson, *Rudeness & Civility* (New York: Hill and Wang, 1990), 37, 54, 200.

12. On "kitchen," see E. Estyn Evans, *Irish Folk Ways* (London: Routledge & Kegan Paul, 1957; reprint, New York: Routledge, 1989), 83, 251, and Roger J. McHugh, "The Famine in Irish Oral Tradition," in *The Great Famine: Studies in Irish History 1845–52* with a new Introduction and Bibliography by Cormac O Grada, R. Dudley Edwards and T. Desmond Williams, eds. (Browne and Nolan, 1956; reprint, Dublin: Lilliput Press, 1994), 392. Cormac O Grada, *Ireland: A New Economic History 1780–1939* (Oxford: Clarendon Press, 1994), 85, provides the 1839 data. O Grada, 91, and E. Margaret Crawford, "Food and Famine," in *The Great Irish Famine,* Cathal Poirteir, ed. (Dublin: Mercier Press, 1995), 62, discuss the Irish diet. See also A. (Asenath) Nicholson, *Ireland's Welcome to the Stranger or An Excursion through Ireland in 1844 &1845, for the purpose of personally investigating the condition of the poor* (New York: Baker and Scribner, 1847), 247.

13. Evans, *Irish Folk Ways,* 46, 59, 85–99; Alan Gailey, "Changes in Irish rural housing 1600–1900," in *Rural Ireland 1600–1900,* O'Flanagan et al, ed, 97, 99, 100, 101; Nicholson, 186, J. J. Lee, "Women and the Church since the Famine," in *Women in Irish Society: The Historical Dimension,* Margaret Mac-Curtain and Donncha O Corrain, eds. *(Dublin: Arlen House, The Women's Press, 1978; reprint, Westport, CT.: Greenwood Press, 1979), 37–38;* Joanna Bourke, *Husbandry to Housewifery: Women, Economic Change and Housework in Ireland 1890–1914* (Oxford: Clarendon Press, 1993), 201, 212–213, 217, 221–228; and Miller, Doyle, Kelleher, " 'For love and liberty' " 48–49.

14. Mr. and Mrs. S. C. Hall, *Ireland: Its Scenery, Character & c,* vol.1, A new edition. (London: Virtue and Co. 1860[?]), 233; Ibid., vol. 2, 55, 272; Colum, 419; Nicholson, 75, 98, 187, 387, 393, 406, 420; Madame (Anne Marie) De Bovet, *Three Months Tour in Ireland,* translated and condensed by Mrs. Arthur Walter (London: Chapman and Hall, 1891), 174, 223; and Synge, 83, 113, 114, 116, 123, 144, 146. Rhodes, 295, cites information indicating Irish girls knew Irish clothing would not do in America.

15. Diner, xiv; Nicholson, 302; Peig Sayers, *The Autobiography of Peig Sayers of the Great Blasket Island,* trans. from the Irish by Bryan MacMahon (Dublin: Talbot Press, 1973; reprint, Syracuse, NY: Syracuse University Press, 1974), 204; Peig Sayers, *An Old Woman's Reflections: The Life of a Blasket Island Storyteller,* trans. from the Irish by Seamus Ennis (Oxford: Oxford University Press, 1962), 71.

16. Sayers, *An Old Woman's,* 81.

17. Robert Ernst, *Immigrant Life in New York City 1825–1863* (New York: King's Crown Press, 1949; reprint, Syracuse University Press, 1994), 67; McKinley, 162; Patricia Kelleher, "*Gender Shapes Ethnicity: Ireland's Gender Systems*

and Chicago's Irish Americans" (Ph.D. diss., University of Wisconsin-Madison, 1995), 433; Dennis P. Ryan, *Beyond the Ballot Box: A Social History of the Boston Irish, 1845–1917* (East Brunswick, NJ: Fairleigh Dickinson University Press, 1983), 101; and *The Boston Pilot,* January 8, 1870, 6.

18. Nicholson, 148; Grace Neville, " 'She Never Then After That Forgot Him': Irishwomen and Emigration to the United States in Irish Folklore," *Mid America: An Historical Review* 74, no. 3 (October 1992), 277.

19. Levine, 62–63; Daniel E. Sutherland, *Americans and Their Servants: Domestic Service in the United States from 1800–1920* (Baton Rouge: Louisiana State University Press, 1981), 40; McKinley, 34–35, 166; Harriet Spofford, *The Servant Girl Question* (Boston: Houghton, Mifflin, 1881; reprint, New York: Arno Press, 1977), 32–33; Dudden, 69–70; Ernst, 67.

20. Spofford, 59–60, the quote is found on 60.

21. Mary Ann Rowe, 29 October 1888, letter quoted in Miller and Wagner, *Out of Ireland,* 76.

22. Catharine E. Beecher and Harriet Beecher Stowe, *The American Woman's Home* (New York: J. B. Ford, 1869, reprint, Hartford, CT: The Stowe-Day Foundation, 1994), 327.

23. First two quotes are from Clarence Cook, *The House Beautiful: An Unabridged Reprint of the Classic Victorian Stylebook* (New York: Charles Scribner's Sons, 1881; reprint, New York: Dover Publications, 1995), 271; Sutherland, 40; next two quotes are from Spofford, 56, while last quote is from Spofford, 37.

24. Mona Hearn, *Below Stairs: Domestic Service Remembered in Dublin and Beyond 1880–1922* (Dublin: Lilliput Press, 1993), 1; McKinley, ii, 8–9, 35–36; Dudden, 1, 115, 126–127, 138–145, 148; Katzman, 46, 49, 269–270; and Alice B. Neal, " 'Fetch' and Carry," *Godey's Lady's Book and Magazine,* February 1857, 113.

25. Diner, 85; Dudden 48, 60; Colum, 171; Synge, 65; Rhodes, 269–270; Miller, Doyle, Kelleher, " 'For love and liberty,' " note 41, page 63; Fitzpatrick, "The Modernisation of the Irish female," 164; and idem, " 'A Share of the Honeycomb,' " 181.

26. The quote is from Schrier, 29. See also Hearn, 15; Bourke, 69; Diner, 85; Katzman, 44; Lucy Maynard Salmon, *Domestic Service* (New York: Macmillan, 1897), 163; Sutherland, 3–5.

27. Helen Campbell, *Prisoners of Poverty: Women Wage-Earners* (Boston: Roberts Brothers, 1887), 225.

28. On American money see Schrier, 110, 112–122 and on the American letter see Schrier, 40–42.

29. Dudden, 179, 194–195; Katzman, 110–111; McKinley, 31–33.

30. The quote is from Blessing, 27; Diner, 51–52; Dudden, 208–209; Katzman, 241, Nolan, 79, 80; Salmon, 103, and Schrier, 130–131.

31. New York State, Executive Department, State Board of Charities, *Record of Inmates, Rensselaer County Poor House, under Act Chapter 140, Laws of 1875,* A1978, Roll 171, New York State Archives, Albany, New York.

32. Irish domestic Mary Ann Rowe called her employers were "very nice people" and said that her "mistress is so very careful of me," see Miller and Wagner, *Out of Ireland,* 76.

33. Hannah Collins was a domestic servant in Elmira, New York in the late 1800s who corresponded with her fellow domestic, Nora McCarthy. The originals of her correspondence are in the possession of Dr. Patricia Trainor O'Malley, Bradford, MA, transcripts of which Dr. O'Malley kindly shared with me. Campbell, *Prisoners of Poverty,* 229, quotes a servant who said, "she [the employer] had no more thought for me than if I had been a machine. She'd sit in her sitting-room on the second floor and ring for me twenty times a day to do little things, and she wanted me up till [*sic*] eleven. . . ."

34. Quote from Schrier, 26, idem, 131, on the fortune.

35. K. Miller, "Assimilation and alienation," 104.

36. "I had to laugh at Tim. So he did not forget about my feet being so big but you tell him I wear shoes now every day which makes them smaller" so wrote Hannah Collins to Nora McCarthy, 8 October 1899.

37. In 1870, Irish domestic Anastasia Dowling wrote from Buffalo, New York that "thare [*sic*] is no end to fassions [*sic*]," see Schrier, 30. Irish domestics' love of fashion was such that their fellow Irish criticized them for dressing too well for their station in life, see Ernst, 67–68, and notes 47 and 48 on p. 245.

38. Ellie Driscoll was the name of a relation of Hannah Collins. Beecher and Stowe, 226–227; McKinley, 14–15.

39. Evans, *Irish Folk Ways,* 59, 72. The quote is from 76 and 91. The word "delph" is colloquial for crockery, probably from Delft.

40. Beecher and Stowe, 226–227, 369.

41. Ibid., 369–370.

42. Campbell, *Prisoners of Poverty,* 227.

43. First quote, Hannah Collins to Nora McCarthy, envelope dated 29 July 1898; second quote, Collins to McCarthy, envelope dated 22 July 1899; re: last quote, on 9 June 1898 Hannah wrote to Nora that , "I am working every day and feels tired I dont [*sic*] have them Idle times like I used to in old Ballinlough . . . ." And, she also wrote to Nora that "I aint got any home here," envelope dated 22 July 1899.

44. Spofford, 39; A. J. Downing, *The Architecture of Country Houses* With a New Introduction by J. Stewart Johnson (D. Appleton, 1850; reprint, New York: Dover, 1969), 278, 309, 326, 350, 360; Campbell, *Prisoners of Poverty,* 230; McKinley, 236–267; Sutherland, 30–34.

45. Kitchens were generally not the clean, bright, cheerful places they are often portrayed to be in historic house museums, see McKinley, 245; Spofford, 38. Evans, *Irish Heritage,* 15, notes that the Irish called the potato the "praty." Nicholson saw children eating potatoes out of their left hand while they held a cup of soup in their right hand. On 234, she remarked that she had seen the Irish in America eat potatoes in a similar manner. When eating potatoes out of hand, the potato skin was peeled away, using the fingers or thumbnail, see Nicholson 169, 247 and McHugh, 392. On May 24, 1899, Hannah Collins

wrote to Nora McCarthy, "I was glad you left that hard place." On the food given to servants, see Dudden, 196; Katzman, 110; and McKinley, 215–216.

46. Keeping in touch with their fellow Irish domestics was important to Irish servants, see Spofford, 58–59. Some employers permitted, while others forbade, domestics' gathering in employers' kitchens, see Dudden, 199. On saying the rosary, see Mary Sadlier, *Bessy Conway,* 152. Rosary beads are displayed hanging from bedposts in the turn-of-the century (nineteenth to twentieth) houses one can visit in the Bunratty Folk Park near Limerick City, Ireland.

47. Spofford, 56, mentions that Irish domestics grew shamrocks.

48. Schrier, 112, says the principal use made of American money was to pay the rent on tenant farms. Mary Malone McHenry, Middle Granville, New York, to her parents in Ireland, 11 April 1870, wrote, "Dear father and mother and brother I take the pleasure of writting [*sic*] these few Lines to ye hoping to find ye in good health as this Leaves us in at preasant [*sic*] thanks be to god . . . " On 1 December 1891, she wrote that, " as now Chrismas [*sic*] is coming I taught [*sic*] I would send ye two pounds for a preasant [*sic*] so ye would have a good Christmas of it." The originals and transcripts of these letters are in the author's hand, donated by Anne Shalvoy Graham, Spring Lake, New Jersey.

49. Domestic Hannah Collins noted that she postponed considering marriage in order to send remittances to her parents in Ireland. Letter, Collins to McCarthy, envelope dated 21 February 1900, courtesy of Dr. O'Malley. Diner, 96, indicates that teaching school, not domestic service, was the chief occupation of American-born (second generation) Irish women.

50. Beecher and Stowe, 38–41, 69–76, 334, 446; Dudden, 142–143, Sutherland, 42, and Spofford, 32.

51. "The Life Story of an Irish Cook," in *The Life Stories of Undistinguished Americans, As Told by Themselves,* ed. Hamilton Holt (New York: Young People's Missionary Movement, 1906), 145.

52. Blessing, 25–26; Dennis J. Clark, "The Irish Catholics: A Postponed Perspective," in *Immigrants and Religion in Urban America.* Randall M. Miller and Thomas D. Marzik, eds. (Philadelphia: Temple University Press, 1977), 59; idem, "Irish women workers and American labor patterns: the Philadelphia story" in *The Irish World Wide.* O'Sullivan, ed. 117; Diner, 51, 94, 140; Katzman, 171; Kelleher, 56, 442; Nolan, 74–75, 94; Colleen McDannell, "Going to the Ladies' Fair," in *The New York Irish.* Ronald H. Bayor and Timothy J. Meagher, eds. (Baltimore: Johns Hopkins University Press, 1996), 248; and idem, *The Christian Home in Victorian America 1840–1900* (Bloomington: Indiana University Press, 1986), 11, 73, 103. For a contrasting view, see Dudden, 230.

53. Kathy Peiss, *Cheap Amusements: Working Women and Leisure in Turn of the Century New York* (Philadelphia: Temple University Press, 1986), 8, suggests that cultural transmission can be a two-way process.

54. Diner, xv; Kelleher, 1, 45, 51 — this is Kelleher's thesis, as indicated in her title, "Gender Shapes Ethnicity."

SUGGESTED READINGS

Catharine E. Beecher and Harriet Beecher Stowe. *The American Woman's Home.* New York: J. B. Ford and Company, 1869. Reprint: Hartford, CT: Stowe-Day Foundation, 1994. Good source of information on household chores and American domesticity.

Elizabeth Clark-Lewis. *Living In-Living Out: African American Domestics and the Great Migration.* New York: Kodansha International, 1994. A basic study on the lives of African American domestic workers.

Hasia Diner. *Erin's Daughters in America: Irish Immigrant Women in the Nineteenth Century.* Baltimore: Johns Hopkins University Press, 1983. The landmark book on Irish women in America.

Faye E. Dudden. *Serving Women: Household Service in Nineteenth-Century America.* Middletown, CT: Wesleyan University Press, 1983. A very readable account of nineteenth-century domestic service.

Hamilton Holt, ed. "The Life Story of an Irish Cook" in *The Life Stories of Undistinguished Americans, As Told by Themselves.* New York: Young People Missionary's Movement, 1906.

David M. Katzman. *Seven Days a Week: Women and Domestic Service in Industrializing America.* New York: Oxford University Press, 1978. Includes information on Irish domestics, African Americans, and other immigrants in domestic service.

Margaret MacCurtain and Donneha O'Corrain, eds. *Women in Irish Society: The Historical Dimension.* Dublin: Arlen House, The Women's Press, 1978. Reprint: Westport, CT: Greenwood Press, 1979. Provides excellent background information on Irish women.

Colleen McDannell. *The Christian Home in Victorian America, 1840–1900.* Bloomington: Indiana University Press, 1986. Compares Protestant and Catholic versions of domestic ideology in Victorian America.

Kerby A. Miller and Paul Wagner. *Out of Ireland: The Story of Irish Emigration to America.* Washington, D.C.: Elliott & Clark Publishing, 1994. General account of the Irish coming to America.

Janet A. Nolan. *Ourselves Alone: Women's Emigration from Ireland, 1885–1920.* Lexington: University of Kentucky Press, 1989. One of the few books on Irish women written by an American historian.

Rita M. Rhodes. *Women and Family in Post-Famine Ireland: Status and Opportunity in a Patriarchal Society.* New York: Garland Publishing, 1992. An important book on women in post-Famine Ireland.

Mrs. J. Sadlier [Mary Anne Madden Sadlier]. *Bessy Conway; or the Irish Girl in America.* New York: D. & J. Sadlier, 1863. A novel written for and about Irish domestics. <http://avery.med.virginia.edu/~eas5e/Bessy/Bessy.html>

Arnold Schrier. *Ireland and the American Emigration, 1850–1900.* Minneapolis: University of Minnesota Press, 1958. Immigrant letters are one of the sources for this often-cited work.

Harriet Prescott Spofford. *The Servant Girl Question.* Boston: Houghton Mifflin, 1881. Reprint: New York, Arno Press, 1977. Contains considerable detail about Irish domestics.

Chapter 7

SHE'S IN THE GARDEN: FOUR TURN-OF-THE-CENTURY WOMEN AND THEIR LANDSCAPES

Nancy Mayer Wetzel

Women's stories are writ large on the landscape where we never thought to look before. Garden sites tell us a great deal about women's lives that is often overlooked. What have gardens meant to women? What do gardens reveal about the women who cultivated them? How have women interacted with the landscape and what are some significant examples of women's garden sites?

A visitor can begin to learn about the lives of women of the past by examining three sites where four women gardened at the turn of the nineteenth to the twentieth century: Sarah Orne Jewett, Celia Laighton Thaxter, Emily Davis Tyson, and Elise Tyson Vaughan—all plantswomen of southern Maine. Guests to the properties of these women are usually drawn to the buildings there—Jewett House and Hamilton House which are museums in South Berwick, and the Shoals Marine Laboratory on Appledore Island. But those who follow the garden path are rewarded. Standing in their home grounds, a visitor can appreciate the vital connection between these women's landscapes and their lives.

Although the Maine gardens serve as models for interpretation, historians of women's past are not restricted to them. There is a long tradition of women gardeners and a rich variety of landscapes that reveal details about the daily lives and values of women. Women have kept kitchen gardens; cottage gardens; estate gardens; meditation, market, and medicinal gardens; study gardens. There have been gardens for survival, gardens of confinement. Flower gardens, which women created for pleasure and art, were also sanctuaries for old, out-of-style plant stock; laboratories of selection and breeding; and showcases for exotics and new hybrids. Various examples of women's landscapes from all over the United States are described in the last part of this chapter. Other sites exist in every town and city in the country.

The gardens of Jewett, Thaxter, Tyson, and Vaughan were shaped by the Colonial Revival in American design.[1] Colonial Revivalists saw the vestiges of colonial gardens disappear as the Victorian trend for open lawns, curving flower beds, and carpets of new annuals in two-dimensional plantings gained popularity. Jew-

Figure 7-1. Author Sarah Orne Jewett, right, and Emily Tyson admire the garden at Hamilton House, South Berwick, ME, in 1905. (*Courtesy of the Society for the Preservation of New England Antiquities.*)

ett, Thaxter, Tyson, and Vaughan, however, identified with a different trend that gave free reign to romantic evocations of colonial gardens, retaining an enclosed proximity to the house, beds with straight lines, and the three-dimensional spatial quality of old-time perennials. Traditional in character and famously the realm of female gardeners, these inventive "colonial" gardens were called—then and now—old-fashioned or grandmother's gardens.[2]

Gardens fulfill a desire in those who make them for a private place, a public place, and an abiding place. Privacy, ever an important garden element, was an essential characteristic of the Colonial Revival garden. A garden room at home offered solitude and expansion of the inner life to women gardeners. They found spiritual solace in nature's cycles of dormancy and renewal. They developed autonomy, assurance, and fulfillment in creativity. Skills honed in the privacy of the garden constituted a preparation and stimulus for related endeavors outside the home.

The move from garden as private place to public place is only a short step. In full bloom, a garden is to be seen. After providing for the pleasure of family and friends in their gardens, many turn-of-the-twentieth century women found ways to share their expertise in the greater community. For instance, some women moved beyond the domestic confines of their gardens (and lives) by publishing garden books and magazine articles, which were often autobiographical. The many garden books published between the late 1800s and the 1940s were, in fact, predominantly by women writers including: Frances Duncan, Helena Rutherfurd Ely, Mrs. Francis King, Louise Shelton, and Anna B. Warner.[3] Their publications were popular, not only for the garden information, which was impressive, but for the personality and life experience disclosed in the garden accounts.

A garden is also an abiding place where memories and associations flourish. The Colonial Revival garden was an abiding place in a changing world, representing continuity with the imagined past. The centennial celebration in 1876 triggered a rampant nostalgia for the simpler preindustrial, pre-Civil war world of the colonial period. Women looked for a connection with their literal and figurative grandmothers in gardens made to look old-fashioned, whether or not they were actually old or brand new.

The abiding place bolstered a slipping class identity. Descendants of the nation's old English families found their position altered by the *nouveau riche,* an emerging middle class, and waves of immigration. In *Old Time Gardens,* 1901, Alice Morse Earle promoted the colonial-style garden as a haven of birth and breeding where even the plants had pedigrees. She cherished the old English flowers of her ancestors that bloomed in an "unbroken chain of blossom to seed" for three centuries.[4]

The Colonial Revival gardens of Sarah Orne Jewett, Celia Laighton Thaxter, Emily Davis Tyson, and Elise Tyson Vaughan illustrate the private, public, and abiding aspects of the garden. Each woman's garden embodied all three aspects, but one salient aspect characterized each site: Jewett's garden was a private place, Thaxter's was public, and the Tyson and Vaughan garden was an abiding place.

*   *   *

Sarah Orne Jewett (1849–1909) achieved enormous success as a writer who immortalized rural Maine in the nineteenth century. Jewett's home grounds surround two houses at the center of South Berwick, the house where she was born and died, and the house where she grew up. The former is a museum owned by the Society for the Preservation of New England Antiquities (SPNEA). When visiting Jewett House, one must look for Jewett outdoors where the atmosphere of her literary gardens is manifest in authentic nineteenth-century landscape spaces; front yard; side, barn and ell yards; backyard garden—all within the sweep of a white picket fence. This landscape was the private place of a woman of renown.

For generations, the women in Jewett's family were gardeners and, until Jewett's middle age, the garden was literally her grandmothers' garden. That word, grandmothers', is plural and possessive. Grandfather Jewett had four wives over his lifetime and three of them could have had a hand in the grounds Jewett knew. In 1888, Sarah and her sister Mary moved into their grandparents' house and updated the backyard of the Grandmothers Jewett in the fashionable grandmother's garden style. In this way, Jewett's garden was a literal and metaphoric connection to the past.

The plants in Jewett's garden were decidedly old-fashioned and she named them again and again. Jewett wrote to a friend, "The garden is so nice—old fashioned indeed with pink hollyhocks and tall blue larkspurs."[5] London pride stood in ranks "most gorgeous to behold, with its brilliant red and its tall straight stalks. It had a soldierly appearance, as if the flowers were out early to keep guard."[6] This colonial plant is still around today, known as Maltese cross, *Lychnis chalcedonica*.

These plants connected Jewett to such women of the colonies and early republic as Martha Ballard, a midwife and healer, who noted in her diary that a "decoction of ye flowers of London pride" relieved her grandson's pain.[7] Like Ballard, the countrywomen in Jewett's literature had gardens that symbolized their lives. Ballard's fictional counterpart in the novel *Country of the Pointed Firs* was Almira Todd, an herbalist, "a renewal of some historic soul," a heroic figure.[8]

As a gardener herself, Jewett was a private figure. Popular as the autobiographical garden books of her contemporaries were, she never exposed her own life and garden in one comprehensive volume. However, others published evocative descriptions. There was a vine-covered arbor where Sarah and Mary breakfasted. Seen through a gateway with ball finials, a great garden of long paths and wide beds was abundantly planted in roses, lilies, peonies, asters, and other favorites of the grandmother's garden. There were also fruit trees and vegetables.[9]

Among the contributions that Jewett did make to the genre of women garden writers was a landscape history of New England villages titled "From a Mournful Villager." This essay is a passionate treatise on the vanishing landscapes that Jewett knew as a child—the front yards, flowers, and fences. She advocated the building of fences to create private outdoor rooms for the family and to keep the garden from the highway, assuring the reserve, separateness, and sanctity of one's home grounds. The reader was offered tantalizing glimpses of a landscape world bounded by a white picket fence where the young Jewett played.[10]

Outside of her fence, on the roads around the Jewett property, were two important buildings. One, a factory with a tall smokestack, she did not allow into her personal garden writing. The qualities Jewett valued were diminished by the advance of industrialization—another reason for the symbolic separation she sought in white picket fences. The other building nearby was a church, and she did compare her garden, with its long central axis, to the church. It is likely that Jewett recounted a fond fantasy of her girlhood in *The Country Doctor,* an autobiographical fiction: "The bees were humming in the vines and as she looked down the wide garden-walk it seemed like the broad aisle in church, and the congregation of plants and bushes all looked at her as if she were in the pulpit."[11]

Jewett took pleasure and comfort in walking the garden path throughout her life. After a carriage accident, she walked the straight, broad aisle, "creeping out into the garden with a stick walking zig-zag and swaying about."[12] In the poem *Flowers in the Dark,* Jewett found solitude in the broad-aisle garden:

> Late in the evening, when the room had grown
> Too hot and tiresome with its flaring light
> And noise of voices, I stole out alone
> Into the darkness of the summer night.
> Down the long garden-walk I slowly went . . .[13]

From this place, Jewett, the nationally respected author, struck a balance between her private life and her cosmopolitan interests. She spent part of the year in Boston attending the literary salon of her companion, Annie Fields, or traveling abroad. While she was in South Berwick, she entertained guests including Willa Cather, Henry James, William Dean Howells, and Rudyard Kipling. "Come some time," she invited, "when the garden is blooming well and we can show you our dear South Berwick with its pleasant look."[14]

Today, the Jewett House stands at a busy crossroads. The factory building remains in the neighborhood; the church is forgotten. Within the white picket fence, the immediate landscape surrounding the Jewett House is preserved. The lattice archway is gone and so is the burgeoning complexity of paths and beds behind the house, but one still crosses a threshold into a separate garden room, following the same broad aisle to view beds of old-fashioned flowers. In essence, the grandmother's garden of Sarah Orne Jewett endures, a private place.

In order to visit her friend Celia Laighton Thaxter (1835–1894), Jewett traveled twenty miles to the seacoast and another ten miles by boat out to the Isles of Shoals. When Jewett reached Thaxter's garden on the resort island, she entered a public place, a destination, meant to be seen. Thaxter was the famous poet of the Isles of Shoals and icon of her times; her image appeared in paintings, post cards, and even on cigar boxes. She was the daughter of the Laighton family of *hoteliers,* wife of Levi Thaxter, and mother of three sons. Although her house and garden on Appledore Island burned in 1914, John M. Kingsbury, director of the Shoals Marine Laboratory, an outpost of Cornell University on Appledore Island, headed up the reconstruction of the garden on its original site in 1976. Miraculously, some surviving plants flourished again. The Shoals Marine Laboratory at Cornell arranges tours of the garden today.

Thaxter's garden was small, but it extended to the vine-clad piazza and flower-filled parlor of her cottage. It was enlarged by a casual swath of plantings outside the fence and down to the sea. Inside the board fence, an explosion of color and form was somewhat contained within a grid of rectangular beds; however, because the garden burst outside the fence and up the sides of the piazzas, it created an impact well beyond its modest dimensions.

While Thaxter was a true plantswoman who tried new exotic plants, she disdained new Victorian planting styles such as carpet beds and ribbon borders. Rather, the beds in her enclosed cottage plot had a right-angle geometry. Like her old-fashioned clothes, her plants included "the old-fashioned flowers our grandmothers loved."[15] Clearly, the colonial ideal had captured her imagination.

Thaxter's spiritual being thrived in a spectacular setting—the dramatic terrain of the island, vast skies, and long views to the sea. To this she introduced artifice in the form of a small garden where she worked determinedly with nature. Thaxter studied the flowers of this cultivated plot through the lens of a pocket magnifying glass, shifting the focus from nature's grandeur to its minute marvels. She scrutinized an *Eschscholtzia* and transmuted the poppy to prose, "lustrous satin sheen . . . infinitely fine lines to a point in the centre of the edge of each petal . . . powdery anthers are orange bordered with gold . . . whirled about the very heart of the flower . . . shining point of warm sea-green. . . beauty of the blossom supreme."[16]

Thaxter's family ran a popular summer resort where people came to enjoy the ease and gaiety of a fashionable island playground. People also came to see Celia Thaxter and her famous garden, absorbing the setting of her poetry and prose just as they would take the sea air. Fragrant white lilies bobbing by her garden fence, blue sweep of sea and sky—these were captured like a souvenir when she wrote, "O lightly moored the lilies lie, Afloat beneath the flowing sky!"[17]

Thaxter's garden was part of the public's view from the hotel, along with tennis courts, swimming cove, boat landing, and the natural landscape and seascape. She raised the tone of this public idyll by presiding over a prestigious salon that attracted her peers in the world of writing, painting, and music. The garden served as a forecourt to her piazza and parlor where John Greenleaf Whittier, Frances Hodgson Burnett, Ross Sterling Turner, Ole Bull, and others gathered.

Painters created a breathtakingly lovely body of work in the garden. Year after year, the painter Childe Hassam returned, inspired to an outpouring of works that

Figure 7-2. A postcard of Celia Thaxter and her cottage on the Isles of Shoals, NH, reveals its garden setting at the turn of the twentieth century. (*Courtesy of the Isles of Shoals Collection, University of New Hampshire.*)

captured the spirit of the place. He wrote to a friend, "Mrs. Thaxter's garden is beautiful, perfectly beautiful."[18]

Thaxter, on the other hand, declared, "I plant my garden to pick, not for show. They [the flowers] are just to supply my vases in this room."[19] Espousing a loose, informal aesthetic in the garden, she used more control in arranging the cut flowers for the salon. Thaxter featured specimens for study and massed flowers in progressions of color. An impressive result was achieved by rising at 5:00 a.m. (Her only private time in the summer garden) and working "like a ploughman" for hours until the arrangements were satisfactory.[20]

Thaxter's garden achieved its most public aspect in her writing. In 1894, she published a classic of garden literature in the autobiographical genre of women garden writers. *An Island Garden* was an account of Thaxter's gardening year in the inspired language her readers had come to expect. The volume is distinguished by the pictures and illuminations of Childe Hassam and a garden plan showing locations of plants, which was recommended by Sarah Orne Jewett. It revealed nitty-gritty garden know-how, glorious description, and the integration of the garden with a fascinating life:

> Yet still the summers come, the flowers bloom are gathered and adored
> . . . Still in the sweet tranquil mornings at the piano one sits playing, also with
> a master's touch, and strains of Schubert . . . soothe and enchant the air. The
> wild bird's song that breaks from without into the sonata makes no discord.
> Open doors and windows lead out on the vine-wreathed veranda, with the
> garden beyond steeped in sunshine, a sea of exquisite color swaying in the
> light air. . . . A thousand varied hues amid the play of fluttering leaves:
> Marigolds ablaze in vivid flame; purple Pansies, — a myriad flowers, white,
> pink, blue, carmine, lavender, in waves of sweet color and perfume to the
> garden fence, where stand the sentinel Sunflowers and Hollyhocks, gorgeously arrayed and bending gently to the breeze . . .[21]

Today, Thaxter's reconstructed garden is a gay dash of color on the island landscape. Head gardener Virginia Chisholm of the Rye Driftwood Garden Club has presided in Thaxter's stead since 1982. Guests who still journey there must imagine the cottage that burned and the plantings outside the fence. Due to an increased population of plant-eating wildlife, the garden is almost completely confined to the dimensions of the fenced area. This has the curious effect of opening the garden to its surroundings, but Thaxter's garden always was oriented to resort life, a public place.

About twenty-five miles away, the salt water that breaks on the Isles of Shoals surges up tidal riverways to Hamilton House, an eighteenth-century mansion with a stunning prospect of the Salmon Falls River in South Berwick, two miles from Jewett House. Today, the buildings and grounds are owned by SPNEA. The estate seemingly stands outside the stream of time as the river flows on to the head of tidewater. The landscape at Hamilton House is an abiding place, consciously redesigned to revere an illustrious past.

Figure 7-3. Head gardener Virginia Chisholm of the Rye Driftwood Garden Club talks to guests about her work in Celia Thaxter's reconstructed garden in 1986. (*Courtesy of Tanya M. Jackson.*)

About 1785 when it was built by Jonathan Hamilton, the place was bustling with commerce. A prosperous sea trade followed the river to wharves, warehouses, and Hamilton's Georgian mansion. One hundred years later, the estate had become a declining farm, and it occupied Sarah Orne Jewett's thoughts. She searched for a buyer in order to block development of the property, and she wrote a historical fiction set at Hamilton House. Using the novelist's prerogative in writing *The Tory Lover,* Jewett created a Revolutionary War legend for the mansion. Time and accuracy were blurred, and the aura of the Colonial Revival settled on Hamilton House.[22]

At Jewett's recommendation, Emily Davis Tyson (1846–1922) and her step-daughter Elise Tyson (1871–1949) purchased Hamilton House for their country retreat. Emily, known for her private literary readings, was the wealthy widow of George Tyson and raised his children by a previous marriage.[23] Elise was an amateur photographer and shared an interest in design with Emily. In middle age she married Henry Vaughan.

The Tysons first came to Hamilton House, not by river, but by the only other access, a country lane. "When we came, of course all the prosperity and picturesque finery of its early days had vanished completely . . ."[24] wrote Elise, and therein lay their mission: to revive the property, not Hamilton's enterprise but the perceived romantic charm of his era. This suffused the mother-daughter partnership; their shared vision was to create an abiding place. While renovations were underway in South Berwick, *The Tory Lover* was appearing serially in *The Atlantic Monthly* and later as a book.

The Tyson women worked on an impressive scale, honoring the classical antecedents of the nation's architecture and Hamilton House itself. Following the principles of an Italian Renaissance villa, they extended the house farther into the grounds. Lattice-covered wings opened to a central path which connected several garden rooms. Recognizing the agrarian tradition of this property, the Tysons raised vegetables and fruit and hayed the old fields. Rather than demolish the barn, they relocated it to make space for the formal garden.

The most distinctive feature of the garden architecture was the pergola, a long, vine-draped bower. It formed an arcing border beginning at the entrance gate nearest the house and continuing along the river side of the garden to a secluded sitting room built into the terraced slope. From the pergola, Hamilton's river vista was served to house guests in discreet glimpses right along with afternoon tea.

Although removed from the busy mainstream of the early twentieth century, the Tysons' private retreat was known to the public through magazine articles written by several women. The early articles reveal Emily to be the chief gardener. In 1909, Louise Shelton acknowledged Emily's abilities in *American Homes and Gardens* as those of a nature-lover and artist who fashioned a garden in harmony with the old mansion and ancient elms.[25]

Hildegarde Hawthorne described Hamilton House in a series on New England

Figure 7-4. The Hamilton House garden offers a view of the Salmon Falls River. (*Courtesy of Sandy Agrafiotis.*)

gardens made by women. She published "A Garden of Romance: Mrs. Tyson's at Hamilton House, South Berwick, Maine" in *Century Magazine,* 1910. The plants Hawthorne named in a familiar litany—iris, delphinium, spotted lilies, tall holly-hocks, and more—place Emily among the generations of old-fashioned flower lovers.[26] In writing *The Lure of the Garden* the next year, Hawthorne recalled her time among the Tyson's house guests. After tea, they sat idly by the river, se-cluded by the rose-hung pergola and green arbors; box edging on the grass paths added to the fragrance of the surrounding flowers.[27]

Four issues of *House Beautiful Magazine* featured Hamilton House in 1929. Emily Tyson had died, and Elise Tyson Vaughan had married. Elise had become an excellent gardener in her own right, using color schemes and new hybrids. Writer Edith Kingsbury and photographer Paul J. Weber paid tribute to the gar-dens, by then in their full maturity.[28]

The sophistication of Vaughan's approach to the gardens came in part from memberships in the Garden Club of America (GCA) and local clubs. They linked her to a wider community of women gardeners. In notes for one old garden on a GCA tour, Vaughan wrote, "8th generation *Mother* to *Daughter*."[29] The GCA came to Hamilton House in 1934 on its annual national tour, endorsing the preser-vation of New England's historic properties. Vaughan was in harmony with the club's stance and willed Hamilton House to SPNEA.

Today, visitors to the site will find that many garden elements remain, but the pergola has disappeared, and the old elm trees have died. A recently launched gar-den restoration project required that not only records of the past be scanned but the landscape itself. Just like pentimento—when the original lines show through on an old painting—an abiding past emerges in the present at Hamilton House.

*   *   *

Women's garden sites abound today and, in their great variety, the Colonial Re-vival is but one design influence. The sites are worth a trip, but one should also look close to home. Home gardens are a good place to begin because women's landscape work was mainly domestic well into the twentieth century. Inspect the landscapes at old houses, house museums, and community garden tours. The rem-nants of colonial, Colonial Revival, Victorian carpet beds, or World War II vic-tory gardens may still be evident in plants and architecture. Depressions in the ground and openings in fences or stone walls may indicate garden paths.[30]

Investigation will often vouchsafe a woman's garden story. What is not appar-ent on the surface may have an underlying story. Always ask about the landscape; talk to the guide and gardener. It is important to read the literature, look at old pho-tos and documents, visit websites. Follow link to link where one woman's inter-action with the landscape connects to the next woman's.

As women moved out of the home garden, they moved into landscape archi-tecture, community improvement, education, preservation, conservation, ecol-ogy, botany, and the arts—all fields related to gardening. They formed garden clubs and, in 1913, founded the Garden Club of America which continues to be primarily a women's organization, now addressing such concerns as endangered plant species, biodiversity, clean air and water, and municipal beautification. Thus, today, street planters and town parks; college campuses and planned communities; nurseries, national parks, and parkways; even earthworks are women's landscape sites.

Sarah Orne Jewett expressed the changes for women in 1881 when, looking out on the few remaining front yard gardens of her village, she wrote:

> The disappearance of many of the village front yards may come to be typical of the altered position of woman, and mark a stronghold on her way from the much talked-of slavery and subjection to a coveted equality. She used to be shut off from the wide acres of the farm, and had no voice in the world's politics; she must stay in the house, or only hold sway out of doors in this prim corner of land where she was queen. No wonder that women clung to their rights in their flower-gardens then, and no wonder that they have grown a little careless of them now, and that lawn mowers find so ready a sale. The whole world is their front yard nowadays![31]

Women's gardens continue to provide private, public, and abiding experiences. Women's gardens have come to include not only domestic, but also civic and business locations nation-wide. The following selection of landscape sites are examples.

Montgomery Place, Annandale-on-Hudson, New York was the estate of Janet Livingston Montgomery, resourceful widow of Revolutionary War hero General Richard Montgomery. She built a Federal mansion in 1804, kept up existing orchards and started a commercial nursery. Nineteenth-century descendants developed a landscape of sweeping lawns and picturesque vistas to the river under the guidance of designer Andrew Jackson Downing.

Linked by marriage to this impressive landscape heritage, Violetta Delafield, botanist and garden club member, left her own mark on Montgomery Place in the early twentieth century. She transformed a secluded kitchen garden into a Colonial Revival garden of straight paths and garden rooms with abundant plantings of roses, herbs, perennial flowers, and a wisteria vine at the entrance to a potting shed and greenhouse. One may scan Delafield's "rough garden" for remnants of the original rock garden that she abandoned during the war years. The presence of generations of women is evoked in the orchards, lawns, and gardens at this site.[32]

Stan Hywet Hall, Akron, Ohio, was the estate of Gertrude and Frank Seiberling, founder of Goodyear Tire Company. Warren Manning designed the landscape in 1911 and Gertrude claimed the English garden—walled, hidden, and filled with flowers—for her own private repose. In 1928, Gertrude worked with landscape architect Ellen Shipman, "one of the best, if not the very best, Flower Garden Maker in America."[33]

Shipman, dirt gardener herself, excelled at designing lush flower borders for women clients who found emotional satisfaction in the experience of perennial gardening. In partnership with Gertrude, a painter, and her daughter Irene, Shipman restructured the plantings and settled on a palette of pinks, blues, and yellows. She worked in her signature style, "as if . . . painting pictures, and as an artist would."[34] M. Christine Klim Doell and her partner Gerald Allan Doell, landscape historians, completed a restoration of the garden plantings in 1992. The restored English garden is the only Shipman garden open to the public.

Dumbarton Oaks, in the Georgetown section of Washington, DC was the estate of Mildred and Robert Bliss, a diplomat in the State Department. In 1921 landscape architect Beatrix Farrand began a twenty-year collaboration with the Blisses, resulting in one of America's finest landscapes. In 1899 Farrand was the only woman founding member of the American Society of Landscape Architects. Doyenne of her field, she was the first landscape architect to excel in flower planting *and* garden design.[35] Beatrix and Mildred worked closely, addressing one another in correspondence as "Dearest Gardening Twin" and "Dearest Collaborator."[36] Farrand's assistant Ruth Havey became Garden Advisor after Farrand's retirement.

Dumbarton Oaks was given to Harvard University in 1941, and, in order to provide a resource for maintenance. Farrand wrote the *Plant Book* for Dumbarton Oaks. Every conceptual and practical detail was explained for the features of this site—vistas, terraces, allees, pools, rose garden, flower border, open air theater, and more. Diane Kostial McGuire, landscape architect and garden advisor at Dumbarton Oaks, edited the book in 1980.[37]

Joshua Tree National Park in southern California was the vision of Minerva Hamilton Hoyt. Hoyt's personal mission to protect the desert paralleled the GCA's stance on protecting the environment. Mutual concerns were served when Hoyt used the club's exhibit space at the 1928 International Flower Show in New York for a Mojave Desert tableau (with fresh desert flowers flown in daily) targeted to win support for desert preservation. The scope of her campaign quickly expanded to the formation of the International Desert Conservation League.

In this country, Hoyt focused on preserving a specific area of Joshua tree habitat until President Franklin D. Roosevelt proclaimed 825,340 acres as the Joshua Tree National Monument in 1936. The Joshua Tree Women's Club quoted Hoyt's feelings about the desert on a plaque they placed at the highest point in the monument, "I stood and looked. Everything was peaceful, and it rested me." In 1994 the site was expanded to become a national park.[38]

Timberline Lodge, Government Camp, Oregon was hand-built by the Federal Works Projects Administration in 1936. Today, it is a National Historic Landmark located in the Mount Hood National Forest ski area, a year-round recreational site. In the early 1990s, Barbara Fealy, landscape architect, worked with a team of long-time associates, a government agency, volunteer organizations, and lodge staff to improve the grounds.

Fealy's design concept, to make Timberline Lodge look as if it were growing up out of the mountain, was achieved by repositioning huge local boulders and bringing the native forest carpet, flowers, and shrubs up to the building.[39] In her late eighties at the time of this commission, Fealy first learned about plants as a child in her father's wholesale nursery. Known for superb plan composition, carefully crafted details, use of boulders and mounds, Fealy's work conveys space, simplicity, and timelessness.[40]

Greenwood Pond: Double Site, Des Moines, Iowa is a wetland sanctuary for people and wildlife in an urban center. From 1989 to 1996, the site was restored by a coalition of local organizations and agencies. The Des Moines Founders Garden Club raised money, including a 1994 Founder's Fund Award from the GCA, for the purchase of plantings that reflect Iowa's botanical heritage. The Des Moines Garden Club members planted 12,000 themselves and take shared responsibility for continuing to watch and care for the site.[41]

An environmental sculpture was designed by Mary Miss, an artist in the evolving tradition of women and landscapes. Miss said that in this electronic age we must reintroduce the actual physical and psychological experience people had in places like gardens.[42] Her structures at Greenwood Pond give such accessibility to the wetlands, prairie, and woodlands on the site. A Miss walkway allows one to stand out on the pond or go below the earth's surface to sit at eye-level with the water.

Anne Spencer House and Garden Historic Landmark, Lynchburg, Virginia has a one-room cottage, named Edankraal, set in the garden behind the house. This was the sanctuary of Harlem Renaissance poet and civil-rights activist Anne Spencer. Martin Luther King, Jr., Marian Anderson, James Weldon Johnson, W. E. B. DuBois, and others were the Spencers' house guests. The garden she tended for seventy years is classically configured with garden rooms, central axis, and pergola. Spencer's husband, Edward, built the garden structures, including a blue lattice trellis at the entrance and a concrete pond where a sculpture of an Ebo tribesman was used as a fountain. This landscape was the ideal realm of love, beauty, and purity in Spencer's poetry, which she called "time's unfading garden."[43]

Landscape designer Jane Baber White undertook restoration of the garden in 1983, eight years after Spencer's death.[44] The Hillside Garden Club adopted the project and earned the Commonwealth Award from the Garden Club of Virginia. They reclaimed rose garden, grape arbor, flower borders, and all the rest that tell today's visitor about Spencer's life. In an intimately-voiced poem (Edward's voice, presumably), Anne Spencer offered this broad insight: For those who would know the woman, she's in the garden, her very soul:

> He Said:
> Your garden at dusk
> Is the soul of love
> Blurred in its beauty
> And softly caressing:
> I, gently daring
> This sweetest confessing,
> Say your garden at dusk
> Is your soul, My Love.[45]

Figure 7-5. Anne Spencer stands in her garden in 1925 with Edankraal cottage in the background. (*Courtesy of Chauncey Spencer. Photo by Rawley Martin Long.*)

NOTES

1. Sarah L. Giffen and Kevin D. Murphy, eds., "*A Noble and Dignified Stream:*" *the Piscataqua Region in the Colonial Revival, 1860–1930* (York, ME: Old York Historical Society, 1992), xi. Murphy in his introduction explains the Colonial Revival in the geographical area where the gardens of this chapter are located: "The renewal of interest in the material culture of the colonial period gained momentum with the celebration of the centennial of American independence in 1876, but . . . this concern with the tangible vestiges of the colonial period was already emerging in the Piscataqua region well before that date. As the national fascination with the fine art, architecture, literature, diet, dress, and domestic furnishings of the eighteenth and early nineteenth centuries—everything before 1840 being considered equally 'colonial'—mounted, the Piscataqua region provided imagery of the past far out of proportion to its geographic size."

2. Perhaps because the gardens of this essay are located in an area where the onset of the Colonial Revival was early and potent, current exposition considers these old-fashioned, grandmother's gardens to have been clearly identified with the colonial. See Alan Emmet, *So Fine A Prospect: Historic New*

England Gardens (Hanover, NH: University Press of New England, 1996), 180–81: "A 'colonial' garden was by then considered an essential adjunct to a colonial house. . . . the Tysons had the Jewett garden as a local model and were surely familiar with other people near Boston who were planting 'old-fashioned gardens'." See also: Lucinda A. Brockway, "Tempus Fugit: Capturing the Past in the Landscape of the Piscataqua" in Giffen and Murphy, eds., *"A Noble and Dignified Stream,"* 84, 106: "She [Thaxter] extended her door yard with trellises and framed her garden with flowers, such as phlox and peonies, from her grandmother's time" and "Even in her choice of plant material, she followed the trend of the colonial revival to stress both aesthetic interest and historic precedent."

3. The following are exemplary titles from the publications of these authors: Frances Duncan, *The Joyous Art of Gardening* (New York: Charles Scribner's Sons, 1917); Helena Rutherford Ely, *A Woman's Hardy Garden* (New York: Macmillan, 1903); Mrs. Francis King, *The Well-Considered Garden* (New York: C. Scribner's Sons, 1915); Louise Shelton, *Continuous Bloom in America* (New York: Charles Scribner's Sons, 1915) Anna B. Warner, *Gardening by Myself* (New York: A. D. F. Randolph, 1972).

4. Alice Morse Earle, *Old Time Gardens* (New York: Macmillan, 1901), 4.

5. Sarah Orne Jewett to Sarah Wyman Whitman in Richard Cary, ed., *Sarah Orne Jewett Letters* (Waterville, ME: Colby College Press, 1967), 157.

6. Sarah Orne Jewett, "The Confession of a House-Breaker" in *The Mate of the Daylight* (Boston: Houghton Mifflin, 1893), 240–41.

7. Martha Ballard in Robert R. McCausland and Cynthia MacAlman McCausland, eds., *The Diary of Martha Ballard, 1785–1812* (Camden, ME: Picton Press), 550. See also Laurel Thatcher Ulrich, *A Midwife's Tale: The Life of Martha Ballard, Based on Her Diary, 1785–1812* (New York: Vintage Books, 1991).

8. Sarah Orne Jewett, *The Country of the Pointed Firs and Other Stories* (Garden City, NY: Anchor, 1956), 14. It was first published in 1896.

9. John Eldridge Frost, *Sarah Orne Jewett* (Kittery Point, ME: The Gundalow Club, Inc., 1960), 77; "Sarah Orne Jewett—A Visit to Her Home," *Bangor Daily Commercial,* 20 December 1901.

10. Sarah Orne Jewett, "From a Mournful Villager" in *Country By-Ways* (South Berwick, ME: Old Berwick Historical Society, 2001), 68–69. The book was first published in 1881.

11. Sarah Orne Jewett, *A Country Doctor* (New York: Meridian, 1986), 40. The book was first publlished in 1884.

12. Sarah Orne Jewett to S. Weir Mitchell quoted in Paula Blanchard, *Sarah Orne Jewett: Her World and Her Work* (Reading, MA: Addison-Wesley, 1995), 350.

13. Sarah Orne Jewett, "Flowers in the Dark" in *The Complete Poems of Sarah Orne Jewett* (New York: Ironweed Press, 1999), 20. The poem was first published in 1880.

14. Quoted in Patrice Todisco, "By Pen and Spade," *Hortus* 14 (Summer 1990): 43.

15. Celia Thaxter, *An Island Garden* (Ithaca, NY: Bullbrier Press, 1985), 44.

16. Ibid., 76–77. *An Island Garden* was first published in 1894.

17. Celia Thaxter, "On Quiet Waters" quoted in Jane E. Vallier, *Poet on Demand: The Life, Letters, and Works of Celia Thaxter* (Portsmouth, NH: Peter E. Randall, 1994), 206.

18. Childe Hassam to Woodbury, quoted in David Curry, *Childe Hassam: An Island Garden Revisited* (New York: Norton, 1990), 30.

19. Maud Appleton McDowell in Oscar Laighton, ed., *The Heavenly Guest . . .* (Andover, MA: Oscar Laighton, 1935), 126.

20. Ibid.

21. Thaxter, *An Island Garden,* 102–03.

22. See Sarah Orne Jewett, *The Tory Lover* (South Berwick, ME: Old Berwick Historical Society, 1975). *The Tory Lover* was first published in 1901.

23. Robert Grant, *Fourscore* (Boston: Houghton Mifflin, 1934), 283.

24. Elizabeth R. (Tyson) Vaughan, "The Story of Hamilton House," typescript, SPNEA Archives, n.d.

25. Louise Shelton, "The Garden at Hamilton House," *American Homes and Gardens* 6 (November 1909): 422.

26 Hildegarde Hawthorne, "A Garden of Romance: Mrs. Tyson's at Hamilton House, South Berwick Maine," *Century Magazine* 80 (September 1910), 779–86.

27. Hildegarde Hawthorne, *The Lure of the Garden* (New York: Century, 1911), 101–02.

28. See "The House in Good Taste," *House Beautiful* (January 1929): 61–64; "The Garden in Good Taste," *House Beautiful* (March 1929), 313–16; Edith Kingsbury, "Hamilton House: A Historic Landmark in South Berwick Maine," *House Beautiful* (June 1929): 783–87; Edith Kingsbury, "Suggesting Long Holidays: The Cottage at Hamilton House in South Berwick, Maine," *House Beautiful* (December 1929): 690–95.

29. Elizabeth R. (Tyson) Vaughan, notes for Garden Club of America tour of Mrs. Cooke's garden near Philadelphia, SPNEA Archives, n.d.

30. Rudy J. Favretti and Joy Putnam Favretti, *Landscapes and Gardens for Historic Buildings* (Nashville, TN: The American Association for State and Local History, 1978): 87–90.

31. Jewett, "From a Mournful Villager" in *Country By-Ways,* 62–63.

32. I am grateful to Historic Hudson Valley and Susan Leve, horticulturist, for access to landscape documents. See Ogden Tanner, *Gardens of the Hudson Valley* (New York: Harry N. Abrams, 1996).

33. Warren Manning to Frank Seiberling quoted in Judith B. Tankard, *The Gardens of Ellen Biddle Shipman* (Sagaponack, NY: Sagapress, 1996), 117.

34. Ellen Shipman, quoted in Anne Petersen, "Women Take the Lead in Landscape Art," *New York Times,* 13 March 1938.

35. Eleanor Perenyi, "Woman's Place" in *Green Thoughts: A Writer in the Garden* (New York: Vintage Books, 1983), 269.

36. Quote in Jane Brown, *Beatrix: The Gardening Life of Beatrix Jones Farrand, 1872–1959* (New York: Viking, 1995), 176.

37. See Diane Kostial McGuire, ed., *Beatrix Farrand's Plant Book for Dumbarton Oaks* (Washington, DC: Dumbarton Oaks, 1980).

38. Polly Welts Kaufman, *National Parks and the Woman's Voice: A History* (Albuquerque: University of New Mexico Press, 1996), 36–39.

39. For sharing her recollections, I am grateful to Linn Adamson, curator at Timberline Lodge, who assisted Fealy on the project.

40. I am grateful to Linda S. Long, manuscripts librarian, Special Collections and University Archives, University of Oregon Library system, Eugene, for the use of a manuscript in progress on Barbara Fealy.

41. I am grateful to Barbara J. Lyford, chairman, Des Moines Founders Garden Club Greenwood Pond Double Site Committee for a history of the club's involvement in the project.

42. Mary Miss, "On a Redefinition of Public Sculpture" in *Prospecta: The Yale Architectural Journal* 21(1984): 60. See Christian Zapatka, *Mary Miss: Making Place* (New York: Whitney Library of Design, 1997).

43. Anne Spencer, "Rime for the Christmas Baby (At 48 Webster Place, Orange)" quoted in J. Lee Greene, *Time's Unfolding Garden* (Baton Rouge and London: Louisiana State University Press, 1977), 178.

44. See Jane Baber White, "Restoration of a Poet's Garden," *American Horticulturist,* 66 (October 1987): 27–31.

45. Anne Spencer, "He Said," quoted in J. Lee Greene, *Time's Unfading Garden,* 183.

SUGGESTED READINGS

Virginia Tuttle Clayton, *The Once and Future Gardener—Garden Writing from the Golden Age of Magazines: 1900–1940.* Boston: David R. Godine, 2000. Clayton sets the historical background for the "literature of amateur gardening" found in periodicals; then presents articles and photographs on themes including old-fashioned gardens with biographical information on the writers, most of whom are women.

May Brawley Hill, *Grandmother's Garden: The Old-Fashioned American Garden, 1865–1915.* New York: Harry N. Abrams, 1995. This account traces the development of a vernacular garden style, beautifully evoking the legacy of principally women gardeners in primary sources, period paintings, and photographs.

The Influence of Women on the Southern Landscape. Winston-Salem, NC: Old Salem, 1997. The proceedings of the Tenth Conference on Restoring Southern

Gardens and Landscapes, 1995, encompasses gender, race, and class in a comprehensive model for understanding women's various roles in landscape history.

Sarah Orne Jewett, *Country By-Ways*. South Berwick, ME: Old Berwick Historical Society, 2001, originally published in 1881. These evocative essays of 1881, turn on Jewett's rambles in her home environs—a cruise on the tidal river, a horseback ride down deserted tracks, a view of village gardens, a walk across fields to visit two old women, a carriage drive up a nearby mountain—all with ruminations on the passing of time and its impact on the places Jewett knew best.

Starr Ockenga, *Earth on Her Hands: The American Woman in Her Garden*. New York: Clarkson Potter, 1998. The horticultural life-work, continuous learning, and community endeavors of eighteen contemporary women gardeners from across the country is documented in life stories, photographs, property schemes, plant lists, and practical tips.

Eleanor Perenyi, "Woman's Place" in *Green Thoughts: A Writer in the Garden*. New York: Vintage Books, 1983. This is an eye-opening feminist view of landscape history, a history that Perenyi considers "the two-thousand-odd years of women's incarceration in the flower garden."

Edith A. Roberts and Elsa Rehman, *American Plants for American Gardens*. Athens: University of Georgia Press, 1996. First published in 1929 by Roberts, a professor of botany at Vassar College, and Rehman, landscape architect, this pioneering book integrates ecology with landscape design, suggesting native plant associations for progressive American gardeners.

Celia Thaxter, *An Island Garden*. Ithaca, NY: Bullbrier Press, 1985. This lyrical telling of Thaxter's garden story is her paean to the gardening life. Published in 1894, it is a superb early example of women's autobiographical garden literature. The Bullbrier Press edition includes historic and contemporary photographs of the garden site.

Louise Beebe Wilder, *The Fragrant Garden: A Book About Sweet Scented Flowers and Leaves*. New York: Dover, 1974. Wilder's book on fragrance in the plant world contains wide-ranging research, personal anecdotes, and horticultural expertise conveyed in engaging prose. First published in 1932 as *The Fragrant Path*, it is one of ten garden books that Wilder wrote.

Chapter 8

CALLED HOME:
FINDING WOMEN'S HISTORY IN
NINETEENTH-CENTURY CEMETERIES

Katharine T. Corbett

Five miles north of the shimmering Gateway Arch on the St. Louis riverfront lies Bellefontaine Cemetery. The quaint limestone gatehouse and massive iron gates at the entrance stand in sharp contrast to the crumbling brick flats and vacant storefronts just across busy Florissant Avenue. Once inside the cemetery gates, however, the city seems far away. Narrow winding roads, shaded by century-old oaks, lead past thousands of monuments carefully arranged on gently rolling hills that overlook the Mississippi River. From the entrance gate a visitor can follow the twisting route to Woodbine Avenue and the Henry T. Blow family lot. Two large monuments dominate the grave site. A rectangular block of granite marks the grave of Henry, a prominent nineteenth-century industrialist and civic leader. His wife Minerva's slightly smaller cylindrical monument, adorned with four crumbling urns, is crowned with a weatherbeaten classical female figure holding an infant. In the corner of the lot shaded by Henry Blow's monument, a small stone marks the grave of his daughter, Susan. Founder of America's first continuously operating kindergarden and a pioneer in early childhood education, Susan Blow was the only member of the family who left a mark on the national culture.[1]

Every town in America has a least one cemetery where monuments, often as modest as Susan Blow's, identify women significant to the history of that community, if not the nation. Although most traditional cemetery tours and guidebooks, like most town histories, still focus on businessmen, politicians, and military leaders, some now include stops at the graves of prominent women. Few, however, interpret the nineteenth-century cemetery itself as a site specific to a historical period, a place to discover changing realities and attitudes about life, death, domesticity, and gender roles. Cemeteries are everywhere accessible, richly revealing but seldom used for exploring the place of women in nineteenth-century American culture, for teaching the history of individual women, and for making abstract demographic data about women's experience immediate and tangible.[2]

Bellefontaine, founded in 1849, was the first Rural Cemetery west of the Mississippi. The Rural Cemetery Movement influenced the appearance of most Amer-

Figure 8-1. Cemetery tours like this one at Bellefontaine Cemetery, St. Louis, MO, introduce the public to local women's history and to the role of women in nineteenth-century American life. (*Courtesy of author.*)

ican cemeteries founded after the mid-nineteenth century. If students and teachers who visit local cemeteries looking for the grave sites of individual women broaden their inquiry to include the design of the grounds and style of the monuments, they will enrich their understanding of the gendered culture in which these long-dead women lived.

The American Rural Cemetery Movement began in 1831 with the founding of Mount Auburn Cemetery in Cambridge, Massachusetts, across the Charles River from Boston. It spread rapidly as city after city broke with past burial customs and opened new cemeteries designed to meet changing needs. European cemeteries had been places for the temporary burial of the urban poor; the wealthy usually had more permanent grave sites on their own property or under churches. Americans not buried on their farms and plantations were often interred in church or community grave yards. By the end of the eighteenth century, however, civic leaders in Europe and America were eager to move cemeteries out of the path of urban progress, not only to free up land for the living but also to promote public health. Before the discovery of germ theory, physicians believed miasmas—vapors rising from decaying matter—spread disease and made proximity to cemeteries foolhardy. As old cemeteries filled up or were abandoned, civic leaders sought new locations away from densely populated cities.[3]

At the same time that burial space was becoming scarce in America's growing cities, the demand for grave sites was increasing. By the mid-nineteenth century, industrialization had created an expanding urban middle-class of prospering families who could afford permanent burial sites. New cemeteries sold large family lots suitable for impressive monuments to nearly any Caucasian buyer; in most cases the only restriction was the ability to pay. The typical American rural cemetery was a nonsectarian, nonprofit organization of lot owners, called proprietors, governed by a self-perpetuating board of civic leaders. Located on the outskirts of cities, these "rural" cemeteries were quintessentially "urban" in context and "suburban" in locale.[4]

While issues of health and urban growth spurred communities to create cemeteries away from city centers, changing social attitudes influenced how these new institutions would look and function. Founders were remarkably forthright and articulate about the ideas that underlay their rural cemeteries. Cemetery plans and regulations conveyed assumptions about the relationship between nature and death, the primacy of family and private property, and the definition of civic identity.

Complex and interrelated changes in attitudes—especially notions about salvation, spirituality, and sentimentality—help explain the special character of the rural cemetery. The names of Bellefontaine's winding roads, Willow, Laurel, Vista, and Hope, reflect an early nineteenth-century shift in beliefs about the relationship between life and death, particularly among the elite, white Protestants who founded this and similar civic cemeteries. Early Protestant theology, which consigned most sinners to hell, did not encourage people to linger in graveyards where deaths heads carved on rows of tombstones stood as reminders of a vengeful, judging God. By the early nineteenth century, however, ever more American Protestants were embracing "free grace," the notion that redemption was available to all; the forgiven could look forward to heavenly reunion with loved ones who had already been "called home." Ministers who preached that families would be regathered and friends reunited in heaven encouraged cemetery visitation. Spiritualism, the belief that the living could communicate with the spirits of the dead, also attracted grieving survivors to their loved ones' burial places. The influence of Romanticism, a late eighteenth-century and nineteenth-century movement known for sentimental expression in literature and art, encouraged cemetery planners to adopt a picturesque aesthetic for these places of consolaton.[5]

Although founded, governed, and designed by men, the appearance of new cemeteries also reflected the cultural values of their wives and daughters. In America more women than men were church members engaged in religious introspection; more women wrote and read romantic, sentimental literature. In 1846, the poet Emily Dickinson wrote of Mount Auburn Cemetery that "it seems as if Nature had formed the spot with a distinct idea of its being a resting place for her children." Planners carefully positioned trees and shrubs on a gently rolling terrain to emphasize naturalistic vistas reminiscent of large English gardens. They deliberately designed cemeteries to be sculpture gardens where tasteful, individual monuments would embellish the pastoral landscape.[6]

Visitors to Bellefontaine see a crowded sculpture garden, but they also encounter what appears to be a symbolic community of private homes. This resemblance to a residential community is not accidental. Like other rural cemeteries, Bellefontaine was founded to be a city of the dead. When Professor Truman Post, minister of the Third Presbyterian Church of St. Louis, dedicated Bellefontaine Cemetery in 1850, he declared it would become "the last home for families, and friends." Material evidence of this domestic vision is everywhere on the landscape. Stone steps and gateposts, some inscribed with surnames or lot numbers, lead into family plots fronting on paved streets. In the oldest sections of the cemetery, lots are at least four hundred square feet, with space to inter many family members together. For thirty years, the cemetery association required owners to enclose their lots, as most did their homes, with either iron fencing or stone curbing. Few fences survive, but steps and curbing still mark the perimeters of older lots. On each lot, one or two large monuments, often inscribed with a family name, tower over the smaller memorial stones arranged inside the fence line. Tucked away along the edges of the cemetery are single lots designated for "strangers," people who had died far from home and family.[7]

Nineteenth-century Americans were more at home with death than Americans had been previously or have been since. Until the nation industrialized, home was a workplace for most families where men, women and children all had responsibilities essential for economic survival. Every illness was potentially life-threatening and every family experienced untimely deaths. Caring for the sick and dying was a traditional female responsibility; women usually preformed the swift and simple final rituals of death.[8]

By mid-century, however, industrialization was upsetting traditional patterns of work and family life in American cities. Income producing jobs took most men out of the house. Domesticity, women's work, took on new meaning in a home that was no longer the economic center of the family. Urban middle-class families began to view their homes as private, sheltering havens for keeping the complex and confusing outside world safely at bay. The home became the center of a new kind of family life, one where women preserved and nurtured values considered necessary for survival in the industrial city. Domestic rituals, such as those surrounding death, became more important, elaborate, and time-consuming. The large family lots in rural cemeteries like Bellefontaine are material expressions of changing gender roles, the growing importance of domesticity, and a fear of social disorder that characterized this period in American history.[9]

Nineteenth-century family lots in rural cemeteries gave material expression to the domestication of death and the idealization of the patriarchal family. Visitors in search of women's history will find that the design and size of monuments, memorial inscriptions, and the placement of grave markers all reflect nineteenth century attitudes about women's place in the family and in the culture.

Figure 8-2. The large, ornate monuments surrounded by smaller stones on this fenced family lot in Bellefontaine Cemetery are typical features of cemeteries in American cities that were influenced by the Rural Cemetery Movement. Founders created symbolic communities of private homes on the outskirts of their growing cities. (*Photo by Ruth L. Bahon.*)

Consistent with the ideological distinction between the public male world and the private female world, ownership of the cemetery lot and the duties of proprietorship fell largely to men. The head of the family usually marked his plot by erecting a monument inscribed with the family name. Obelisks were popular choices. A traditional symbol for commemorating important personages, the soaring column was an unambiguous affirmation of patriarchy. Occasionally two obelisks, one shorter than the other, rose from the lot encircled with a carved wreath to signify the enduring bonds of matrimony.[10]

Cemetery literature encouraged men to commission before their deaths tasteful monuments of original design in keeping with the sculpture garden motif. Over time, however, fashions changed: earlier highly carved soft marble or limestone sculpture gave way to more durable, massive, granite monuments. By 1878 when Bellefontaine regulations outlawed fences on new lots, a scion of industry was likely to set himself apart by interring his family in a large private mausoleum, truly a "home away from home."[11]

Women's contribution to the new rituals of death grew out of their changing domestic role. The rigid division of labor that characterized urban middle-class marriage and gave increasing importance to domesticity came at a time when fewer children and more female immigrant servants made traditional homemaking less arduous. Only a small percentage of Americans actually lived the middle-class life, but its ideology had widespread influence. As guardian of the home, a middle-class wife was responsible for creating a well-running, attractive sanctuary that reflected her husband's success in business. Magazines like *Godey's*

Lady's Book reenforced the domestic ideal, setting new standards for taste, etiquette, and fashion. Home embellishment became a moral imperative as manufacturers flooded the market with household furnishings and mass-produced art objects. The home was where a good wife and mother preformed her civic duties, rearing her children to be productive, useful citizens. Charged with instructing her sons in civic responsibility and her daughters in domestic piety, she turned for advice to popular sentimental novels and religious tracts that romanticized home and family, both in this world and the next. Lydia Maria Child, author of popular domestic advice books, encouraged mothers to take children to visit cemeteries and to tell them that going to heaven was "like going to a happy home."[12]

England's Queen Victoria, who ruled from 1837 to 1901, spent forty years in formal mourning after the death of her husband Albert, in 1861. Victoria not only gave her era its lasting name, but her behavior set its standards for fashionable deportment. Devoted to family and propriety, the queen set an example of domesticity that made extensive, elaborate, and ritualized public grief the mark of a proper middle-class woman in England and America. The Victorian etiquette of death included an array of fashions for each prescribed period of mourning as well as black-bordered stationery and specialized black jewelry often set with faceted jet, a form of coal. Grieving women and girls used snippets of the deceased's hair to make memorial wreaths and jewelry; they embroidered intricate mourning pictures replete with symbolic willow trees shading family graves. Elaborate home funerals with massive floral tributes became the norm for those who could afford them. During the Civil War, many American women sought solace in these customs, putting on black for fallen fathers and sons and publicly expressing their private grief in a manner consistent with their expanding roles as citizens and consumers.[13]

Cemetery lots offer tangible middle- and upper-class evidence that in death, as in life, a women's primary identity was domestic. In most instances, a married woman was memorialized only as the wife of a lot owner, her first name, middle initial, and dates carved into the family monument beneath his. Monuments often listed a succession of wives in this manner. Individual gravestones also reflect the patriarchal family structure: women were identified as "wife of," men were seldom "the husband of." "Mother" and "Father," however, appear frequently on headstones and the names of both parents were usually carved on the gravestones of sons and daughters who died unmarried. Large family lots were often the extended family seats in eternity, holding the graves of unmarried sisters and of married sons buried with their wives and children. Some family cemetery lots, like family homes, sheltered a variety of relations. Seventy-one individuals from seven generations of Kinglands lie together in their huge Bellefontaine lot. In general, however, the male head of a household paid to establish a separate "home away from home" for himself and his dependents.[14]

Occasionally a woman's maiden name appears on her tombstone, particularly if she came from a family of equal or greater prominence than her husband's. A man's grave in a lot belonging to his wife's family could be a sign that he had joined her family's business or that his social status came from their union. Hyphenated family names on monuments usually indicate the joining of two equally prestigious families in marriage.[15]

The iconography and inscriptions on grave markers in family lots reflect an increasingly consoling attitude toward death. Motifs carved from nature suggest hope: ivy for memory, poppies for sleep, oak for immorality, and acorns for life. Inscriptions reenforce optimistic and comforting themes of heavenly family reunion. Tombstones in a small cemetery established in 1853 in Gorham, Maine, display verses typical of those selected by grieving families in many civic cemeteries of the period. Julia Blake Thomas, who lost two infants, a seventeen-year-old daughter, and a twenty-four-year-old son before her own death at age 54, lies under a head stone that reads:

> Oh the hope, the hope is sweet,
> That we soon in heaven shall meet
> There we all shall happy be
> Rest from pain and sorrow free

When Arthur H. Jaques died shortly after the deaths of two sons, aged nineteen and twenty, his widow and surviving children found solace in placing this verse on a richly ornamented white Zink family monument:

> Dear Father with a reverent hand
> This to thy memory given
> While one by one thy household band
> God reunites in heaven.[16]

Figure 8-3. The Rural Cemetery Movement influenced nineteenth-century cemeteries in many small towns. The domestic ideal is reflected in the stairs leading to this family monument in Gorham, ME. (*Photo by author.*)

Although some families or colleagues listed a deceased man's public accomplishments on his monument, they seldom extolled his virtues as a husband or father. In contrast, the highest praise for a woman was that she had been a successful in her domestic role. Susannah Putnam's husband commended his wife on her Mount Auburn monument:

Having discharged with unwearied fidelity and devotion
the duties of this relationship as well as those of a daughter and a mother,
she sank into the sleep of death with the hope of full immortality."[17]

Most women share family monuments with their husbands and children or, like Susan Blow, lie under simple headstones despite their public accomplishments. In nearly every cemetery, however, a few women were memorialized with elaborate individual markers. Minerva Blow's Bellefontaine monument is nearly as large as that of her husband. Married at nineteen, Minerva had six living children when she died in June 1875 at the age of fifty-four. She had been a board member of "The Home for the Friendless," an institution for destitute women founded by her sister, Charlotte Charless. Her husband's brother, Taylor Blow, was the last owner of Dred Scott and had pursued the slave's unsuccessful legal battle for his freedom in the 1850s. As an ardent Unionist and member of the Ladies' Union Society during the Civil War, Minerva had helped to raise funds for war relief. Unlike the deaths of most women, Minerva Blow's was noted in the local press because of her husband's prominence. Her obituary described a woman who was "not only a devoted wife, mother, and friend, but delighted in doing good to all, regardless of sect, color, or station in life." The *Missouri Republican* concluded that although her mind was "highly cultured, her mental characteristics will be, perhaps less remembered than those of her benevolent and most charitable heart. . . . She filled her sphere with grace and elegance, but the motive underlying all was a delicate sense of duty."[18]

Less than three months after Minerva Blow's death, her husband Henry died unexpectedly while vacationing. The papers printed long, effusive obituaries chronicling his many accomplishments as an industrialist, civic leader, and former ambassador to Brazil. Hundreds of St. Louisans gathered at the family home to view his casket resting under a canopy of white flowers set next to a full-length portrait embellished for the funeral with "a delicate ornamentation of flowers . . . of good taste." A carriage bore his body through the city to Bellefontaine Cemetery where he was interred next to his wife. Visitors to the cemetery can see embodied in the style of the Blow's individual monuments evidence of the same nineteenth-century attitudes about men and women that underlie the stories the local newspaper published when Henry and Minerva died.[19]

Since there is no single family monument on the Blow lot, Susan and her siblings may have selected memorials for each of their parents, although Henry, who died three month after his wife, could have chosen Minerva's elaborate, expensive monument. Most large civic cemeteries contain impressive monuments commissioned by grieving husbands. In 1892 Louis Sullivan, designed a delicate clas-

Figure 8-4. Susan Blow's small rectangular monument in Bellefontaine Cemetery is to the left and slightly in front of the large memorial to her father, Henry T. Blow. The tall memorial topped by a figure on the right marks the grave of her mother Minerva. (*Photo by author.*)

sical tomb in Bellefontaine for Charlotte Dickson Wainwright, the young wife of a local brewer for whom the architect had just completed a downtown office building. Both structures are considered masterpieces of late nineteenth-century architecture. When Kate Brewington Bennet died at age thirty-seven, ostensibly from consuming small quantities of arsenic to retain her fashionably pale completion, her husband ordered placed on her grave a statue of a sleeping woman under a Gothic canopy of white marble attended by a female servant.[20]

Although few statues of women in Bellefontaine are as sentimental as the one honoring Kate Bennett, female figures embellish many monuments. The mother and infant crowning Minerva Blow's monument is a typical motif. While obvious representations of the Virgin Mary were decidedly Roman Catholic, more generic representations honored the maternal ideal and reinforced the omnipresent domestic theme. The large Bellefontaine monument to Annie Wallace Luke depicts a mother sitting with two children at her knees and makes clear the importance of her maternal role to the surviving Lukes.[21]

Trustees and cemetery designers exercised little control over the statuary owners erected on their private lots, but they actively discouraged weeping angels and other religious iconography considered inappropriate for a democratic, nonsectarian cemetery. Allegorical female statuary, however, was in harmony with the approved classical symbols of republicanism. Often cut and chiseled by artisans on the East Coast or in Europe, these impressive figures symbolized emotions associated both with women and with death. Large somber stone women representing grief, faith, and hope dot the cemetery landscape.[22]

Mourners, who most often purchased memorial statuary from catalogs, made selections that reflected their desire to chose proper, tasteful monuments and, at the same time, to honor specific individuals. Cemetery guidebooks sometimes include stories that explain the relationship between a monument's allegorical figure and the life of the deceased, but in most cases there is no record of the selection process and visitors are left to speculate on the intended personal symbolism. Rebecca Sire is buried alone in Bellefontaine beneath a life-sized classical statue of a woman holding a fallen torch. Sire, widowed in 1854, lived to 1903; only nieces and nephews survived the eighty-three-year-old woman. During the Civil War, Sire ardently supported the Southern cause in a bitterly divided Union city under martial law. Authorities assessed Confederate sympathizers to pay for

Figure 8-5. A symbol of an extinguished life, this allegorical figure marks the grave of Rebecca Sire in Bellefontaine Cemetery. It was a particularly appropriate memorial for Sire who was a passionate supporter of the defeated Confederacy. (*Photo by author.*)

refugee relief and publically humiliated those who resisted. Rebecca witnessed her confiscated piano and mahogany sofa being sold for a pittance at public auction. If years later Rebecca Sire chose for her monument the woman with a fallen torch, a classical motif for an extinguished life, it would have been in harmony with her personal and political sympathies for the defeated Confederacy.[23]

The graves of children were most often marked with sentimental domestic and religious iconography. The late nineteenth century was still a perilous time for children; family lots are sprinkled with grave sites of young sons and daughters. Stone angels watch over sleeping stone infants with lambs nestled at their feet to signify sacrifice and innocence. Consolation literature assured mothers they would see their children awake from the temporary sleep of death once the family reunited in heaven. Elaborate, expensive memorials to children may indicate that falling birthrates and less infant mortality made individual children more precious and their deaths more difficult for grieving families, but these monuments are also evidence that new cemeteries gave affluent parents the opportunity to express their natural grief in a socially acceptable permanent setting. In Calvary Cemetery, a St. Louis Roman Catholic cemetery adjacent to Bellefontaine and modeled after it, Adele Morrison commissioned realistic monuments to two children who died when they were five and three years old. A life-sized statue of her sleeping son sits in a stone sleigh; a replica of his younger sister rests in a cradle nearby. Their mother regularly changed the toys around the statues with each new season and in winter erected a shelter over the graves.[24]

Cemetery landscaping and upkeep followed the conventions of middle-class homes and neighborhoods. Cemetery associations expected proprietors to beautify their lots with tasteful plantings and to care for them as well; perpetual care became a requirement of ownership only late in the century. Crumbling vases copied from classical urns and garden-style benches still adorn old family lots. In many instances, these domestic embellishments are all that remain of a lot owner's extensive nineteenth-century landscaping. Andrew Jackson Downing and other domestic architects gave suggestions for cultivating trees, shrubs, and plants on burial lots that closely followed their plans for home landscaping. Although some families hired gardeners, most tended their own grave sites. Women, who were used to expressing themselves creatively through domestic gardening, took on this responsibility more often than men did. In 1887, a St. Louis newspaper reported that women "sit beside a grave all day untiringly giving their attention to little details of beautification that would escape the eyes of a man."[25]

Because nineteenth-century attitudes about death and domesticity infuse the landscape of the rural cemetery, a visitor to Bellefontaine can easily imagine a grieving family gathered on its lot to mourn and remember the relatives buried there. But the rural cemetery was also a cultural institution with a very specific social purpose for the larger community. On any pleasant Sunday afternoon ordinary St. Louisans would have strolled the winding roads of Bellefontaine, enjoying the well-planned vistas and admiring the impressive monuments of the city's elite families. The civic leaders who founded the new cemeteries intended them to serve this dual purpose: to be both private places of family remembrance and public spaces for inculcating personal and civic virtues.

When in mid-century, European immigrants began flocking to St. Louis and other American cities, the local elite feared social disorder and loss of cultural control. They created public schools and other institutions to transmit their values to these newcomers. Cemeteries were also community classrooms for educating new Americans in aesthetics, middle-class morality, civics, and local history. In his 1850 dedication speech, Professor Post hailed Bellefontaine Cemetery as "a great interest of civilization, a perpetrator of social life and order" where "the wise, the gifted, the eloquent, the good, the heroic" are gathered together in a "Pantheon of historic virtues." While the emphasis was on honoring male statesmen, military heros, successful businessmen, and religious leaders, Post also praised women whose lives exemplified cultural values of piety, domesticity, and benevolence. Like other cities with civic cemeteries, St. Louis promoted Bellefontaine as a tourist attraction where citizens and visitors alike could absorb local history by reviewing the biographies of influential men.[26]

By the early twentieth century public parks and museums were replacing cemeteries as destinations for family outings. Except for the recently bereaved, birdwatchers, or genealogists on a quest, few people today consider cemeteries fitting sites for casual Sunday strolls. But the cemetery as a local history classroom is still a viable concept. Historical tours of nineteenth-century cemeteries are increasingly popular with the public. There is a growing market for richly illustrated cemetery guidebooks.[27]

Recent books on two Massachusetts cemeteries, Mount Auburn and Forest Hills, could serve as models for guidebooks that use current scholarship in women's history and the Rural Cemetery Movement. Most cemetery tours and guidebooks, however, are based on traditional local history resources. They focus on men and highlight only a few nationally known women: the grave sites of poet Sara Teasdale and novelist Kate Chopin appear in all St. Louis cemetery guides. Occasionally other women make the list: some, like Wainwright, because their monuments are significant, others, like Bennet, because interesting anecdotes are associated with their deaths. St. Louis' most recent cemetery guide lists sixty-seven people buried in Bellefontaine and Calvary cemeteries, only three of whom are women. Only 12 grave sites of women are among the 244 stops on a walking tour published in a recent history of Detroit's Elmwood Cemetery.[28]

Because women are as well represented in family lots as men, cemeteries are great untapped resources for teaching local women's history. The school where Susan Blow opened her first kindergarten is maintained as a museum and historic landmark, but tours that include her modest monument in the Blow family lot help bring her story to a different audience. Some women acknowledged to be historically significant—including Virginia Minor, the St. Louis suffragist who was the first women to take her demand for the vote to the U.S. Supreme Court—have no permanent memorial sites other than half-forgotten tombstones.

The civic purpose of rural cemeteries was to celebrate community achievement and to set a moral example of good citizenship for future generations. Because nineteenth-century Americans considered public achievement to be a male virtue, citizens honored accomplished men and attributed civic progress to them. But scholarship in women's history is rapidly uncovering the role of middle-class and elite women in shaping America's cities. The civic cemetery, the final resting place of the city's most prominent families, is an appropriate site for promoting a more complete, more balanced, and less gender-biased view of local history.

Virginia Minor's legal challenge was just one tactic used by American women to secure the vote. In nearly every community women organized to fight for suffrage. They held public meetings, lobbied legislatures, and fought to persuade reluctant men to grant them full citizenship. Although there are few reminders of this struggle on the urban landscape, the names of many of these now forgotten women are inscribed on monuments in family cemetery lots throughout the country.

Cemetery tours and programs frequently focus on Civil War statesmen and soldiers, but most ignore the wartime activities of the wives and daughters buried next to them. Women in St. Louis organized to raise thousands of dollars for medical relief, served as paid and volunteer nurses, and administered homes for refugees and ex-slaves during the war. Many of these same women established social service institutions for destitute women and children in a time before government welfare programs. St. Louis is hardly unique: in every community there were female social activists, writers, artists, business owners, and philanthropists whose inclusion would enrich existing cemetery tours.

Although many grave sites of influential women are located in civic cemeteries, others are scattered throughout a community's religious, ethnic, and smaller secular graveyards. Rows and rows of identical crosses fill the lots of women's religious orders in Calvary Cemetery, the large Roman Catholic cemetery adjacent to Bellefontaine. These are the graves of women who founded and administered dozens of schools, orphanages and hospitals in this historically Catholic city. In the nineteenth century, the Daughters of Charity and the Sisters of Mercy each constructed huge red brick convents and hospitals; all are gone from the urban landscape. Few St. Louisans familiar with St. John's Hospital, a sprawly modern medical complex in the St. Louis suburbs, know that it started with six determined Sisters of Mercy who arrived in 1880 to care for the immigrant poor. Truly hidden from history, the Daughters of Charity are now few in number and their work in the local community largely forgotten. Adding the burial lots of religious orders to cemetery tours not only acknowledges the place of nuns in a city's history, but also offers an opportunity to compare the domestic vision expressed there to the secular symbols of domesticity in family lots.[29]

African American women who were successful businesswomen, educators, artists, and civil rights leaders have monuments in St. Peter's Cemetery a few miles away. Notable St. Louis women buried there include Julia Davis, a local historian and public school teacher who promoted African American history for more than seventy-five years, and Marion Oldham, a founding member of the Congress of Racial Equality (CORE). Racial restrictions in American cemeteries

Figure 8-6. Gravestones cover the Calvary Cemetery plots of the Sisters of Loretto and the Sisters of St. Joseph of Carondolet, two of the most active teaching orders in St. Louis. The rows of identical tombstones reflect a different domestic ideal from that represented on family lots in the same cemetery. (*Photo by Mary Seematter.*)

varied by location; northeastern cemeteries frequently sold lots to anyone who could pay for them; southerners and midwesterners were more racially restrictive. In St. Louis, segregation did not end with death, but since its founding by white Protestants in 1855, St. Peters cemetery has permitted African American burials. As local scholars work to ensure that women of every race, class and ethnicity become part of their community's historical memory, citywide cemetery tours that include African American cemeteries publically demonstrate inclusiveness and reach out to new audiences.[30]

Rural cemeteries are not just nineteenth-century cultural landscapes and tour sites for women's history. The family lots within their gates are also starting points for research that can expand and deepen our understanding of women's experience. Careful examination of names and dates on monuments makes abstract demographic data immediate and tangible. Even naming patterns over time offer clues to internal family dynamics and generational changes in outlook. The great grandmother of Kate Austin, a late nineteenth-century feminist anarchist, was named Submit, but the name on her aunt's tombstone was Reform.[31]

A close examination of the material evidence on a single family lot in Bellefontaine Cemetery illustrates rich possibilities waiting in every American community. Families who bought large lots and who over time interred many relatives usually left paper trails as well as stone markers. Starting with the monument and working back through the available records, a researcher can uncover information about individual women and gain insight into the domestic, economic, and social history of the community.

A massive, rectangular granite monument with names and dates engraved on all four sides dominates the large Bellefontaine lot of George Collier. Identical stone medallions centered on the monument's two long sides state that he was born in 1796 and died in 1852. On the side facing the street, two lists of family members, each headed by the names of one of George's two wives, flank the medallion. Francoise E. Collier is memorialized with her three young children. Ann, 17 months old, died when her mother was eighteen and her sister Catherine was six months old. A year later, Francoise was either pregnant or had just given birth to a daughter, Louisa, when Catherine died at nineteen months. On August 30, 1835, both Francoise, now twenty-five, and six-year-old Louisa died.[32]

Within five years George married again. Sarah, his second wife, who is commemorated on the monument to the right of her husband, died in 1885 at the age of seventy-three. She too buried three young children. Her daughter Francoise, named in memory of her husband's first wife, died in 1846 at age four. An eleven-month-old daughter, Elizabeth, died in 1850. Sarah's four-year-old son Henry died in 1855, three years after the death of his father. Two other unmarried sons interred with Sarah, Thomas and John, lived to be twenty and thirty-five years old.

This glimpse of the Collier family gleaned from their cemetery monument is a poignant reminder of the fragility of life on the urban frontier. Although the Collier family was one of the wealthiest in St. Louis at mid-century, Francoise and Sarah were as powerless as poor mothers to save their children. Infectious diseases and pneumonia claimed most young lives; postpartum infection killed mothers, many already weakened by tuberculosis. Francoise and her daughter Louisa, who died on the same day in 1835, may have succumbed to cholera, an infectious disease spread by poor sanitation which claimed St. Louis lives nearly every summer. In 1800 the average native-born white woman had seven children in her lifetime; by 1900 the average had dropped to less than four. Birth control measures account for some of this decline in the birthrate, but gains in sanitation and health care made at the end of the century resulted in more children living to adulthood and more mothers surviving childbirth.[33]

The name of Nelly Warren, an African American woman who died in 1857 at the age of eighty, appears next to the medallion on the monument's long side. Along with her name, age, and date of death, the Colliers had chiseled: "Aunt Nelly" and "(colored)." Although Bellefontaine Cemetery did not sell burial plots to black St. Louisans, proprietors could bury African Americans in their private lots. Nelly Warren, identified simply as "colored" on the monument, was entered in the cemetery records as a slave in 1857 when the Collier family interred her body.[34]

Because George Collier was successful in business and died a wealthy man in 1852, he appears in narrative histories of St. Louis, but the women whose names are etched on the Collier monument do not. Approaching family burial plots with an eye to seeking out information about everyone buried there will ensure that women have a role in local history. Women's history research begun in the Col-

Figure 8-7. Nelly Warren, an enslaved African American woman, is memorialized on the George Collier family monument with members of the extended Collier family. The names of Collier's two wives, Francoise and Sarah, and those of their children are inscribed on the other side. (*Photo by Ruth L. Bahon.*)

lier lot not only produced a more complete and balanced view of these elite St. Louisans, but also helped to explain George's success.

Catherine Collier, George's widowed mother, was buried on the lot. Her husband Peter was a Maryland farmer who died about 1810 leaving Catherine to educate young George and his older brother John. A slave owner, she managed the family farm herself, earning enough money in agriculture and trade to send her sons to school in Philadelphia. In 1816 John moved west to St. Charles, Missouri, where he opened a mercantile business. Catherine and George followed two years later and the two brothers formed a successful partnership with offices in St. Charles and nearby St. Louis. After John's death in 1821, George expanded his business interests to include investments in steamboats and lead shipping. Catherine supervised a number of African American women, probably her own slaves, in making shirts and other garments for sale. She also organized a school in St. Charles. When she died in 1835, some of her estate went to the school for training Methodist ministers, but most, nearly $70,000, she placed in trust for George's children. Catherine also made provisions in her will for her four slaves. Three were to be freed gradually over ten years, but "Nelly," because of her age was not to be freed. Catherine instructed George to use money from her estate to take "proper care of" Nelly for the rest of her life.

Francoise Pettus, the daughter of a successful St. Charles merchant, was only sixteen years old when she married George Collier in 1826. Shortly after Francoise's death in 1835, George formed a banking partnership with her brother. George's second wife, Sarah Bell, was a merchant's daughter from Pittsburgh. The firm of Collier and Pettus prospered in international trade, but failed with many other businesses in 1842, a depression year. George founded another company with Francoise's brother-in-law. Alone and in partnership, George invested in land, railroads, utilities, mining, and rental property. In 1851 he became the principal investor in the Collier White Lead & Oil Company managed by Henry T. Blow.

George left an estate worth more than $500,000 when he died in 1852. He owned seven slaves valued at $2,000 including "Nelly," listed in the inventory as having no monetary value at age seventy. Sarah Collier chose, as was her legal right, to reject the provisions George made for her in his will and instead claimed her dower right of one-third of the estate. She inherited the large family home on a downtown street ripe for commercial development. After she had the house torn down and replaced by a business block, Sarah moved to a fine new home on Lucas Place, the city's first private residential street.[35]

The Collier monument commemorates male prominence and female domesticity, but the story is more complex. Catherine's business ventures helped to launch her son's successful career. George benefited from marriage into established mercantile families and Sarah added to the family fortunes after her husband's death. Nelly Warren spent her life as an unpaid worker for the Collier family: she probably made garments that Catherine sold and later took care of several generations of Collier children. Sarah considered it appropriate that her slave accompany the family to its heavenly home.[36]

Research on the Collier family began with cemetery records. Like other civic cemeteries, Bellefontaine kept excellent records because the founders were self-conscious proponents of family and community history who provided adequate funding for professional administration. Local historical societies often have information about the owners of large cemetery lots. The Missouri Historical Society library contained information about George's childhood and business career. The only Collier information in the society's manuscript collection, however, was a copy of George's will and information on the St. Charles school founded by Catherine Collier. Although it was not true in this case, collections from prominent families often contain correspondence of female family members that provide glimpses of domestic life, including slave owners' treatment of their slaves.

There was no information about Nelly Warren at the historical society. Her name did not appear on a slave bill of sale, nor could she be identified on census records. Documents, wills, and inventories in George Collier's probate records located at the St. Louis City Courthouse proved to be the most useful source for information about Nelly Warren, although there was no clue to the origin of the name Warren that appears on the monument. The probate files also made possible the reconstruction of Catherine and Sarah's financial history.

Finding family lots rich with artifactual information is relatively easy in a large urban cemetery like Bellefontaine, but may be more difficult in smaller cemeteries. In most, however, there are some family lots with impressive monuments and in all there is ample evidence of high nineteenth-century death rates for mothers and children. Visitors will notice, however, that the newer sections of old rural cemeteries more closely resemble cemeteries founded in the twentieth century. By the turn-of-the-century considerations of maintenance, changing standards of taste, and attitudes about the rituals of death were influencing the appearance of newly opened sections. Moreover, even at the height of the Rural Cemetery Movement, some small public cemeteries and church yards did not fit the pattern described here.[37]

Although the Rural Cemetery Movement influenced most American cemeteries, ethnic burial places remained distinct. The appearance of Jewish cemeteries reflected religious and cultural traditions very different from nondenominational Protestantism. African Americans seldom could afford permanent monuments or perpetual care for cemeteries that too often were later neglected or obliterated for development. The abundant variety of existing ethnic cemeteries invite comparative studies of iconography related to gender by those steeped in or willing to learn their traditions.[38]

Large, urban Roman Catholic cemeteries established in the late nineteenth century reflect the influence of the Rural Cemetery Movement. In 1854 Archbishop Peter Kendrick of St. Louis purchased land for Calvary Cemetery adjacent to Bellefontaine partly in response to the popularity of the new civic cemetery. Although the Archdiocese discouraged lot owners from erecting expensive secular grave markers and insisted on religious iconography, Calvary too has winding roads and substantial monuments on large family lots. Countless crosses and other religious statuary, however, set Calvary apart from its neighbor. Statues of the Madonna, visible from every direction, are clear expressions of the traditional place of women in Catholicism while reinforcing attitudes about women's piety, submissiveness, and maternal role that permeated nineteenth-century American culture.[39]

Roman Catholic cemeteries modeled on the civic rural cemetery promoted American uniformity over ethnic variety, chastising people who insisted "on bringing their national customs and prejudices to our modern cemeteries." Some ethnic groups, however, were able to practice their own burial customs. Beginning in the 1850s, Italian-Americans expressed their vision of heavenly domesticity in New York City's Calvary Cemetery by planting flowers in front of family monuments and vegetables behind them. St. Louis families of Irish, Italian, and Southern European heritage also chose monuments for their sections of the cemetery that expressed different memorial traditions.[40]

In spite of its sectarian emphasis, the Calvary landscape is more varied than Bellefontaine. The founders of Bellefontaine compared their cemetery to a city. Calvary with its own neighborhoods and ethnic pockets was more representative of the city of St. Louis, although, with the exception of Dred Scott, few African Americans were buried there.

Nineteenth-century cemeteries are rich sites for teaching, researching, and promoting local women's history. Pre-visit lesson plans and on-site activities for field trips that focus on landscape and iconography can guide students of every age to discoveries about gender in nineteenth-century America. Moreover, by helping students read the cultural messages expressed in the design of a cemetery and its monuments, teachers can sensitize them to the importance of material culture in understanding the past. Nineteenth-century mortality rates take on new meaning for middle-school students who have analyzed a monument like the Collier family's at Bellefontaine or have searched family lots for sentimental verses on the gravestones of long-dead children. The experiences of the women in the Collier family are not atypical, but local histories seldom include anything about female family members in the biographies of prominent men. Students need to learn where and how to find the women. By starting with family lots, high school and undergraduate classes in women's history or research methodology could learn to use a variety of primary and secondary sources.[41]

Public historians and others who develop historical tours of cemeteries either can revise existing tours to give a more accurate account of women's roles in nineteenth-century life and death, or use new research in local and national women's history to create female-focused tours. A group of high school or college students might research the lives of a number of women in a single cemetery to develop a tour, guidebook, or even first-person dramatic presentations. Decisions about whom to include would require investigations into the history of women's activities in many areas of community life. Studying the cemetery as a cultural institution could help students understand the values and attitudes that shaped the lives of the women chosen for the tour. Inclusion of local cemeteries from other ethnic, racial, and religious groups would help to broaden their knowledge of community history. A local business or foundation might even underwrite the cost of publishing a guidebook, particularly if it were analytical, well written, and illustrated with good student photographs.[42]

Research for a guidebook or cemetery tour can lead to activism. Susan Wilson's interest in identifying graves of significant women in Boston's Forest Hills Cemetery inspired her to organize a group of people to restore the grave of Susan Dimoch, a promising young physician at Boston's New England Hospital for Women and Children who drowned in a shipwreck off the coast of England in 1875. In St. Louis, the crumbling mausoleum of Ann Lucas Hunt, who gave thousands of dollars to support Catholic orphanages, schools, and hospitals, awaits attention from a public only now becoming aware of her significance to the community.[43]

Rural cemeteries are women's history sites where subtle textures of class, race, and gender are manifest in the tangible artifacts and emblems of death and remembrance. Middle-class Americans designed their civic cemeteries to reflect and promote a domestic vision of the good life, one which centered on being "called home," both here on earth and after death. In communities all over America, it is still possible to pass though iron gates, walk down winding roads, and find on shaded lots material evidence of the complex worlds of nineteenth-century women.

NOTES

1. The author thanks Patricia L. Adams, Howard S. Miller, Mary Seematter, Sarah Turner and Ruth L. Bohan for research, editing, and photographic assistance. For a brief history of Bellefontaine Cemetery in the context of the Rural Cemetery Movement and the history of St. Louis see Katharine T. Corbett, "Bellefontaine Cemetery: St. Louis City of the Dead," *Gateway Heritage,* (Fall 1991). For Susan Blow, see Dorothy Ross, "Susan Blow," *Notable American Women, 1607–1950,* vol.1 (Cambridge, MA: Belknap Press, 1971), 181–183 and Katharine T. Corbett, *In Her Place: A Guide to St. Louis Women's History* (St. Louis: Missouri Historical Society Press, 1999), 108–109.

2. The Carondelet Historical Society owns the Des Peres School, the location of Susan Blow's first kindergarten. Volunteers maintain a collection of artifacts related to Blow's work and the St. Louis public schools. Thanks to their efforts and to St. Louisans interested in the history of women, tours of Bellefontaine Cemetery today more often extol her accomplishments than those of her largely-forgotten father.

3. For a history of Mt. Auburn Cemetery see Blanche Linden-Ward, *Silent City on a Hill: Landscapes of Memory and Boston's Mount Auburn Cemetery* (Columbus: University of Ohio Press, 1989). For burial customs and attitudes about death in Western culture see Philippe Aries, *The Hour of Our Death,* trans. Helen Weaver, (New York: Knopf, 1981), 450–530. For the European cemetery reform movement and the invention of the secular bourgeois cemetery, see Frederick Brown, *Pere Lachaise: Elysium as Real Estate* (New York: Viking Press, 1973). See David Charles Sloane, *The Last Great Necessity: Cemeteries in American History* (Baltimore: Johns Hopkins University Press, 1991) for a comprehensive history of American burial practices.

4. For American attitudes about death and the development of the cemetery as an American cultural institution see Stanley French, "The Cemetery as Cultural Institution: The Establishment of Mount Auburn and 'The Rural Cemetery Movement,'" in David Stannard, ed., *Death in America,* (Philadelphia: University of Pennsylvania Press, 1975), 69–71. See also Richard E. Meyers, ed., *Cemeteries and Gravemarkers: Voices of American Culture* (Ann Arbor: University of Michigan Research Press, 1989); James J. Farrell, *Inventing the American Way of Death, 1830–1920* (Philadelphia: Temple University Press, 1980); and David Charles Sloane, *The Last Great Necessity.* J. J. Smith, *Designs for Monuments and Mural Tablets Adapted to Rural Cemeteries, Church Yards, Churches and Chapels* (New York: Bartlett & Welford, 1846) was a popular guidebook for the founders of rural cemeteries. Smith advised founders to have regard for the wealth and taste of people who will use the cemetery, but not to devote the cemetery to any one class: the ability to pay should be the only criteria. For cemetery board membership as a civic duty of the male elite, see Sloane, *The Last Great Necessity,* 69.

5. See Ann Douglas, *The Feminization of American Culture* (New York: Knopf,

1977), 200–226 and "Heaven Our Home: Consolation Literature in the Northern United States, 1830–1880" in Stannard, ed., *Death in America* for the impact of changing religious beliefs on the domestication of death.

6. Margaret J. Darnall, "The American Cemetery as Picturesque Landscape: Bellefontaine Cemetery, St. Louis," *Winterthur Portfolio 18* (Winter, 1983). See also Sloane, *The Last Great Necessity,* 51. Ann Douglas, *The Feminization of American Culture,* 202–203. Douglas argues that women and Protestant ministers promoted the cult of death to bolster their status. Emily Dickinson's comment on Mount Auburn is from a September 8, 1846 letter to Abiah Root, quoted in Sloane, *The Last Great Necessity,* 36.

7. See Sloane, *The Last Great Necessity* and Ruth L. Bohan "A Home Away from Home: Bellefontaine Cemetery, St. Louis, and the Rural Cemetery Movement," *Prospects 13* (1988) for a detailed analysis of the relationship between domesticity and the material culture of rural cemeteries. Truman Post, "Address of Professor Post," in *Dedication of the Bellefontaine Cemetery* (St. Louis: T. W. Ustick, 1851), 17. J. J. Smith in *Designs for Monuments,* stated that the family focus of rural cemeteries made it appropriate to segregate single graves.

8. See Laurel Ulrich, *Good Wives: Image and Reality in the Lives of Women in Northern New England, 1650–1750* (New York: Knopf, 1982) for a discussion of women's work and family life in pre-industrial America.

9. See Sara M. Evans, *Born for Liberty: a History of Women in America* (New York: Free Press, 1989), 119–143 for the impact of industrialization on urban middle-class women. See also Stuart Blumen, *The Emergence of the Middle Class: Social Experience in the American City, 1760–1900* (Cambridge: Cambridge University Press, 1989); Mary Ryan, *The Cradle of the Middle Class: The Family in Oneida County, New York, 1790–1865* (Cambridge: Cambridge University Press, 1981); Harvey Green, *The Light in the Home: An Intimate View of the Lives of Women in Victorian America* (New York: Pantheon Books, 1983); and Katharine T. Corbett and Howard S. Miller, *St. Louis in the Gilded Age* (St. Louis: Missouri Historical Society Press, 1993).

10. Information on regulations and suggestions to lot owners is from *Bellefontaine Cemetery Association Original Charter, Amendments to Charter, Together with the By-Laws and Rules and Regulations of the Bellefontaine Cemetery and Suggestions to Lot Owners, Etc.; also Containing an Historical Sketch* (St. Louis: Commercial Printing Co., 1896), a compendium of Bellefontaine publications dating from 1850 to 1896. Cemetery administrators used monument company catalogs and guidebooks such as J. J. Smith, *Design of Monuments* to assist proprietors in choosing appropriate monuments. See also Linden-Ward, *Silent City on a Hill,* 220. Men also left instructions in their wills for erecting monuments on previously purchased lots. See "Last will and testament of John Collier," July 8, 1852, Gamble Collection, Missouri Historical Society (MHS). For changing grave marker motifs and their symbolism see James Deetz, *In Small Things Considered* (New

York: Anchor Press, 1977); Sloane, *The Last Great Necessity,* 77–79; Michael S. *Frank, Elmwood Endures: History of A Detroit Cemetery* (Detroit: Wayne State University Press, 1996), 205.

11. Mark Twain and Charles Dudley Warner characterized the era in *The Gilded Age: A Tale of Today* (New York: Harper, c.1915) in part because industrial capitalists flaunted their wealth by purchasing pretentious homes. *Bellefontaine Cemetery Association,* 1878; "Styles of Classical Architecture Shown in Mausoleums Lately Erected at Bellefontaine," *The St. Louis Republic,* January 18, 1903. See also Kenneth Ames, "Ideologies in Stone: Meanings in Victorian Gravestones," *Journal of Popular Culture* (Spring 1981): 641–656. Ames considers erection of Victorian gravemarkers "elaborate forms of avoidance behavior" by people unwilling to accept the finality of death.

12. Nancy Woloch, *Women and the American Experience,* 3rd ed.(Boston: McGraw-Hill, 2000), 103–130. See also Evans, *Born for Liberty,* 138–139; Douglas, *The Feminizaton of American Culture,* 220–245; Corbett and Miller, *St. Louis in the Gilded Age,* 19–23. Lydia Maria Child quote from Mrs. Child, *The Mother's Book,* reprint of 1831 edition (New York: Arno Press & *The New York Times,* 1972), 81.

13. Thomas J. Schlereth, *Victorian America: Transformations in Everyday Life* (New York: Harper Collins Publishers, 1991), 290. See Green, *The Light in the Home,* 165–179 for an illustrated discussion of mourning customs. For the relationship between the Civil War and mourning customs, see Douglas, *The Feminization of American Culture,* 371, note 6.

14. Susan Wilson, *Garden of Memories: A Guide to Historic Forest Hills* (Boston: Forest Hills Educational Trust, 1998). Wilson, who located many notable women buried in this Boston cemetery, notes that women were identified as "wife of" even when they had records of individual achievement. Bohan, "A Home Away from Home," *Prospects 13:* 162–169.

15. Bohan, "A Home Away from Home," *Prospects 13:* 162–169.

16. Epitaphs quoted are from gravemarkers in the North Gorham Cemetery, founded in 1853 in Gorham, Maine. See Barbara Rotundo, "Monumental Bronze: A Representative American Company," in Meyer, *Cemeteries and Gravemarkers* for a description of Zink monuments, popular for a short time in the late nineteenth century.

17. Linden-Ward, *Silent City on a Hill,* 243.

18. See Corbett, *In Her Place* for information on the Blow family, St. Louis women's charitable activities, and the relationship between Dred Scott and the Blow family. Quotations from *Missouri Republican,* June 30 and July 1, 1875.

19. *Missouri Republican,* September 12 and 19, 1875.

20. Bellefontaine's nineteenth century records do not reveal when monuments were placed on lots, making it impossible to ascertain who selected them and when. Signed monuments are easier to trace. *A Walk Through Bellefontaine Cemetery* (St. Louis, Bellefontaine Cemetery Association, 1944) states that

Mary Augusta Bissell and Angelica Yeatmen were buried under monuments commissioned by their grieving husbands from Robert von der Lavenity, a New York sculptor. Women sculptors also received cemetery commissions: Harriet Hosmer created a statue of Puck for Forest Hills, Wilson, *Garden of Memories,* 24; *Tombstone Talks: Landmarks Tour of Bellefontaine Cemetery* (Landmarks Association of St. Louis, Inc., 1970), 18, 21. Landmarks emphasized that Sullivan's unique 1892 design did not follow current fashion, being neither Gothic nor Egyptian Revival. See also John Gary Brown, *Soul in Stone: Cemetery Art from America's Heartland* (Lawrence: University of Kansas Press, 1994).

21. Bohan, "A Home Away from Home," *Prospects 13:*165.

22. *Bellefontaine Cemetery Association Original Charter. . . . ;* Michael S. Frank, *Elmwood Endures,* 20; Smith, *Designs for Monuments,* discouraged allegorical figures in favor of classical and gothic designs. See also David Robinson, *Saving Graces: Images of Women in European Cemeteries* (New York: Norton, 1995).

23. "Rebecca Sire," MHS, "Necrology Scrap Book" vol. 2P: 21. See Corbett, *In Her Place,* for treatment of Southern sympathizers and an 1862 *Missouri Republican* article preserved in the MHS, "Civil War Scrapbook: 5," for report of the auction of Sire's furniture. The overturned torch was an Egyptian symbol for a life extinguished and appeared as a motif in monument company catalogs. Richard O. Reisem, ed., *Forest Lawn Cemetery: Buffalo History Preserved* (Buffalo: Forest Lawn Heritage Foundation, 1996), 104.

24. Sloane, *The Last Great Necessity,* 73; Elizabeth Stuart Phelps, *The Gates Ajar* (1868) and Theodore Cuyler, *The Empty Crib* were typical of consolation literature describing heavenly domestic life. See also Douglas, *The Feminization of American* Life, 223–226 and Green, *The Light in the Home,*166–167, 177–179. See also Ellen Marie Snyder, "Innocents in a Worldly World: Victorian Children's Gravemarkers," in Meyer, ed., *Cemeteries and Gravemarkers,* 11–29. Some cemeteries had special sections for children's graves when young parents could not afford family lots. Reisem, *Forest Lawn Cemetery,* 58; *Tombstone Talks: Landmarks Tour of Calvary Cemetery* (Landmarks Association of St. Louis, 1970),15.

25. Sloane, *The Last Great Necessity,* 53; Douglas, *The Feminization of American Culture,* 212–213; *Saint Louis Globe-Democrat,* September 18, 1887, quoted in Bohan "A Home Away from Home," *Prospects 13:* 153.

26. Post, "Address of Professor Post," 18.

27. See, for example, Wilson, *Garden of Memories;* Reisem, *Forest Lawn Cemetery,* and Frank, *Elmwood Endures.*

28. Wilson, *Garden of Memories.* The grave sites of Sara Teasdale and Kate Chopin appear in *Tombstone Talks: Landmarks Tour of Bellefontaine Cemetery* and *Tombstone Talks: Landmarks Tour of Calvary Cemetery.* Kevin Amsler, *Final Resting Place: The Lives and Deaths of Famous St. Louisans* (St. Louis: Virginia Pub., 1997); Franck, *Elmwood Endures,*179–201.

29. Corbett, *In Her Place,* passim for specific information about women religious in St. Louis. See also Mary Ewens, *The Role of Nuns in Nineteenth Century America* (New York: Arco Press, 1978) and Carol K. Coburn and Martha Smith, *Spirited Lives: How Nuns Shaped Catholic Culture and American Life* (Chapel Hill: University of North Carolina Press, 1999)

30. Shirley Wotawa, *History of St. Peter's Cemetery* (Normandy, MO: S.A. Wotawa, c.1999); Corbett, *In Her Place,* 291, 289–291; Sloane, *The Last Great Necessity,* 83. See Ann Morris, *Sacred Green Spaces: a Survey of Cemeteries in St. Louis County* (St. Louis: s.n., 2000) for an example of a historical survey of local cemeteries, including African American and ethnic burial places.

31. Howard S. Miller, "Kate Austin: A Feminist-Anarchist on the Farmer's Last Frontier," *Nature, Society, and Thought,* 9, #2 (1996): 189–209.

32. George Collier purchased his 2050 sq.ft. lot on Lawn Ave., Bellefontaine Cemetery, St. Louis, Missouri, in 1850 and reinterred the remains of his first wife and several children shortly afterward. His will, written shortly before his death in 1852, stipulated that his executors spend $2,500 to erect a "plain, neat, substantial, and unostentatious" monument on the lot. "Last Will and Testament of George Collier," July 8, 1852, MHS.

33. Nancy Woloch, *Women and the American Experience,* 605–606; Schlereth, *Victorian America,* 288; Green, *The Light in the Home,*165–166.

34. *Bellefontaine Cemetery Association Original Charter. . . . ;* Bellefontaine Cemetery Association office maintains a record of burials on the George Collier lot.

35. Information on the Collier family history is from the following sources: William Hyde and Howard Conard, *Encyclopedia of the History of St. Louis* (New York: The Southern History Company, 1899), 423; George Brooks, ed., "A Reminiscence from the St. Louis Critic, 1885," (*MHS Bulletin* XXIX):105; Frederick L. Billion, *Annals of St. Louis in its Territorial Days* (St. Louis, 1888), 291–293; Henry Hitchcock, "George Collier," (unpublished manuscript, MHS Library); Federal Census of 1830, 1840 and 1850 for St. Louis and St. Charles Counties; Probate Records of the Estate of George Collier, St. Louis, Missouri 3778, Box 3-A, 17 files; Scott McConachie, "Public Problems and Private Places," (*MHS Bulletin* XXXIV): 93–94.

36. Although there is no direct evidence that Nelly Warren was one of the African American women who sewed the garments Catherine Collier sold, it is unlikely Collier hired free labor. Of 488 black women enumerated in the St. Charles County 1830 census, only 13 were not enslaved.

37. The 1867 St. Louis City Directory listed twenty cemeteries, the majority affiliated with churches. Historical societies and genealogical groups frequently survey local cemeteries. Like Morris, *Sacred Green Spaces,* they often provide information about cemetery history and locations. See Sloane, *The Last Great Necessity,* 157–215 for a discussion of the decline of the Rural Cemetery Movement and the rise of the commercial memorial park.

38. See Richard E. Myer, ed., *Ethnicity and the American Cemetery* (Bowling

Green, Ohio: Bowling Green State University Popular Press, 1993) for essays on Italian-American and Ukranian-American cemeteries, Jewish cemeteries, and funeral customs of Czech and Irish families; also see Kathy McCoy, "Afro-American Cemeteries in St. Louis," (*Gateway Heritage* VI-3): 30–37.

39. Calvary Cemetery Association, *Charter, By-Laws and Rules* (St. Louis: Calvary Cemetery Association, 1878).

40. Calvary Cemetery Assn., *Charter,* 58. Joseph J. Inguanti, "Domesticating the Grave: Italian American Memorial Practices at New York Calvary Cemetery," *Markers* 2000, 17: 8–31. John Matturri, "Windows in the Garden: Italian-American Memorialization and the American Cemetery" in Meyer, ed., *Ethnicity and the American Cemetery* argues that despite pressures to conform, ethnic differences persist in American cemeteries. Spring Grove Cemetery in Cincinnati suggested that plot owners plant ethnic trees rather than erect ethnic monuments. See also Kenneth T. Jackson and Camilo Jose Vegra, *Silent Cities: The Evolution of the American Cemetery* (New York, 1989), a richly illustrated volume that analyzes the impact of race, ethnicity, religion, class, and fashion—but not gender—on the history and appearance of American cemeteries.

41. See Ann Palkovich, "Teacher's Corner: Exploring Historic Cemeteries," *AnthroNotes,* vol. 20, no.2, (Winter 1998) for a lesson plan on interpreting a rural cemetery. Palkovich focuses on material culture in leading students to consider issues of class and gender. The lesson can be adapted for middle school to undergraduate classes. Penny Coleman, *Corpses, Coffins, and Crypts: A History of Burial* (New York, Henry Holt, 1997), a history of death and burial practices for young people, contains curriculum for using cemeteries to teach women's history and a list of burial sites of famous women.

42. A volunteer organization in Portland, Maine, developed a tour brochure, "Notable Women at Evergreen Cemetery," available from Friends of Evergreen, P.O Box 11015, Portland, ME 04104.

43. Wilson, *Garden of Memories,* 44; Corbett, *In Her Place,* 58.

SUGGESTED READINGS

Blanche Linden-Ward, *Silent City on a Hill: Landscape of Memory and Boston's Mount Auburn Cemetery.* Columbus: University of Ohio Press, 1989. This well-illustrated history of the first American rural cemetery is an excellent source to use when looking for the influences of the Rural Cemetery Movement in local cemeteries. Linden-Ward explains the origins and philosophy of the movement in the context of Victorian culture and urban, middle-class values.

David Charles Sloane, *The Last Great Necessity: Cemeteries in American History.* Baltimore: Johns Hopkins Press, 1991. Sloane traces in detail the history if American cemeteries from the colonial period through the twentieth century. The book is particularly helpful for comparing the landscape and material culture of nineteenth century cemeteries with what came before and after.

Susan Wilson, *Garden of Memories: A Guide to Historic Forest Hills*. Boston: Forest Hills Educational Trust, 1998. Colorful, clear, and well researched, this is a model for integrating women's history into a cemetery guidebook. Wilson embeds the history of Forest Hills in local and national culture and includes the graves of many women in the six walking tours.

Harvey Green, *The Light in the Home: An Intimate View of Women in the Victorian America*. New York: Pantheon Books, 1983. Based on the domestic collections of the Margaret Woodbury Strong Museum in Rochester, New York, this older, but excellent, book examines mourning customs and artifacts of death in the context of Victorian ideology and the material culture of middle-class women.

Chapter 9

REVISITING MAIN STREET: UNCOVERING WOMEN ENTREPRENEURS

Candace A. Kanes

At a busy intersection in downtown Buffalo, New York, across the street from the Buffalo Convention Center, a plaque on the corner of the Statler Hotel notes that here in 1919, the Zonta Club, an international organization of business-women, was born. The plaque might be surprising or confusing to passers-by who never heard of Zonta or its members. In the near distance one can see the large in-dustrial structures that are reminders of Buffalo's golden era of steel production, flour milling, and other manufacturing. Buffalo enjoyed prominence because of the Erie Canal, railroads, and its geographical advantages. But business *women*? Who were they and what were they doing in Buffalo in 1919?

To find out what the plaque signifies, one might wander into the local history room of the Buffalo and Erie County Public Library where a question about Zonta or businesswomen would turn up stories of Marion DeForest, a lifelong Buffalo res-ident, newspaper woman, playwright, musical impresario, and Zonta national pres-ident from 1924–1925. DeForest, born in 1864, was ill as a child and spent much of her time reading and writing. She was inspired by Jo in Louisa May Alcott's *Little Women* and, like Jo, sold some stories to magazines under an assumed name. She later became a newspaper reporter, serving for many years as a drama critic. Her business was writing. She wrote the first stage version of *Little Women* as well as several other plays that received considerable attention in the 1920s. In addition, she was committed to the organization of businesswomen that she helped create and is still remembered within the organization by a fund and an award that bear her name.

The search inspired by the Zonta plaque might also lead to the Archives of the University at Buffalo, where records of the Buffalo Zonta Club are housed. Among the more than 150 founding members of the Buffalo Zonta Club were social work-ers and tea room operators, women with advertising agencies and owners of retail businesses, doctors and clerical workers, corporate managers and insurance agents, milliners, and the head of women's prisons. The archives include copies of newsletters, national magazines, and scrapbooks full of newspaper clippings that

Figure 9-1. Maud F. Storey operated her millinery shop on Congress Street in Portland, ME, from about 1913 to 1926. This photo was taken at Christmastime about 1913. (*Courtesy Maine Historical Society.*)

Figure 9-2. Members placed the Zonta International plaque near the entrance to the Statler Hotel in Buffalo, NY, on the fiftieth anniversary of the founding of the organization which had meeting rooms in that hotel. (*Photo by author.*)

detail the successes of club members. The records suggest that businesswomen were not unique to Buffalo, nor to Zonta.

Concealed within cities and towns throughout America are similar stories of women engaged in mostly small—or perhaps tiny—business enterprises. These women generally were not the builders and operators of steel mills and canals, of railroads or manufacturing plants. But they saw themselves as businesswomen and they had an impact on their communities. The streets where they conducted business might be re-envisioned as sites of women's history, with maps, interpretive panels, or plaques noting where women had businesses and when. First, though, the women and the sites must be identified.

The existence of businesswomen has been largely obscured for several reasons, even though women have been engaged in business activity since colonial days.[1] The focus of much of the history of business has been on big business and thus has helped to hide women's involvement; most women's businesses have been small. Also, we have assumed that if *most* women were involved in domestic pursuits, or excluded for other reasons from the business world, then we do not have to look further to find if *any* women were included. We have missed the ways in which many women over generations were able to combine domestic responsibilities with business, or the ways in which women have capitalized on women's interests and needs in developing businesses aimed at other women. We often have assumed that if women's roles were domestic, then the Main Street business district was the province of men, or perhaps only of women as consumers. In addition, when we see men and their experiences as the norm, we have concluded that women did not have a significant part in the economic development of the country.

Finding women in business, understanding their importance, and designating sites requires both research and shedding assumptions about men, women, and business. This chapter will discuss several women in several cities who remind us of the importance of small enterprise, and help us to rethink how we look at main streets of cities and towns. It also will offer some suggestions on sources for finding these women.

"Business" has come to mean big enterprise. Since the 1830s, more and more capital has been necessary to finance larger and larger business concerns such as cross-continental rail lines and massive factories. Especially since the advent of schools of business management in the 1890s, the "businessman" has been the financier or the top management of large enterprises. The separation of labor from the decision-making process, the growth of management as a discrete skill, and the integration of many market functions into single large firms often are cited as the most significant business developments of the nineteenth century.[2] Because these developments have come to be equated with "business," when we look for people or sites to recognize in our communities or when we seek to reconstruct our history, we frequently look toward huge enterprises. This effort most often leads to wealthy and influential men.

We might be disappointed to find that there are few women among these managers, financiers, and entrepreneurs. And we might conclude that women were not involved in business (at least until the 1970s or so), that such business careers were closed to them, or that they "failed"(for a variety of reasons) to achieve success in such male-dominated pursuits. Or we might find a few notable women, such as Lydia Pinkham who, along with her sons, developed and began marketing a popular tonic the 1870s; or Elizabeth Arden who created a cosmetics empire in the twentieth century, or Madame C. J. Walker, whose hair care products for African Americans made her a millionaire in the early twentieth century. Having found a few notable women, we are then convinced that they are worthy examples of what women might do, but nevertheless are exceptions, and that, in business enterprise, notable men are the rule. Such conclusions tacitly support the notion that (white) men and men's experiences are the norm by which to judge all experiences.

But the Zonta records remind us that many more women *were* involved in business. Zonta saw itself serving executive women, women who were entrepreneurs or who held independent decision-making positions. The records detail a number of women in the first half of the twentieth century who directed successful and long-term business enterprises. Recognizing the existence of women prompts a reevaluation of the history of business and of the factors that make particular persons or activities significant.

While the earliest members of Zonta and similar groups whose lives are detailed below were white, not all women entrepreneurs were white, and certainly not all were elite or from middle-class backgrounds. The club itself brought together college-educated women and those with little or no education. Members might have been from poor or working-class backgrounds or from elite households where success in business was expected, albeit only for sons.[3]

Regardless of the impact of huge business on the American economy, on workers, and on consumers, that is clearly not the entire story of American business, nor of entrepreneurs. Main Street businesses continued to dominate towns and cities through much of the twentieth century, despite the presence of chains or of huge industrial enterprises. Daily life, along with the economy of many communities, has centered on local businesses. It has been on Main Streets where people gather, where they discuss local events, where they meet friends, where they take care of necessities to observe transitions like marriages, births, deaths, graduations, the opening of the school year, holidays, and so forth.

In immigrant or African American neighborhoods or communities, these local businesses have been particularly crucial. They have provided an alternative to sometimes hostile white or native-born merchants and provided local gathering places that have created community solidarity and safe havens. In African American communities, especially, some black-owned businesses were the only choice for certain services. White funeral homes, hairdressers, and some related businesses often would not serve African American customers.[4] Neighborhood grocery stores and small bars or lunch rooms often were owned by residents of the neighborhood and therefore matched the racial or ethnic composition of the area.

Within many communities, businesses can be found that were owned by African Americans or members of particular immigrant groups.

All local businesses and the community networks they often foster, regardless of the ethnicity or race of the owners, have been important to American towns and cities for many generations for social as well as economic reasons. Main Street businesses keep local money in the local economy. They hire local workers. And they often support local schools, clubs, and organizations in their activities. It is here, on Main Street and within various surrounding neighborhoods, that many American women entrepreneurs have made their mark.

A map of the major streets in downtown Buffalo and the West Side retail area could be marked with the locations of businesses that were owned by some of the founding members of the Buffalo Zonta Club. These streets are not just sites of businesses that come and go, of places to stop for coffee or to accomplish errands. They are sites of women's history, of the efforts of women to be recognized as competent, serious, and career oriented. In 1919 alone, the buildings in the area were teeming with hardworking and ambitious women. The map or markers along the streets could feature Bessie Bellanca, an Italian immigrant, who was a florist. Bellanca was well known within the Buffalo community through the Colonial Flower Shop, which she began about 1914 and which she operated until her retirement in 1958. Bellanca also was involved for several years in a musical impresario business.

Other sites on a 1919 Buffalo map could include Elizabeth C. Duggan who owned and operated Betty's Colonial Sweets, a candy making and sales business. In 1914, Duggan worked in a downtown office. She started making candy for fun. At Christmas, she decided to sell some candy to eager friends. The demand was so great that she gave up her office job and opened a candy business in the back of her home. She closed her business during World War I because sugar was not available and she was unwilling to use sugar substitutes. But by the mid-1920s, she was open again and employed about a dozen people. Her confections were sought for most of Buffalo's "elaborate parties and social affairs."[5]

The map could include owners of a silk and specialty shop, a textile weaving business, a lace and embroidery shop, and white china store. It could feature women in advertising, including Wilhelmine A. Hamelman, vice president of the Moss-Chase firm. Hamelman left school to become an office girl for a new venture started by J. C. Moss. She worked her way up until she became vice president and treasurer of the firm, which represented many industrial and business concerns in Buffalo.[6]

Among the proprietors of apparel stores was Mary E. Carr, president and treasurer of M.E. Carr Co., a retail glove business. Carr had been involved in the glove business all her working life, as a saleswoman and then buyer for retail dealers. In 1912, when she was about thirty-seven, she decided to open her own business. By the early 1920s, she added hosiery and lingerie to her store. She closed the store and retired in 1927. Remembering her decision to open a shop of her own, Carr recalled a feeling among many people "that women were still not strong enough to carry on the hardships of having a business of one's own." Many people told her it was a mistake to give up a weekly salary for the uncertainties of entrepreneurship, but Carr persisted for fifteen years, outgrowing several spaces.[7]

A rather unusual business owner was Fennella G. Crowell, of the F. G. Crowell Co., which manufactured boiler tube scrapers. Crowell had been a concert pianist, but hurt her arms and was unable to continue that career. In 1911, she bought the firm that made boiler tube scrapers, learned the business, and served as the only manager. She continued in business into the 1930s. "The modern woman can adapt herself to any situation," Crowell said about her experiences.[8]

Another woman in manufacturing was Mary Cass, manager of F. N. Burt Co., Ltd., the world's largest paper box manufacturer. She had been general manager for twenty-four years, and would remain so for another decade, developing new products and winning the loyalty of hundreds of employees. She had started as an office girl in 1881, when the company had but eight employees. Cass was known within the box industry and within the Buffalo community. Besides running a profitable and efficient business, Cass adopted a young boy and reared him.[9]

A number of Zonta members were in business for many years, and therefore were well-known and often well-respected and important community members. Unlike our image of most working women in the early twentieth century, the women who founded Zonta were not young women working until they married.[10] The average age of the founding members was forty and many women remained in business for decades. A magazine article about Buffalo Zonta members in 1925 highlighted about two dozen who had been at their jobs for twenty years or more.

These are but a few examples of the business women who were early members of Zonta. A map of Buffalo's retail areas, even one limited to 1919–1930, would be impressive for the numbers and varieties of businesses owned and operated by Zonta members, as well as for the longevity of many of the businesses. It would be a visual reminder that women were involved, in relatively large numbers, in the economic life of Main Street-type businesses. The map might have more impact than would detailed stories of one or two especially prominent women, for it would help dispel the notion that women in business were an exception.

Zonta was not the only organization for businesswomen, and Buffalo far from the only city where such stories may be found. In fact, women had been organizing into clubs aimed at promoting their interests as businesswomen since the late nineteenth century. Some clubs were purely local, while others attempted to be national by forming chapters in a number of cities.[11] Shortly after World War I ended, businesswomen started a number of organizations, most of which remain active today. In 1919, the year Zonta was formed, two other organizations also began, the Quota Club and the National Federation of Business and Professional Women's Clubs. The latter sought to incorporate existing clubs of businesswomen into a national federation to help expand opportunities for businesswomen, to provide various types of support for them, and to generally improve the status of businesswomen. Although many of the original clubs were those that had existed previous to 1919, the federation also helped to organize new clubs where none existed. Within a few years, others clubs followed such as the Pilot

Club, Soroptimist, and a revised Altrusa Club.[12] All of the groups were national, and eventually international; although at first, all tacitly or overtly limited membership to whites. Local organizations of African American businesswomen existed during this period, although no national groups apparently did. Many thousands of women who identified themselves as businesswomen joined these organizations in the 1920s and beyond.

In Portland, Maine, a passer-by might not see plaques on buildings that suggest the existence of businesswomen, but anyone pursuing old newspapers would be struck by headlines like "These Sisters Run Establishment on a Definite Plan," and "Prosperous Business Woman; Member of Local Club Whose Earnings Were $8,000 Last Year."[13] Headlines like these appeared frequently in the daily newspapers and lead the reader to some of the community's businesswomen and the organization they formed, the Portland Business and Professional Women's Club. In cities like Portland, many businesswomen's groups had weekly columns in local papers. They used the forums to communicate with club members and to announce their activities and successes to the larger community. One *Portland Daily Press* column features a large headline, "Business Women's Club Has Firm in Its Membership." The story discusses BPW members Abba Harris and Ruby Jackson, who bought Anna Robertson's stenography and multigraphing business in 1910. At the time, Jackson was a private stenographer to a partner in a downtown business firm. Harris worked as a stenographer at a manufacturing company. Neither had any experience in owning or running a business. Nevertheless, they invested their savings, took out a small loan, and bought the business. Within a decade, they had increased its output five- or sixfold. They employed six women and had a reputation in Portland for efficiency. The further story of the business and the proprietors can be followed through city directories that list businesses as well as individual residences, through club publicity, through marriage and death records, and through real estate transactions available at county offices. Harris married and left the business in the mid-1920s, but Jackson continued to operate it until the 1940s.[14]

Like the businesswomen in Buffalo, those in Portland, a much smaller city, operated many ventures in locations that still can be spotted throughout the retail district. Mapping the locations, creating a trail that follows the activities of the club's members as well as the locations of its meeting rooms, or placing plaques on particularly significant buildings in the area can help tell the story of women's history in a community where such history is hidden from everyday view. The Portland Women's History Walking Trail, which includes a booklet for self-guided tours, features some of these sites, helping to uncover and remember the activities of women in the city's past.

Other sources of information about Main Street entrepreneurs are local historical societies or other archives, including college or university collections. The Maine Historical Society in downtown Portland is the repository for records of the Portland Business and Professional Women's Club; the University of Maine in Orono holds the Maine BPW records. Both contain valuable resources such as

Figure 9-3. Nearly hidden in the upper left of this 1913 photograph is the millinery sign of the Congress Street shop operated by Ethel M. Flye for many years. Like the sign, women's businesses are often hidden from view today. (*Courtesy Maine Historical Society*).

membership lists, histories, and scrapbooks. The information contained in such archives often provides the seeds for locating particular sites that have been important to women's business history. Uncovering further details then requires mining sources already mentioned such as city directories, newspapers, probate records, and real estate records. The manuscript U.S. Census also is an especially valuable source of information because it details living arrangements and ages and marital status of women, as well as providing information about home ownership, ethnic background, and the neighborhood in which the women worked and lived.[15]

Most of those records were helpful in uncovering the story of Lillian Cheney, a short-time businesswoman, but one whose efforts could well be remembered on a map or marker at the site. In 1913, Cheney's husband died, leaving her with two children to support. She had no business experience but decided to open a neighborhood grocery store. She figured it would allow her time with her children and enough income to support them. She selected a location in South Portland and opened a store attached to her home. She closed at noon to prepare lunches for the children when they came home from school. She managed to run the store alone, keep house herself, and keep the family going.[16] Her store was a popular stopping place for children and adults alike. When Cheney remarried a few years later, she gave up the operation of the successful business.

Records of businesswomen's clubs, especially those formed after World War I, are excellent sources for learning about the activities of entrepreneurs, executives, and women involved in other business pursuits. From the clubs comes the sense of the prevalence of women in local business, both as entrepreneurs and as employees working their way up career ladders. Many of the local chapters of business-women's organizations still exist, and members may know the location of histori-cal records that list club members' names and occupations from earlier years. In ad-dition, businesswomen's organizations in the 1920s and 1930s encouraged local clubs to recruit journalists and to gain weekly columns in local newspapers. Most clubs had active publicity programs and newspapers often contain detailed stories about individual businesswomen or about club activities as a whole.

These organized businesswomen had considerable economic impact on their communities. They also worked, through publicity and other means, to increase public awareness of their activities and successes. They served as role models for many younger women and girls and helped create new opportunities for women. As clubs, they also had an effect on their communities. Many clubs had club rooms; some purchased club houses that offered space for other community ac-tivities. Clubs often became involved in various community events as well.

Clubs are not the only source of information about women entrepreneurs. Even though the clubs and their members were visible in many cities and towns across the country, not all women entrepreneurs joined such organizations. In addition, women were active in business pursuits long before the clubs were formed in the early twentieth century. Even in colonial America, women were engaged in busi-ness enterprise.

There are fewer obvious physical reminders of the business activities of colo-nial women. These women sometimes escape notice because of the dominance of the ideology of domesticity and our failure to recognize that women could be "do-mestic" and still be involved in business. Until the mid-nineteenth century, most women lacked legal rights to control property, to control wages or earnings, and to do business in the same way men did. But those restraints did not keep women out of the economy or from entrepreneurial pursuits. By uncovering these women's activities, we can further fill in the literal and figurative maps of our communities to explore how people lived, how different parts of the community might have been connected, and what women's roles really were.

For instance, some women in colonial New York state kept account books that suggest they operated stores attached to their homes, supplying particular goods or serving particular clientele. In most cases, these women's husbands also oper-ated stores, or supply houses. Yet the women kept different items, and sometimes sold to different customers. They kept separate account books as well, offering a window into their activities.[17] Joan Jensen has documented strategies of women in the Mid-Atlantic states in the late eighteenth to mid-nineteenth centuries to en-sure family survival. Women, who generally were in charge of milking and re-lated activities and of small farm animals like chickens, might sell milk, butter, or eggs at all times, but might step up that production and sales to aid the family when other agricultural crops did not produce enough income.[18]

Laurel Thatcher Ulrich uncovered a separate female economy in New England during the same time period. Girls and young women often worked in other households, doing laundry or spinning or weaving. Women produced cloth goods, baked items, and eggs, butter, cheese, and other dairy items, all of which could be used in barter for other goods. In addition, women like Martha Ballard worked as midwives, earning their own income in money or trade, and keeping separate accounts from their husbands or other men.[19] Martha Ballard's work and activities live on not only in Ulrich's book about her, but in "The Maine of Martha Ballard: A self-guided tour." This pamphlet produced by the Maine Humanities Council provides some general historical background, then leads the reader through maps, photos, and descriptions to sites of Ballard's activities in the late eighteenth and early nineteenth centuries. The self-guided tour, like many walking tours, leads the traveler to privately owned locations that are not tourist sites open for inspection or maintained in period authenticity, but are visual and physical reminders of women's important activities in the past.

Ballard and the other colonial women mentioned might not be Main Street entrepreneurs, but their experiences give us a more complete picture of women's roles, as well as provide evidence of the unbroken thread of women's enterprises. These entrepreneurs can be more challenging to locate than women in the late nineteenth and early twentieth centuries. However, clues exist in a number of locations. Historical societies and other state and local repositories of historical records are a good place to begin. They often hold diaries, account books, or similar private records that provide the basis for studying women's economic activities. As Ulrich's *A Midwife's Tale* demonstrates, diaries do not necessarily reveal their secrets easily. Sometimes, it is necessary to read between the lines as well as conduct considerable additional research. Community histories sometimes indicate women who have been active in various enterprises, as might tax rolls, deeds, and similar public documents. Newspapers also are excellent sources of information. News columns generally focused on men's activities, but advertising columns sometimes provide information about women's shops, schools, or other pursuits.

Sometimes the clues to the existence of these businesswomen are more apparent. In Brunswick, Maine, for instance, a restaurant bears the name "Narcissa Stone." The name is a memorial to a prominent nineteenth-century businesswoman who lived at the site of the restaurant and inn. If the name prompts curiosity, the owner of the inn (named for Stone's father) and restaurant can provide a few details. His source of information and where the search would lead are a history of Brunswick written in 1878, a year after her death, and the local historical society.[20] Community lore might also lead to the story of Narcissa Stone because a large rock outcropping in the Androscoggin River is known as the Narcissa stone. In fact, Narrcissa Stone, born in 1801, the eldest of ten children of a local merchant and community leader, was a locally well-known businesswoman. Further information about her life is available from her obituary in the local newspaper, and from property deeds and other legal documents. The least expected source, though, is a collection of deeds, letters, and other papers at the Portland, Maine, Museum of Art. Stone saved many of the letters, deeds, and other paper she accumulated during her life. Although she never married, the items found their way after her death to a relative who happened to be part of the McLellan (also McClellan) family. The McClellan home is part of the Portland Museum of Art, which acquired a number of the relative's papers and other belongings from an auction in the Midwest. Without those somewhat serendipitous events, less would be known about Narcissa Stone and much less would be known about business in a small Maine town in the nineteenth century.

Stone was a significant businesswoman in part because her many independent business transactions were unusual for a woman in the nineteenth century. Stone sometimes operated her father's shop where she apparently learned the basics of business. After his death, she ran the store for several years. From the 1820s until her death in 1877, Stone bought and sold property, invested in a local hotel and manufacturing firm, and began her own manufacturing operations.[21] She remained single throughout her seventy-six years. A newspaper article published when she died noted that she was "a woman of great intelligence, of thorough business habits."[22] She reportedly left an estate of $60,000, a considerable sum in 1877. When she died, only one sibling remained alive. Most apparently died fairly young. Stone's remaining brother, Daniel H. Stone, also was prominent in Brunswick business circles, but his activities did not outshine those of his oldest sister. She was the child who seemed to have inherited much of her father's interest and skill in business, as well as his confidence. It was Narcissa Stone who appeared to keep the family together after the parents' deaths, and who helped to support many important business ventures, the physical structures of which are remembered and discussed in Brunswick, even though they may not be standing.

It is important, though, not to rely on community lore as a method of remembering and recognizing this or other businesswomen. Narcissa Stone's grave in a local cemetery is listed on a small map of graves of notable women in Brunswick. Her name graces the restaurant, but there is no particular connection between her and a restaurant. Further marking could be made of the sites of her various business ventures and the church she attended and supported. She also is remembered in a local women's history walking trail, but for Stone and others like her who made a difference to the economic history of their communities, physical markers or interpretive panels are rare.

Visual clues, albeit obscure ones, exist for other women's business ventures as well. A magnificent Queen Anne style house and a neighborhood store in Penobscot, Maine, are reminders of the economic influence and importance of Abby Grendell Condon. She had the house built with proceeds of her business and she and her husband built a general store, still the site of the store in Penobscot. A teacher before her marriage, in 1864 she took advantage of Civil War era economic conditions to profit from the lack of available manufactured goods. She bought fifty pounds of yarn in Boston, hired women from her community of Penobscot to knit mittens from the yarn, then sold the mittens back to the Boston yarn dealer. By 1874, the war had ended, but Condon's business had grown. She employed about 250 women to knit mittens. Eventually, she bought knitting machines that she put in women's homes. Women hired by Condon reportedly knitted 180,000 pairs of mitten in 1880, a number that would have translated into the women earning a total of about $11,000.[23]

Condon's business apparently spawned a similar venture operated by merchants in the neighboring town of Castine. There, women knitted for a local market and for sale to ship crews. Instead of being paid in cash, the women who knit for the store traded finished mittens for store merchandise. Some women apparently supported themselves by knitting, while others produced mittens when they needed extra spending money.[24] The knitting business took advantage of women's skills and women's domestic responsibilities, allowing them to work at home and, in many cases, choose the pace and amount of work they would do.

Condon's activities were recorded by an area woman in her diary. In addition, one of Condon's knitters was interviewed in the 1930s and the area newspaper later wrote a story about Condon. Mention of her business also exists in the records of the R. G. Dun & Co. that are located at the Baker Library of Harvard Business School. The records are a rich source of information on selected nineteenth-century businesses.[25] The other knitting business is detailed in extant company records. A variety of sources can come together to help revive the memory of notable business activity.

Several types of women-owned businesses that represent significant women's history sites were common on Main Streets across America from the Civil War through the early twentieth century. Dressmakers, milliners, and corsetieres all were essential in supplying the wardrobes of many ordinary and most elite women in the era before ready-made clothing was common. These were businesses often owned and operated by women, and with women customers. Historian Wendy Gamber calls the millinery and dressmaking trades from 1860 to 1930 the "female economy." As Gamber points out, women may have been "slaves" to fashion, but the need for some women to have dresses and hats that followed the latest styles created occupational opportunities for other women. Dressmaking and millinery trades provided a decent living and a chance for economic independence for some women, although others were unable for a variety of reasons to maintain lucrative businesses. Eventually, the dressmaking, millinery, and corset-making trades disappeared, replaced by factory-made products. What were frequently women-dominated businesses in the eighteenth and nineteenth centuries became larger corporations, generally owned and managed by men. The jobs women were then able to get in such industries were wage labor positions, which rarely afforded the same economic independence or security as had the earlier trades.[26]

One often readily available source of information about women trades is city or town directories. Such directories were published in many communities, especially beginning in the last half of the nineteenth century. At the back of most of these directories is a list of people engaged in various occupations, and sometimes small advertisements for local businesses. Among the listings are usually "dress

Figure 9-4. Emma Mayo (probably the woman in white) ran the Eastern Steamboat House on the Portland, ME, waterfront from 1879 to 1896. The hotel catered to people in the maritime business. The man to Mayo's right is probably her husband Alphonso. (*Courtesy of the Maine Historic Preservation Commission.*)

makers," "corset makers," and "milliners." Other listings often include teachers, nurses, music teachers, public stenographers, court reporters, and other occupations held by women. Women engaged in many of these occupations often owned their own businesses, and frequently employed other women. The directories are a useful starting point.

For example, the 1884 city directory for Portland, Maine, lists more than one hundred dress and cloak makers in its classified section, along with at least twenty-five milliners. Only one name among the hundred listed could be a male dress or cloak maker. There were likely other women in those trades who were not listed for various reasons. Along the city's major retail street alone, there were at least thirty dressmakers and fifteen milliners in 1884. Most of the remaining shops also were downtown, within a few blocks of the main street. Some of the milliners and dressmakers were single, some married. Some appeared to be sisters, a few might have been mother and daughter. More investigation might reveal the nature of the shops, how long they remained in business, and some of their specialities. Miss Caroline P. Ingraham is the only dress and cloak maker among the long list for whom a specialty is indicated. She made children's clothing. Another directory category lists "tailoresses." About a dozen names appear there. In many communities, dressmaking and millinery were occupations open to women of all racial, ethnic, and class backgrounds. Although department stores, many offices, and other retail businesses did not hire African American women as clerks, stenographers, or in other positions in which they might come into direct contact with white customers, the clothing trades offered opportunities for black women and various immigrants.[27]

One might imagine walking down the main street in a city such as Portland in the late nineteenth or early twentieth centuries and encountering department stores with women clerks, a growing number of offices with women clerical workers, and scores of small shops owned and operated by women. Women would have been an integral part of the economic and social health of the city. Women's history trails, historical pamphlets about women's history sites, interpretive markers, or plaques on buildings all are reminders of the richness of women's economic contributions to our communities. We can further remember these women and their business activities through curricula in elementary and secondary schools as well as in colleges and universities. Students at all levels could help to research women in business in their communities. Such research, by students or by historians, could enrich local history curricula in schools, could be grist for women's history month observances, or could provide interesting ideas for displays at historical societies, museums, or in the Main Street buildings where many of the women's business activities occurred.

Besides permanent plaques, memorials, or women's history trails, photographs from newspapers or historical collections along with interpretive information could help to remind communities about the significant economic contributions of women. We can use our imagination to think about earlier centuries, but we can use our community resources and the skills of women's historians to ensure that these histories live on.

Although we are familiar with women as consumers, and especially with women's domestic roles, neither gives a complete picture of women's relationship to the economy now or in past centuries. Women have contributed to the family economy and the community economy as producers, entrepreneurs, employees, and in most other roles, both as temporary measures taken when needed to ensure family survival, and by choice in long-term careers. Before the Civil War, fewer women's enterprises lined Main Street; many women carried out their ventures from their homes. As the nineteenth century proceeded, women's presence on Main Streets increased. Their activities in both venues requires us to think about public spaces and private spaces, about the commercial aspects of colonial and early national residences, and, especially, about Main Streets. Women's presence as entrepreneurs and executives along Main Streets and other retail segments of communities gives those spaces new meaning. In Portland, Maine, one downtown building was occupied almost exclusively by women's offices, ranging from medicine to dressmaking. Women's presence as employers and as independent business operators is significant, both economically and as a piece of the history of women moving into spaces and positions often thought of as male.

When we walk through commercial and some residential districts, we can be reminded by maps, walking trails, plaques, or other historical notations about the women whose businesses once occupied many of these buildings, how women helped the buildings come alive, and how women's businesses helped support Main Streets, the women themselves, and others in the community. We can remember how Main Streets have been important sites of women's business activities, as well as important as meeting places for women workers, as sites of important networking activity for women, and as centers in some instances of a nearly separate women's economy.

NOTES

1. For examples of colonial women involved in production, selling, and other enterprises, see Aileen Agnew, "Silent Partners: The Economic Life of Women on the Frontier of Colonial New York" (Ph.D. Thesis, University of New Hampshire, 1998); Caroline Bird, *Enterprising Women* (New York: Norton, 1976); Joan M. Jensen, *Loosening the Bonds: Mid-Atlantic Farm Women, 1750–1850* (New Haven CT: Yale University Press, 1986).
2. See, for example, Alfred D. Chandler Jr., *The Visible Hand: The Managerial Revolution in American Business* (Cambridge, MA: Belknap Press, 1977).
3. Organizations similar to Zonta existed at various times for African American women, one of the earliest being the Colored Business Women's Club that began in Chicago in 1900. See Candace A. Kanes, "American Business Women, 1880–1930: Creating an Identity," (Ph.D. Thesis, University of New Hampshire, 1997), 93–105.
4. Jacqueline Jones, *Labor of Love, Labor of Sorrow: Black Women, Work, and the Family from Slavery to the Present* (New York: Basic Books, 1985), 178–181; and Elsa Barkley Brown, "Maggie Lena Walker and the Independent Order of Saint Luke: Advancing Women, Race, and Community in Turn-of-the-Century Richmond," *Signs* 14 (Spring 1989), 610–633.
5. "Experiment, Tried for Fun, Grows into Indispensable Institution," *Buffalo Courier,* June 6, 1925.
6. Undated newspaper article, Buffalo Zonta Scrapbook, State University at Buffalo Archives, Buffalo, NY.
7. "Mary Carr to Move," *Zonting Zebra* 2:4 (January 1922), 5.
8. "Women in the Public Eye," *Buffalo Courier-Express,* April 13, 1930.
9. *Zontian* 5:2 (January 1925), 9.
10. Julie A. Matthaei, *An Economic History of Women in America: Women's Work, the Sexual Division of Labor, and the Development of Capitalism* (New York: Schocken Books, 1982), 141–142.
11. For information on nineteenth- and earlier twentieth-century groups, see Kanes, "American Business Women," 46–113.
12. Altrusa was started in 1917, primarily as a money-making project by an enterprising man. In the early 1920s, it was reorganized along the lines of the other groups.
13. *Portland Daily Press,* April 30, 1921, 4; March 12, 1921, 3.

14. "Business Women's Club Has Firm in Its Membership," *Portland Daily Press,* April 2, 1921, 9.

15. The manuscript census, available through the National Archives and Records Center, is not released until 72 years after it is taken. The 1920 census was released to the public in 1992 and the 1930 census was released in 2002. These are available on microfilm and an indexing system aids in locating particular individuals. It can be a time-consuming process, however, to locate particular records in the census, especially records of women, who frequently are not heads of households.

16. "Is Only Grocer in the Club," *Portland Daily Press,* March 9, 1921, 4.

17. Agnew, "Silent Partners."

18. Jensen, *Loosening the Bonds.*

19. Laurel Thatcher Ulrich, *A Midwife's Tale: The Life of Martha Ballard, Based on Her Diary, 1785–1812* (New York: Knopf, 1990)

20. George Augustus Wheeler, *History of Brunswick, Topsham, and Harpswell, Maine* (Boston: A. Mudge & Son, 1878).

21. *Brunswick Telegraph,* November 23, 1877, 2.

22. *Brunswick Telegraph,* November 16, 1877, 2.

23. Deborah Pulliam, "Mitten Production in Nineteenth-Century Downeast Maine," in *Textiles in Early New England: Design, Production, and Consumption,* (Boston: The Dublin Seminar for New England Folklife Annual Proceedings, 1997), 132–134.

24. Ibid., 128–131.

25. R. G. Dun & Co. employees wrote commentaries on the business acumen and prospects of some small businesses. When available, these records provide interesting commentary and useful information. After about 1900, the reporting firm altered its methods and similar records are no longer available.

26. Wendy Gamber, *The Female Economy: The Millinery and Dressmaking Trades, 1860–1930* (Urbana and Chicago: University of Illinois Press, 1997).

27. For an explanation of the white-only selling staff rationale, see Susan Porter Benson, *Counter Cultures: Saleswomen, Managers, and Customers in American Department Stores 1890–1940* (Urbana and Chicago: University of Illinois Press, 1986), 209.

SUGGESTED READINGS

Aileen Button Agnew. "Silent Partners: The Economic Life of Women on the Frontier of Colonial New York." Ph.D. diss., University of New Hampshire, 1998. Using account books, Agnew pieces together a picture of women's economic activities, examining how women's businesses were related to those operated by their husbands. She discusses how race and gender affected the businesses and customers.

Susan Porter Benson. *Counter Cultures: Saleswomen, Managers, and Customers in American Department Stores, 1890–1940.* Urbana: University of Illinois Press,

1986. Although this book does not deal with women as entrepreneurs, it provides useful analysis of retailing and women's roles in it. The discussion of the stores' attempts to employ sales clerks who matched the class and ethnic background of customers and the implications of those attempts are especially enlightening.

Wendy Gamber. *The Female Economy: The Millinery and Dressmaking Trades, 1860–1930*. Urbana and Chicago: University of Illinois Press, 1997. Gamber examines both the meaning and economic viability of women's businesses. She discusses women as customers and employers and explores how these women's businesses faded with the dominance of department stores and manufactured clothing. A detailed and useful study of how the businesses both affected women's lives and were affected by economic and social change.

Jacqueline Jones. *Labor of Love, Labor of Sorrow: Black Women, Work, and the Family from Slavery to the Present*. New York: Basic Books, 1985. This is an invaluable study for understanding how race has affected women's experiences in the workforce.

Candace A. Kanes. "American Business Women, 1890–1930: Creating an Identity." Ph.D. diss., University of New Hampshire, 1997. Examines various organizations of businesswomen, publications aimed at them, and literature about them to explore how women came to call themselves businesswomen and what they meant by that designation. Also examines how women negotiated the demands of womanhood while forging identities that were outside the norm of expectations for women.

Angel Kwolek-Folland. *Engendering Business: Men and Women in the Corporate Office, 1870–1930*. Baltimore: Johns Hopkins University Press, 1994. This study of the insurance and financial industries explores how gender affected not only workers and managers, but also the very ideas of the industry. Kwolek-Folland discusses the ways in which the industry used and promoted concepts of separate spheres for men and women and how ideas of appropriate behavior of men and women were employed.

———. *Incorporating Women: A History of Women and Business in the United States* (New York: Twayne, 1998). This book provides an overview of women's business experiences from colonial times through the end of the twentieth century. Because it is a survey, it provides limited details on each time period or theme. Instead it traces the development of women's roles as producers, entrepreneurs, and managers. It is a useful resource book.

Lucy Eldersveld Murphy. "Business Ladies: Midwestern Women and Enterprise, 1850–1880." *Journal of Women's History* 3:1 (Spring 1991): 65–89. In 1870, at least 30,000 women in the Midwest ran their own businesses. Murphy looks at some of those women and discusses the reasons for their going into business and their relationships with their communities.

Deborah Pulliam. "Mitten Production in Nineteenth-Century Downeast Maine." *Textiles in Early New England: Design, Production, and Consumption.* Boston: The Dublin Seminar for New England Folklife Annual Proceedings, 1997: 127–134. This brief study discusses how one woman set up a mitten-knitting operation that provided jobs for many community women and provided a considerable income for herself. Another community business also sponsored mitten knitting, again giving work to local women.

Sharon Hartman Strom. *Beyond the Typewriter: Gender and the Origins of Modern American Office Work, 1900–1930.* Urbana and Chicago: University of Illinois Press, 1992. This is one of several books that attempts to explain how clerical work became women's work and what that change meant for women. It, along with Lisa Fine, *The Souls of the Skyscraper: Female Clerical Workers in Chicago, 1870–1930* (Philadelphia: Temple University Press, 1990), is especially helpful in understanding how jobs and careers that seemed so promising for women, offering benefits of better pay and working conditions than many other available jobs, could lose that promise and instead become largely dead-end careers. Because so many women went into clerical work in the late nineteenth and early twentieth centuries, these books are important to any exploration of women's office jobs.

Laurel Thatcher Ulrich. *A Midwife's Tale: The Life of Martha Ballard, Based on Her Diary, 1785–1812.* New York: Knopf, 1990. A masterful examination of Ballard's work as a midwife and her household operations. The book offers insight into the operation of a separate female economy and its interconnections to the male economy.

Chapter 10

"OUR TERRITORY": RACE, PLACE, GENDER, SPACE, AND AFRICAN AMERICAN WOMEN IN THE URBAN SOUTH

Leslie Brown and Anne M. Valk

At the beginning and end of every day in Durham, North Carolina, hundreds of black women tobacco workers wearing blue uniforms flowed through the streets, traveling between the factories and their homes. President Richard M. Nixon, who lived in Durham while he attended Duke University Law School, remarked that black workers "pour[ed] out of the factories like black smoke from a furnace . . . No one really seemed to think of them as individuals."[1] Durham was known internationally as a center of tobacco manufacturing, and what Nixon had witnessed was the daily exodus of African American laborers, mostly women, from the Liggett and Myers tobacco factory located near the Duke campus. On the one hand, his passing impression reflects the anonymity of African American women in urban settings; by his statement one might not know these were women at all, or might assume that the exiting workers were men. With respect to employment at least, African American women were thought of mainly as household laborers. On the other hand, the comment reveals how striking their presence could be, their numbers vast and their routine familiar to city residents. Nixon's observation discloses yet another aspect of black life in Durham: that African Americans, women in particular, were subject to easy insults by whites, especially males who thought little or nothing of their humanity, who viewed them as unsubstantial objects that dispersed into unknown places.

The places to which they dispersed were African American communities, sites of lively engagement and strong institutions where black people tended to their own affairs with very little thought for white folk. Whites possessed minimal knowledge about the black community, except what they assumed from stereotypes or occasional forays into black neighborhoods. But to African Americans during the Jim Crow era—the period of legal segregation from the late nineteenth through the mid-twentieth centuries[2]—Durham was the "Capital of the Black Middle Class." It was renowned, widely written about and touted as the home of

Figure 10-1. African American women workers flowed through the streets at the shift change at the Flower Warehouse of Liggett and Myers Tobacco Company in downtown Durham, NC, about 1935. (*Courtesy of the Durham County Public Library, North Carolina Collection.*)

North Carolina Mutual Life Insurance Company (reputedly the largest black business in the world during segregation), Mechanics and Farmers Bank (strong enough to withstand the banking crisis), North Carolina College for Negroes (the only liberal arts college for African Americans in the state and one of the few in the South), and the National Negro Finance Company (an investment firm). In addition, blacks in Durham owned and operated a textile mill, a cigar factory, a library, a hospital, and scores of churches and other businesses and institutions. That these institutions sprang up within the restrictive context of racial segregation, in a climate that attempted to suppress black progress, made the place all the more remarkable. Durham's black community earned its designation in 1925 when noted sociologist E. Franklin Frazier wrote of this "city of fine homes, exquisite churches, and middle class respectability."

It is not the place where men write and dream; but a place where black men calculate and work. No longer can men say that the Negro is lazy and a consumer. He has gone to work. He is a producer. He is respectable. He has a middle class.[3]

Many, including Booker T. Washington and W. E. B. Du Bois, had preceded Frazier in applauding black Durham, writing in the early twentieth century about its exceptional enterprises.[4] But their observations, like Nixon's, reflect African American women's invisibility. In showering praise on Durham's black community and its prominent leaders, Frazier and others ignored women all together, including their economic and social contributions.[5] Perhaps this oversight is comprehensible within the context of the late nineteenth and early twentieth centuries, when middle-class sensibilities viewed women's public presence as a violation of traditional gender roles. In recognizing Durham's commendable features, the place of women seemed irrelevant. Appreciating the place of women in the upbuilding of black Durham would have undermined the intent of extolling its virtues, which was to prove that African Americans could acquire those qualities that white Americans assumed they could not possess—a middle class and a correlating system of values and mores. Notwithstanding, "fine homes, exquisite churches, and middle-class respectability" related more to women than men. Women's respectable place was, after all, in the home and the church. Yet, African American reformers often deliberately cultivated the association between community uplift and black manhood, putting men forward in order to secure a sense of dignity, progress, and success in the eyes of whites. The advancement of black communities, presented as the accomplishment of men, in effect voided the presence and contributions of women however essential.[6]

Using Durham, North Carolina, as a case study, this chapter argues that African American women occupied an expansive terrain in the segregated urban South. Black women may seem invisible, particularly given the history of racial segregation. Southern perceptions of "place" conveyed social, political, and spatial meanings, shaped by race and further inscribed by gender. Notions of African American women's proper or expected roles, whether held by whites or by black men, translated into race and gender segregation intended to confine African American women to those physical spaces deemed appropriate for them. Through public documents, photographs, oral histories, autobiographies, maps and city directories, this chapter explains the ways that women created and dominated spaces of their own in Jim Crow Durham. Their struggle against the insult of race and gender indignities necessitated their efforts to control the spaces where they led and served their communities, as well as tended to their own needs. Emerging from slavery intent on defining their sense of freedom, African American women claimed as "our territory" not only the places they established, but also the spaces to which they were relegated. Rather than accept these as places where they were to be controlled, African American women turned them into arenas for racial and gendered struggles. By appropriating these physical areas, they actively asserted themselves even in situations designed to deny them control. As reformers, residents, family members, and workers, then, African American women forged public, semipublic, and private spaces for themselves that supported personal and community needs and that resisted Jim Crow. This chapter demonstrates that, although a myriad of transformations have occurred since the mid-twentieth century, it is possible, nonetheless to find these places in the built environment of the urban South.

Even as—and exactly because—Jim Crow laws and customs restricted the lives and activities of African Americans of both sexes, black women played a vital role in city life, as the city's reputation and the geography prove. They outnumbered men. They contributed paid and unpaid labor, time, and vision to establish and maintain the institutions that helped their communities prosper and ensured the survival of their members. Because economic realities demanded it, African American women entered the public realm of work outside the household, despite the middle-class ideologies; the female employment rate for black women exceeded that of white women. Black-owned enterprises and institutions provided numerous employment opportunities for African American middle-class women, creating occupational options other than teaching; the tobacco factories supplied options other than domestic work for those without advanced education. Indeed, the demands of these female workforces facilitated the development of even more retail businesses and services: beauty salons, dress and hat shops, shoe stores, five and dimes, and furniture stores, as well as drug stores, groceries, meat and fish markets, movie theaters, and restaurants, all employing and catering to the city's black female population. Thus, although black leaders and scholars used men's upbuilding of black urban space to challenge whites' perception of African American inferiority, Durham was the "Capital of the Black Middle Class" due to working women's organizational efforts, substantial labor, and buying power.[7]

As women's historians and researchers have shown, between the end of Reconstruction and the end of the Depression, African American women reformers founded and sustained a range of institutions to assure the survival of communities that suffered extensive racial indignities. Their organizations appeared in urban centers and small towns throughout the nation, compensating for public services that provided second-class treatment or that were denied outright. African American women's associational life in Durham mirrored the activities of women throughout the country. Working individually and collectively, they demonstrated initiative, raised money, staffed and served as volunteers, and organized programs for libraries and schools. They built and supported churches, small businesses, and such private social service institutions as orphanages, nurseries, homes for the blind, reformatories, and facilities for women workers.[8] Among the best known, Nannie Helen Burroughs, extending her work with the Women's Convention of the National Black Baptist Church, established the National Training School for Girls in Washington, D.C. Along with Lucy C. Laney's Haines Normal and Industrial Institute in Augusta, Georgia, it served as a model facility, inspiring similar efforts in other locations and training hundreds for occupations.[9]

Women were critical to the formation and maintenance of the one institution all African Americans could call their own, the black church, where they served as the core constituency and congregation. One of Durham's most celebrated churches, White Rock Baptist, was founded in the home of Margaret Faucette. Molly Markham, a free-born missionary, ran the Freedmen's Bureau school and founded St. Joseph's AME Zion, another prominent church. Within these institutions, women worked in Sunday schools, Bible study, choirs, missionary societies, sewing circles, and youth groups. From there they moved outward, linking sacred and secular activities. Durham resident Minnie Pearson, for example, steered the effort to found the Harriet Tubman Branch of the YWCA in Durham. She also presided over the North Carolina Federation of Colored Women's Clubs, bringing together her work with the North Carolina Women's Convention of the Baptist Church and a local affiliate of the National Association of Colored Women's Clubs. The Efland Home, an institution for deliquent and dependent girls, was among the NCFCWC's core projects.[10]

These institutions operated in multiple ways. On one level, many were voluntary and social reform efforts that reflected a middle-class impulse to inculcate respectability and thereby "uplift" the race. Just as often this constituted efforts to socially control the behavior of the less privileged classes. For example, the Efland Home, later called the State Industrial Home for Colored Girls, aimed to save adolescent girls from delinquency by offering them housing, literacy, and occupational training, though mostly in household labor. The Tubman Y similarly offered job-training programs to black women, again, mostly training young women for jobs in domestic service. The Tubman Y trained women for household labor to appease the white female board of the main branch of the YWCA, but it also disseminated information on banking, insurance, beauty culture, literacy, and voting, and provided recreational options and opportunities for travel that were otherwise closed or limited for its constituency. On another level, then, the Y and such institutions supported programs to educate and empower African American women. Similarly, the Scarborough Nursery served as a World War II childcare center, accepting state funding to address local industries' need for black women laborers. Founded by another of Durham's prominent club women, it was originally called the Scarborough Home, operating as an emergency shelter for families made homeless by fire or other misfortune. The Home later became a nursery, expanding to include a preschool or kindergarten and daytime and evening classes in parenting, nutrition, literacy, and politics for mothers. A versatile institution, Scarborough Nursery served people whose needs were ignored or denied in the culture of Jim Crow.

Finding African American women in the built environment of the South is a much more complex task than identifying the location of the well-known institutions they established. They occupied other territory as well, and the case of Durham magnifies the difficulties of and opportunities for defining other kinds of places or spaces associated with them, especially given racial segregation. Meager sources yield little information about African American communities during the period of segregation. Between 1880 and 1960, the southern culture of racial oppression and white supremacy equivocated the place of African Americans in the "official" public sphere. Documents such as segregation laws and ordinances, newspapers, court records, or archived papers may refer only to the activity of those considered exceptional for their leadership positions or their alleged criminal activity. Until recently, few libraries collected the papers of African Americans. Groups such as the National Association of Colored Women and the National Council of Negro Women maintained their own archives, and from these sources, researchers have been able to recover the rich history of African American women's community service.[11] But black women occupied a place in the city that was both more extensive and more diverse than the commonplace domain of church, civic organization, and community institution building, and more complex and fascinating than obvious explanations might indicate. That place, however, is obscured by the peculiar history of external and internal factors that plague historians' attempts to recover and understand the place and spaces of African American women.

Most strikingly, the physical structures occupied by black city dwellers have vanished or have been transformed dramatically over time. Urban renewal and highway construction, the ambiguous legacies of desegregation, and municipal neglect have contributed to the razing of most buildings and districts that housed black activities before World War II. The tobacco factories of Nixon's memory, some now abandoned and others remade into upscale lofts and condominiums, obscure the places where so many African American women worked. Similarly, the demolition of black school buildings has decimated the domain of black teachers, and the disintegration of original church buildings removed from sight the women who managed these institutions' affairs. Vacant overgrown lots lie where community centers, small shops, stores and cafes, boarding houses and apartment buildings, playgrounds and nursery schools once stood—the long-gone places where African American women congregated, resided, or exerted control. The deteriorated residences still standing in black neighborhoods leave only echoes of lively conversation, club meetings, and organized activity, of front porches where neighbors visited and passed news among themselves, of gardens where women demonstrated their creativity, or pathways they trod from kitchen to kitchen where they solved problems and fed neighbors. Without these structures and their surroundings, black women's past can be easily overlooked and forgotten.[12]

Researchers must consider the expectations of white southerners, the ambiguous responses to black women reformers, and the absence of remaining physical structures as indications of women's place in southern society. These features reveal clues as to the secondary status that black southerners occupied and women's organized response to that treatment. At the same time, however, black women's place in southern cities extended beyond the restrictions of segregation and the institutions established by middle-class club women. The built environment must be reconstructed with the notion of women's lives at the center, a difficulty amplified by the fact that most remaining sources exclude women. What other evidence, then, establishes African American women in public, private, and liminal space in the segregated city? Surprisingly, one might begin retrieving this lost presence by digging into sources considered among the most mundane. With African American women's past at the core of the inquiry, census data, maps, and city directories cultivate new understandings of Durham's black neighborhoods as gendered places. Because segregation was legal, and thus coded and recorded, census data, county maps, fire insurance maps, and city directories all manifest the ways that black communities were organized and contribute considerable information about African American life during the Jim Crow era. These public documents uncover an astonishing amount of information about how the city's layout affected the home life and work of black women, in turn illuminating written sources which then come to life in the language and memories of Durham residents.

The decennial census clearly reveals the expansion of the black female population in southern cities. African American women predominated among the population of tobacco workers in cities like Durham, North Carolina; Louisville, Kentucky; and Richmond, Virginia. In fact, in virtually every southern city in the decades before World War II, African American women outnumbered African American men, and their population increased at a faster rate. According to the federal census, between the end of the Civil War and the Second World War, African American women dominated the migrant streams that moved out of rural areas and into southern cities.[13] The census also provides rough data about urban life. For example, the birth rate for black women fell below that of white women, and the death rate for African American women, especially those of childbearing age, exceeded that of black men, white men, or white women. Lastly, African American women were more often single, divorced, or widowed than white women.

Each of these points raises questions about the life of African American women in the city. Why were so many single? Why was the death rate so high? Why did more women than men migrate to the city? This last question becomes particularly important because it contradicts common understandings of gender roles: that men departed from rural areas, with women and families following later. While this may have been true in the industrial North, it is misleading to assume the same pattern also prevailed in the South. Instead, women were the primary migrants from the rural to the urban South because the requirements of agricultural life for African Americans compelled them to leave the farm. African American farm families struggled against sharecropping and renting systems that stymied their income-earning potential. Ruthless landlords, rural violence, rising costs, and falling incomes created barely surmountable barriers. Women with male kin were released from farming, a gender-segregated enterprise, by their families' needs for income and their ability to find paid employment more easily than men. Because landlords seldom rented to families without male kin, widowed, divorced, or abandoned women found few places to make a living in the country and had no choice but to find work in cities. Consequently, African American women converged on urban areas in search of opportunities: employment, education for themselves and their children, and safety from racial and sexual abuse. In cities, as the census also shows, they found occasional, seasonal, and permanent employment in household labor and select industries like tobacco processing.

The manuscript census offers information at the household level, including age, race, marital status, and place of birth.[14] According to the 1920 manuscript census of Durham, single women rarely lived alone; they lived or boarded in both male- and female-headed households. For example, on Proctor Street, in one black neighborhood, Julia Logan, aged nineteen from Virginia, and Nannie Spence, aged seventeen from New York, both showgirls, boarded with Andy Blue and his wife Mary. Nearby, Priscilla Reade, aged fifty-five, widowed and a cook, lived with her forty-two-year-old single sister, Magnolia, who took in laundry. On Fayetteville Street, Lydia Merrick, widow of a North Carolina Mutual cofounder, lived with her son, a manager at the Mutual, her daughter, and her son-in-law, a doctor. Up the street, the household of Aaron Moore, another cofounder of North Carolina Mutual, included himself and his wife, his daughter, his son-in-law who was a teller at the bank, and Maggie Lennon, his widowed cousin who was the family housekeeper.[15] For the most part, southern neighborhoods were segregated by race, with white Protestants and Roman Catholics living in some sections of town, and blacks in other sections. People who fell along the margins lived in black neighborhoods. Next door to the Moores lived a family of white shopkeepers, Simon Levy and his wife Sarah, both Russia-born Jews, their three single daughters, aged fifteen to twenty-five and born in North Carolina, and a granddaughter, aged five, all of whom spoke Hebrew as their first language.[16] And among the showgirls who lived with the Blue family, the census taker counted one Japanese woman.

City directories can furnish further information about black women's places in cities. Published on a regular basis, often annually, city directories listed not only the names of heads of households and their occupations; the street-by-street organization of the directory reflected residential patterns, locating the main thoroughfares of areas, owner-occupied homes and rental units, and businesses and institutions. Churches, schools, unions, cemeteries, and lodges were usually included. In southern cities (and some northern cities, too), these listings included a racial designation, symbolized with a *, ©, or (col), denoting "colored" residents and businesses. Directories also contained a business section that listed persons engaged in various occupations and advertisements for local companies. The city directories thereby provide a wealth of information about a community's occupational, residential, and cultural life. Although they do not explicitly relate women's status, the city directories allow researchers to trace women's roles and some of their activities as Durham grew from a small town to a large city. The 1887 city directory, for instance, listed only one black clerical worker, male; in 1906, the directory listed thirty black clerical, sales, and kindred workers, mostly women, as well as a boarding house, a dress shop, and a grocery run by African American women. By 1917, the listings of businesses run by black women grew to include a boarding house, confectionary, eating house, two groceries, and three dress shops, as well as one midwife and one nurse. By the time the 1937 city directory was published, 253 black clerical workers, virtually all of them women, called Durham home. Thus the city directory not only indicates the growth of women-owned enterprises and the expansion of businesses requiring clerical labor, but also tracks the shift of clerical work from a male to a female occupation.[17]

Despite the Depression, the growth of black businesses in Durham by 1937 had boosted the economic and social lives of many women (mostly single) who were employed therein or whose family members worked in these establishments. Hayti, Durham's most prominent African American neighborhood, could claim among its establishments several banks and other black-owned financial institutions, real estate agencies, myriad stores and small businesses, the city's only black high school and college, apartment buildings, fraternal organizations' halls, a country club and tennis club, and numerous homes, many owned by women. In one block of Fayetteville Street alone, twenty-one businesses, all but four owned and operated by African Americans, could be found. In addition, the 1937 directory lists several residences like the Rosalie Apartments, owned by Hattie Pearson, where single employed women lived together in shared apartments.

Analysis of manuscript census and city directories indicate that African Americans lived in clusters, grouped together on sets of intersecting streets. This observation is confirmed by a 1937 map commissioned by the county that marked the streets where mostly African Americans lived. Indicating residential segregation patterns, the map made clear the racial designation and location—or lack—

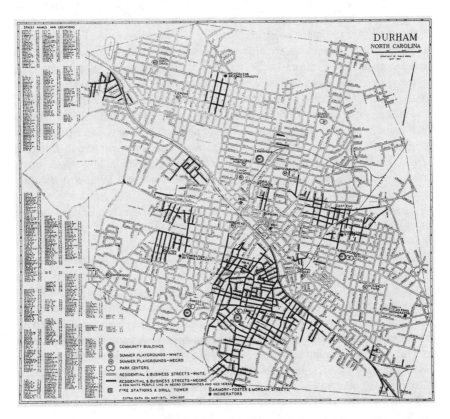

Figure 10-2. The locations of the black neighborhoods in Durham, NC, in 1937 are clearly marked on this county map. The largest area in the southeastern section is Hayti. The West End is located to the west surrounding Lyon Park. The black neighborhood farthest to the west is Hickstown. The map is reproduced in B. F. Lemert, Economic Maps of Durham, North Carolina (Durham: Chamber of Commerce, 1938). (*Courtesy of the Perkins Library, Duke University and reproduced with the permission of the City of Durham.*)

of facilities like schools, playgrounds, community buildings, or fire and police stations. In addition to marking off segregated neighborhoods, county maps suggest the quality of life for African Americans. According to the 1937 county map, few of the city's fire departments and police stations or playgrounds and community centers—the latter designated by ((N)) or ((W)) for Negro or White respectively—were situated in black neighborhoods. But all of the city's incinerators, garbage dumps, and drainage ditches were located there. In the black section of town called the West End (also known as Lyon Park), drainage ditches carried waste from unpaved streets; just beyond, the incinerator burned the city's trash and sent polluted smoke into the air; and from the garbage dump not far away, a terrible stench must have risen, all in proximity to the school.[18]

Fire insurance company maps yield further details on all of the above, making it possible to locate structures and to project patterns of use. These more specialized maps, some created by the Sanborn Map Company, were used to assess the value of properties for insurance purposes. They display detail about the building structures, construction materials, condition of streets, and location of fire alarms and fire hydrants in an area. Drawn to scale, Sanborn maps also enable comparison of the size and proximity of buildings, as well as determination of an area's population density, the identification of residences, businesses, and other types of buildings, and uses of structures. In Durham, narrow, wood-framed shotgun houses clustered on the side streets and alleyways of black neighborhoods, unpaved and distant from fire alarms.[19] Maps from successive years demonstrate how these settings changed over time.[20] Dunbar Street, where a number of newly married middle-class couples lived, for instance, was paved before Poplar Street, where a number of tobacco workers had settled early in the century.

African American women's residential patterns, therefore, can be discerned by using manuscript census, city directories, and maps in combination, and from these indicators of the built environment, researchers can determine other details about black women's lives. For example, African American women of given occupational groups often lived in the same area. This neighborhood characteristic sheds light on the process of employment referrals, which were necessary given the fact that white newspapers did not advertise positions available to African Americans. Neighbors referred each other to jobs in factories and white homes as well as to institutions and services. According to the manuscript census and the city directory, laborers and household workers composed the main population in the neighborhood where Priscilla Reade, the cook, and her sister, the laundress, resided. Almost all of the professionals and businesspeople lived on or just off of Fayetteville Street in Hayti, near the Moores and the Merricks. From there they traveled together to the black business district of downtown Durham where the main offices of North Carolina Mutual and Mechanics and Farmers Bank were located. Many teachers shared apartments or other kinds of group housing. Many of Durham's black washerwomen resided in the Brookstown section and used the stream for which the area was named as the place to gather water. They too shared a common pattern of movement and labor: traversing the city to gather wash on Mondays, returning it

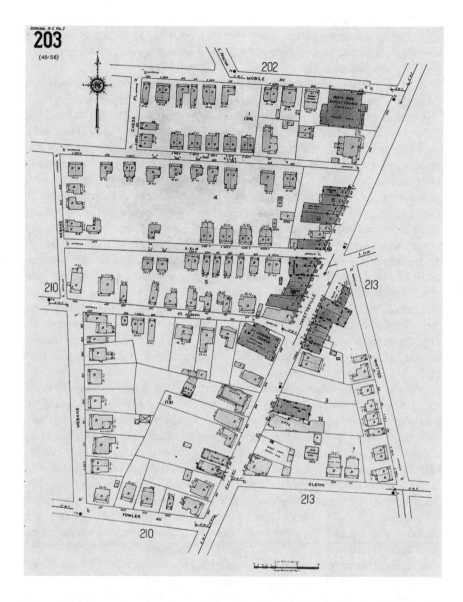

Figure 10-3. The northern boundary of the residential section of the Hayti neighborhood is anchored by the White Rock Baptist Church and intersected by Fayetteville Street as shown in Section 203 of the 1937 Sanborn Fire Insurance Company map of Durham. [*Copyright (1937) Sanborn Map Company, The Sanborn Library, LLC. All Rights Reserved. This Sanborn Map has been reproduced with written permission from The Sanborn Library, LLC. All further reproductions are prohibited without prior written permission from The Sanborn Library, LLC.*]

to white families on Saturday, and patterning their work—soaking, scrubbing, rinsing, hanging, and ironing—in concert with each other. Of these tasks only ironing was done singly and inside; the other jobs gave women opportunity to interact in their neighborhood spaces.[21]

As maps, city directories, and census data reveal, the notion of a singular black community fails to capture Durham's complex segregation pattern. Rather, black neighborhoods of varying sizes spread throughout the city, each with its own central workplaces, churches, schools, and other institutions. As waves of black migrants settled in the city, they created evocatively named neighborhoods of disparate respectability. "Hayti," founded by ex-slaves and named for the independent black nation, became the city's largest black neighborhood, the home of its most prominent black citizens and institutions. In contrast, "Mexico" squeezed between the edges of Hayti and Durham Hosiery Mill #2, one of the few textile mills in the South that hired African Americans. "Needmore" was cramped between the city dump and Vickers Woods while "Buggy Bottoms" sat on the base of a hill behind a white cemetery. Moreover, where one lived reflected differential access to those facilities that eased the insults of segregation, and revealed a family's status and class. Residents of sprawling Hayti enjoyed the benefits of a park, playground, community buildings, and several schools, some named for prominent black men. In contrast, Hickstown, a small black neighborhood in the northwest corner of the city, contained few such facilities and only one school that went through the elementary grades. To attend beyond the sixth grade, children from places other than Hayti had to travel across town.

Although these sources establish the context of black women's presence in the city, they do not provide direct insight into their experiences; beyond locating the buildings and areas associated with women, one must strive to understand how they used these spaces. The ways that black women experienced urban life, as well as the marks that they made on the city's landscape, varied according to their age, social class, marital status, and neighborhood of residence. That women clustered by occupation, for instance, denotes qualities of life as well as patterns of everyday life. Such analyses are enhanced by first hand accounts that depict black life and offer fuller descriptions of women's experiences and activities. Oral history interviews, memoirs, photographs, black newspapers, fiction, and business and personal papers used in combination with public documents can elucidate the quality of life, class and gender dynamics, and social or cultural shifts that characterized African American community life. In this way, environments such as tobacco factories, school buildings, the North Carolina Mutual Life Insurance Company, and even street corners, typically associated with men, can be reconsidered to illuminate women's place in segregated cities.

Pauli Murray, who became a noted civil rights and women's movement activist, forgot neither the place she grew up, nor the insult inherent to its inferior facilities. Her grandfather had built a home during the period following emancipation in the west end of town, but by 1910, when Murray was born, the area was known as "Buggy Bottoms." In a family history published in the 1950s, she described this neighborhood as "an odorous conglomeration of trash piles, garbage dumps, cow stalls, pigpens and crowded humanity." Residing on the hill just above the Bottoms, Murray remembered the ill-effects of population expansion combined with poverty in the early decades of the twentieth century: "shacks for factory workers mushroomed in the lowlands between the graded streets," imposing themselves on her family's home. "These little communities which clung precariously to the banks of streams or sat crazily on washed-out gullies," she continued, "were held together by cowpaths or rutted wagon tracks."[22] A legal scholar whose writings explained the links among gender, race, class, and oppression, Murray was moved by images of her neighborhood throughout her life's work. Gwendolyn M. Parker, who also became an attorney—but for an investment firm—was similarly moved by her environment. She grew up in an affluent family in the Hayti section of Durham several decades after Murray and recalled a more livable black community, "self-contained . . . with its own schools, banks, grocery stores, drugstores, churches, lodge houses, and funeral homes."[23] Parker's family lived among the bankers, insurance people, lawyers, and doctors listed in the city directory. Murray's family, the less prominent Fitzgeralds, were widowed teachers who lived in West End with tobacco workers, domestics, washerwomen, and the unemployed. Murray remembered, "our distance from the hub of the cultural life and our lack of mobility made me acutely conscious of living outside the elite circle."[24]

Even within neighborhoods, the mitigating influence of social class caused some residents to live in relative comfort while their neighbors coped with inconvenient and unsanitary conditions. Some black residents of prosperous Hayti, especially those who lived on the side streets and alleys, still lived in unsanitary conditions created by muddy streets, no indoor plumbing, poor drainage, and unchecked sewage. Annie Mack Barbee's family of tobacco workers crowded into a two-room house in Hayti that had no private bathroom. "The street was not paved," she remembered, "and when it rained it got muddy and in the fall, the wind blew all of the dust in your eyes and face." Housekeeping was consequently an endless and seemingly futile task. These infrastructure conditions, coupled with inadequate housing, insufficient heat, poor ventilation, and poor sanitation led to characteristic ill health and high mortality in black neighborhoods. Urban hazards—open drainage ditches, incinerators, contaminated wells, and garbage dumps—accounted for the high rates of death and infant mortality among African Americans, especially women. In contact with both the white and black community, working in clusters and with children, they were exposed to diseases that ran in epidemic proportions.[25]

Moving beyond the level of neighborhoods, the city's geography and built environment revealed aspects of women's experiences in paid employment. Nearly half of Durham's black women workers were employed by the city's many tobacco companies. Factory operatives tended to work in proximity to their homes in neighborhoods that surrounded industrial complexes. Once away from their neighborhoods, they became associated with the buildings where they worked. Mary Mebane, a high schooler employed in tobacco work, recalled that in late spring, black women gathered on the steps of the main building of Liggett and Myers in a way that suggested a slave auction block. At the top of the stairs, white foremen appeared to select those who seemed young and strong.[26] Once hired, operatives worked in the large interior rooms where translucent windows at the top of the walls provided the only ventilation and light. Concealed behind brick exteriors, they performed notoriously foul jobs within an environment segregated by both sex and race. While black men moved tobacco from building to building, black women did the standing-still work of "rehandling"—sorting, drying, and stemming leaf and feeding it to machines. In the factories, black women worked in hot, humid, unventilated rooms, drenched with sweat, covered with dust, at risk of contracting respiratory diseases that spread through the factory, and beset by ailments like malnutrition, difficult pregnancies, stillbirths, tuberculosis, fainting, and exhaustion. Foremen engaged in verbal, physical, and sexual abuse, brutal treatment, and inappropriate behavior that the outraged women had little choice but to endure.[27]

Thus the factory floor became a site where black women workers and white male supervisors engaged in the racial and gender struggle that Jim Crow signified. In an interview conducted decades later, Dora Scott Miller distinctly remembered "a one-eyed fella named George Hill" from South Carolina. "He was tight. He'd get on top of the machines and watch you to see if you were working alright and holler down and curse. Curse and we working. That's what we had to undergo . . . You didn't say anything. You said anything, you went out." Terminations came frequently. "Just like you come up there to get a job, they could hire you, if they didn't like the way you do, they could fire you," Blanche Scott stated flatly, "I always tried to do my work right so they wouldn't have to just get on me." Sometimes the factory hummed with the rhythm of women at work; other times the factory floor carried a tenor of madness. Some women worked in a frenzy to avoid contact with the foreman; one worked in loud deliberate motions and intentionally ignored the "big boss" when he appeared; another talked to herself to discourage unwanted advances; yet another screamed when the foreman approached.[28] Annie Mack Barbee took a more direct approach and physically threatened her supervisor. Speaking about the factory setting to an interviewer years later, Barbee's bitterness remained: "if you don't stand up and demand respect they won't give you nothing; you have to demand it and let them know that you are willing to pay the price for it . . . I don't care how low your job is, regardless, it's honest work. You have to put dignity on."[29]

Dignity was exactly what foremen denied and women usurped through their challenges to the foremen's authority. What supervisors sometimes read as poor work habits was in reality perpetual protest through slow downs, absenteeism, and negligence. "They give so much trouble in being unreliable and irregular . . . . They are terribly indolent, careless, and stubborn," one foreman told a researcher, marking a stark contrast between his perception and workers' description of their diligence. Rarely satisfied, foremen justified their condescension with fulsome pride. "Whenever they give trouble," one remarked, "we give them rough treatment and that quells them for a while. Rough treatment is the only thing that will reach them."[30] The calm that foremen demanded often came in the form of song. Supervisors eager to exceed production quotas, encouraged the melodious strains, but black women workers used song to send their message beyond the factory walls. One listener, hearing women's voices outside of the factory, described the tone as "eerie . . . sounds that I shall never forget." She explained, the workers "were not singing from joy, but to ease the monotony of long hours going through the same motions day in and day out."[31]

Song was not intended to entertain listeners. Rather, as it stretched beyond the factory walls, the women's singing also represented collective expression and candor. What women could not say outright, they could say in music; what they could not make the boss hear, they could make passers-by understand. "They would let you sing, but you couldn't do much talking unless you talked low. You had to work!" Mary Bailey recalled. So when supervisors forbade talking on the factory floor, women raised their voices in unison as a form of communication. Song spoke in solidarity against the abuses of Jim Crow and the women's work. Work songs like "The Hamlet Wreck," composed by black workers at Liggett and Myers, recalled a railroad accident that crushed a segregated wooden car carrying dozens of St. Joseph AME church Sunday school members. Lyrics such as "Oh, by an' by I'm goin' to lay down this heavy load" were not simply "soulful chants" that hypnotized white listeners, but threats to quit.[32]

That allegiance forged in song played out in strong friendship circles, working teams, walking buddies, and informal clubs in the factory as well as in neighborhood life. Experienced women recommended and then trained new workers, and women covered for each other when necessary. Bailey remembered colluding with another worker to avoid tasks they disliked, and hiding when they learned their foreman planned to move them to another area. Workers also refused to inform on other workers when asked. "You didn't hire me to tell you who was working and who weren't working," Bailey recounted while describing one confrontation. "You hired me to work. Now if you want to know about them people not working, you look and see for yourself, cause I ain't telling you nothing."[33] Outside of the factory, women gathered in neighborhood spaces, visiting, attending churches, and singing in choirs and gospel groups, working in missionary circles, and serving on deaconess boards together. In times of difficulty they offered help; in times of joy, they celebrated. Linked together by a common identity and by common spaces, black women tobacco workers developed a sense of consciousness engendered by their common condition and goals.[34]

Household labor offered an alternative for those forced by anger, disgust, health, or supervisors to leave the factory. One-third of black women workers in Durham served as household laborers.[35] In the back of segregated buses, mostly on foot, or occasionally by automobile, black women in white maids' uniforms traversed the city in the morning and late in the workday. Like washerwomen, the city's domestics, cooks, and maids traveled long distances and in groups between their own homes and those in white neighborhoods. But doing so long before most of the city was awake, they were among the least visible workers and the least able to claim a space of their own. Indeed, their space was claimed by others. Those who lived-in, for example, resided in places that were not theirs. Traveling during the workday in the company of white children or families, ironically they were the most visible—and perhaps the most identifiable—black women in cities, perceived by whites as subservient and in "their place." Domestic service and tobacco work shared many qualities regarding the use of space. Referrals, for example, often came through women's spaces, among neighbors, friend, kin, or at church. The racial hierarchy played out spatially as well. Just as tobacco workers entered a separate building from whites, when a black woman entered the white home, it was through the back door in a subservient position. In the white household, they occupied an ambiguous place between domestic and public spheres, expected to control white children to whom they answered and to manage a household that was not theirs. Thus restricted and confined, and out of the public eye, they endured isolation, endless days, numerous indignities, exposure to sexual harassment, trying working conditions, with few opportunities for collective action, to complain about or improve their wages or situations.[36]

Like the tobacco factories, schools represented another work site claimed by the women who accounted for over 90 percent of Durham's black teaching force. Their classrooms were their provinces. Pauli Murray recalled that neighborhood children held in awe her aunts, both teachers at the West End School and known to maintain tight control of their classes. Unless intending to extend a compliment, principals spoke to teachers only outside of their classrooms, and they always used the respectable title "Miss." Such co-opted space could be violated easily, however, by white officials who entered the classroom unannounced and inspected students' work. Unlike the black principals, white officials always used teachers' first names. Outside the schoolhouse, teachers reigned in the neighborhood where their sudden appearance could silence the sound of play in the street. Moreover, teachers' work of educating black youngsters extended beyond the classroom and beyond the students themselves. A teacher in a small town, Murray wrote, combined the role of "instructor, social worker, truant officer, psychiatrist, adult education specialist, and community leader." After instructing students during the day, Murray's aunts taught adults at night, Sunday school on Sundays, and literacy at the library.[37]

Corresponding to its neighborhood, the West End School where Murray's aunts taught was overcrowded, in this case by the children of tobacco and service workers. The physical structure of school buildings themselves not only provided evidence of the work life of African American teachers, but also exposed the ultimate insult of segregation and the disparities between black and white. The "dilapidated, rickety, two-story, wooden structure" that Murray remembered occupied a clay yard across the road from the Liggett and Myers complex. A fine dust from the warehouse seeped into the rotted boards of the school building's structure.[38] The building was constructed so haphazardly that it creaked and swayed in the wind. Peeling paint and paint blisters covered the outside walls; inside, bare splintery

floors, leaky plumbing, and broken drinking fountains screamed neglect. Foul water puddled on the floors outside restrooms that were always out of order. In contrast, Murray remembered the closest school for equally poor white children as "a
beautiful red and white brick building on a wide paved street," equipped with a
playground and surrounded by an eight-foot fence topped with barbed wire intended to keep the black children out. Even young children understood the message of inferiority conveyed through the condition of such facilities.[39] Eventually,
West End school was replaced by a new brick building after black teachers raised
money to match those donated by the Julius Rosenwald Fund.[40]

Distinct from poor and working-class families, many elite and middle-class
women enjoyed the privilege of living in primarily residential neighborhoods with
a greater distance from factories and their workplaces.[41] In the 1910s, the most affluent black families in Durham built stately homes on both sides of Fayetteville
Street, the main street through Hayti. Clydie Fullwood Scarborough—the under-
taker's wife and founder of the Scarborough Nursery—owned the most elaborate
dwelling on the street, constructed with Doric columns and Palladian windows
salvaged from old plantation houses. These expansive residences dotted the way
from the White Rock and St. Joseph's Churches, which stood near each other, to
the southern edge of the city. There, crowded out by both the elite and the masses
but affluent enough to move, married teachers and business managers established
a middle-class residential development called "College View." Spreading outward toward the corporate limits of Durham, the bungalows, cottages, and houses
ordered from Sears Roebuck catalogs sat along quiet, winding streets across from
North Carolina College for Negroes. College View still stands, although now well
within city limits, as a continuing testament to the strength of Durham's black
middle class.[42]

The African American-owned North Carolina Mutual and its sister financial institutions were the preeminent employers in Durham. Whereas tobacco, mill, and
domestic workers dealt with abuse from white foremen, and teachers also faced
insults when white officials visited their schools and interfered with their work,
women who worked for the Mutual could shield themselves from the most egregious gendered and racial offenses. The Mutual and its affiliates hired more than
twice as many women as men, employing hundreds of single, female college
graduates as clerks, cashiers, secretaries, and bookkeepers at the home offices.
Claiming a place in Durham's Central Business District, North Carolina Mutual
Life Insurance Company built its main offices downtown, albeit on a side street
set apart from the major white-owned buildings. In the company's early years,
women workers were visible through a street level window, presenting a model
of respectability and hard work meant to counter messages of black inferiority.
Mutual officers boasted that after the company hired its first professionally trained
stenographer, crowds of school children gathered at the main branch to watch "the
flying fingers of the colored girl from the North who typed without even looking
at the keys."[43]

As the Mutual grew, so did its women's workers' distance from the street.

Women worked on the second floor of the building constructed in 1906. In 1922 the Mutual's home office moved to a modern, fire-proof, six-story structure, where its offices took up the top four floors. The second tallest building in town, the Mutual made a statement of purpose, stability, and permanence, and the edifice came to represent black progress, at the same time that the company's separation from the street took its workers out of the public eye.[44] Inside, office workers enjoyed the added benefit of employment in a domain where blacks held all positions, from the most menial to supervisory. Viola Turner, who began work as a secretary at the Durham office in 1924, worked on the third floor with all of the secretaries to the managers, an area she referred to as "our territory." This protected, female-dominated space provided not only a place of camaraderie, but also a buffer against Jim Crow. Occasionally, women workers contended with the insults of white women and men, but Turner and the other women workers refused to be unnerved by contentious interactions with whites. When white visitors or government officials refused to remove their hats in the presence of black women or failed to address them as Mrs. or Miss, both fundamental acts of southern etiquette, African American women were expected to show deference nonetheless. But black autonomy altered the balance of power, and black women could control hostile interactions.

Turner and her fellow female clerical workers challenged whites' license to disparage black women, and responded to the charade of racial etiquette. They acted out a script that reversed the terms of interactions and embarrassed ill-mannered white visitors. Known among her co-workers by her nickname "Brownie" and to others as Miss Turner or Miss Viola, Turner simply refused to answer to the name Viola, unless preceded by "Miss." On more than one occasion, she chastised offenders for omitting respectable titles. When whites who came to the office asked

Figure 10-4. African American women shown working in the Agency Department of the North Carolina Mutual Insurance Company about 1948. The photograph was included in the Golden Anniversary issue of *The Whetsone* (1949), a company publication. (*Courtesy of the Special Collections Library, Duke University. Included in the C.C. Spaulding Papers, Box 2.*)

for "Charlie" or the "preacher," as they might call any black man, Turner would turn to her women colleagues and ask, "Have you seen a preacher here this morning?" or "Charlie? We don't have a Charlie working here do we, ladies?" After several moments of mocking banter she would feign understanding, "Oh! You must mean Mr. Spaulding. I'll tell him that you are waiting. And may I take your hat while you wait?" Penalizing the offender for his rudeness, she would hang up the hat, return to her desk, and never pass on the message. The women referred to improved manners among regular white visitors as their "getting religion," and delighted in converting transgressors' impudent presumptions into polite interaction with black women. As racialized, as well as gendered space, therefore, the office was an effective place to mock Jim Crow.[45]

The Mutual offered other "protected" areas for its female professional staff. In addition to the spread of offices, the company provided a ladies lounge plush enough to rival any downtown department store of the era.[46] Also, the Mutual operated a lunchroom where employees received "splendid luncheons" served "free of charge," a benefit that bolstered the Mutual's sense of noblesse oblige. Surely nonprofessional African American women employees cooked and served these meals. Nonetheless, even the Mutual's cooks were protected from possible humiliation or insult from whites as no employee had to venture into the surrounding white business district for lunch. The lunchroom furthermore protected black women workers from negative reputations that might result from any improper dalliances in the streets of downtown.

In 1921 the Mutual established a home for female clerical workers. No similar provisions were made for men who migrated to the city, or for women on the service staff (cooks, kitchen helpers, or bathroom attendants) suggesting that professional women warranted privileged protections.[47] The single women who came to work at the Mutual needed lodging where their safety could be ensured. With rates of pay lower than their black male and white female counterparts, single black women could seldom afford to purchase their own homes. Company housing, therefore, offered these women an alternative to living among strangers or in questionable circumstances. Viola Turner, who lived in the clerks' home in the 1920s, recalled it as a "two-story house in back of . . . a little shotgun house" that was the dining room for the home. The company boasted that the home for "lady clerks" provided "clean, warm lodging, wholesome food, and a refined atmosphere."[48] Similarly, single female teachers lived together in teacherages, and nurses and nursing students, also single, lived in their residence at Lincoln Hospital.[49]

In devising benefits for their employees, companies such as the Mutual were not solely compelled by concerns for their employees' economic condition or familial status. Rigid codes of behavior and tenacious surveillance provided literal and figurative structures that insulated women from real and potential dangers they faced in less controlled (and controllable) environments: hostile encounters with whites, improper explorations of sexuality, and "bad examples" among the lower classes. African American women were particularly vulnerable to inappropriate sexual advances or abuse from white men, and unremittingly contended with challenges to their respectability.[50] Moreover, the migration of single women to cities, away from the supervision of men, provoked "a series of moral panics": women, especially black women, lacking supervision could be judged "sexually degenerate and, therefore, socially dangerous."[51] Because respectability lay at the core of the Mutual's business philosophy, and because the city's black patriarchs perceived it as their role to protect and defend the reputations of its female employees, company-organized boarding houses provided several protections. First, in supervised housing African American women could avoid having their character tarnished or questioned. Second, Durham's black patriarchs could control their female employees' behavior. Finally, supervised housing created a way to maintain, or restore, moral order. Housed in proximity to the home of the Mutual's president, Charles C. Spaulding, the "lady clerks" remained under his watch even after working hours. "Poppa's [Charles C. Spaulding] house was right next door," Viola Turner remarked, "nothing went on at the Clerk's Home that he didn't know about."[52] And Spaulding knew a lot, including when Turner offended his sensibilities by wearing pants outside on a Saturday.

Acting through their institutions—the schools, the college, the hospital, the bank—Durham's black patriarchs similarly sought to protect women by restricting their mobility, closely monitoring their activities, or offering gender segregated accommodations. At the same time that they offered protection, however, such accommodations also imposed standards of respectability on women, determining appropriate and inappropriate dress, company, and social activities. These standards applied not only to the work environment but also to places of business and recreation. Julia Lucas recalled that women could enter only barbershops where women were employed. At the Mechanics and Farmers Bank, located on the first floor of the Mutual Building, managers set aside space for a Ladies Deposit Room, "where female depositors who come a great distance with their moneys hidden in their attire may be free to unearth their treasure." The room offered more than privacy, however, as the Bank's brochure pointed out: "this room will be greatly appreciated by the ladies who often show hesitancy in entering the main banking room which is filled with men." Although the bank did not require women customers to utilize this room, promotional materials suggested that proper ladies would do so. Female students, too, faced constraints on their activities intended to protect them from harm and solidify their status as respectable women. Before the 1950s, women students at North Carolina College for Negroes could travel only in groups, and then only to places approved by the housemother. Even on the college campus, men and women students not only lived in sex-segregated dormitories, but outside of the classroom, they could not socialize in public spaces, only in supervised living areas.[53]

Concern for the protection of women's reputations and physical well-being reinforced a significant distinction between the public and private worlds of women and men, as well as class-based differences in expectations and circumstances. Women of the elite were subject to the offense of Jim Crow only when it entered their space. Similarly, middle-class teachers met with affront when white supervisors entered their classroom and usurped their authority in their domain. Laborers and household workers, however, were employed in white-controlled space, and therefore confronted racial and sexual assaults even as they tried to wrest a claim on their work space and themselves. Professional women lived in protective enclaves that, no matter how restrictive, provided benefits for their safety and financial well-being that were not extended to their working-class counterparts.

In contrast to the restrictions placed on elite and middle-class women's activities, men of different classes met and mixed in the streets and in "men's" space: the gas station, the barbershops, the taxi stand, the pool hall, the offices of the newspaper. Only those whose reputations were suspect were found in these male places considered off-limits to respectable women. Notwithstanding, such women of questionable repute held power in some of the most dubious places. On the side streets in every black neighborhood and business district, African American women engaged in—indeed provided—popular, albeit illegal, ventures. Numbers running, gambling, and prostitution flourished with demand provided by both black and white men and some women. African American women owned not only the houses of prostitution, but also the "dry" city's drink houses: the Margaret and the Martha, the Pink Palace, Mit Dixon's, and among the most famous, Minnie's, as in "Minnie the Moocher" of Cab Calloway fame.[54] Thus, although middle-class propriety labeled the streets, and specifically street corners, as the realm of men, women seen inhabiting this supposed male space were considered unrespectable, but powerful when they held control. They validated black and white patriarchs' fears about their inability to control their constituents in a city of mostly women.

Since the 1950s, due to both the dismantling of Jim Crow and transformations in urban life, black women's spaces, respectable and not so respectable, have been altered. As public transportation gave way to private automobiles, and as the end of legal segregation opened new neighborhoods, schools, and workplaces, black southerners moved out of their limited place in urban life. In Durham, a few of the physical structures associated with African American women from the segregation period remain. Minnie's drink house remains only in legend and the annals of popular culture; those tobacco factories that have not been converted to upscale lofts and malls stand deserted. West End School (renamed Lyon Park School in the 1930s) closed in 1974; once boarded up and abandoned, it now houses a community center. With the black and white YWCAs unified in the 1970s in a new facility, the Harriet Tubman Y remains weathered and deteriorating on a side street of Hayti. No hint of its past lingers. Even the elegant six-story Mutual building has lost its grandeur in the demise of the downtown business district. A new Mutual structure, an integral part of the Durham skyline, has replaced it. Some structures such as churches remain in use, although the areas surrounding them have changed nearly beyond recognition. These transformations have made it increasingly difficult to identify specific places considered the domain of African American women.

Moreover, African American women's place has altered in modern life, as the dissipation of race and sex segregation has decreased the demand that they claim "our territory." Nonetheless, their presence remains distinctive and at the center of community activities. The Lincoln Hospital site now serves as a community day care and health care center. Even as postwar urban renewal efforts brought housing developments and highways that wiped out black neighborhoods and business districts, some women's businesses remain. Beauty parlors, restaurants, neighborhood markets, and churches—all primarily racially segregated—still dot the urban landscape of old Hayti and other black neighborhoods in Durham. Still, much that was so visible about the lives of African American women in the Jim Crow era has faded in the post-civil rights era. The current built environment bears only remnants of their earlier activities. But researchers can transcend the alteration of the landscape to reconstruct black urban communities and women's spaces in them. Census data, county maps, fire insurance maps, enhanced by oral histories, narratives, and other first hand accounts facilitate a rich discovery and in-depth analysis of the places and people who seem otherwise gone like smoke from a furnace.

NOTES

1. Richard M. Nixon quote cited in *Best of Enemies: Race and Redemption in the New South* by Osha Gray Davidson (New York: Scribner, 1996), 31.
2. The period of legal segregation typically indicates the period between two pivotal decisions of the U.S. Supreme Court: *Plessy v. Ferguson* (1896) with its notion of "separate but equal" sanctioned racial segregation, placing the onus to prove inequality on African Americans; and *Brown v. Board of Education,* (1954) wherein the Court began to dismantle the legal framework that supported segregation. *Brown* established that, in the arena of education, segregation marked African Americans as inferior and, hence, separate could never be equal. At the state and local level, laws were enacted earlier than *Plessy* and often remained in effect well beyond the *Brown* decision. Between 1896 and the 1950s, individual African Americans and civil rights groups continuously challenged the legality of segregation.
3. E. Franklin Frazier, "Durham: The Capital of the Black Middle Class," in Alain Locke, *The New Negro: Voices of the Harlem Renaissance* (New York: Albert & Charles Boni, 1925; reprint, Antheneum/Macmillan, 1992), 333.
4. Booker T. Washington, "Durham, North Carolina, a City of Negro Enterprises," *The Independent* 70 (23 March 1911): 644–648; W. E. B. Du Bois, "The Upbuilding of Black Durham, The Success of Negroes and their Value to a Tolerant and Helpful Southern City," *World's Work* 3 (January 1912): 338–339.
5. Jean Bradley Anderson, *Durham County: A History of Durham County, North Carolina* (Durham, NC: Duke University Press and the Historic Preservation

Society of Durham, 1990), 130–153; William K. Boyd, *The Story of Durham: City of the New South* (Durham, NC: Duke University Press, 1927), 278.

6. Hazel V. Carby, *Race Men* (Cambridge, MA: Harvard University Press, 1998); Evelyn Brooks Higginbotham, "African American Women's History and the Metalanguage of Race," *Signs* 17 (1992): 251–273.

7. Leslie Brown, "Common Spaces, Separate Lives: Gender and Racial Conflict in the Capital of the Black Middle Class," (Ph.D. Diss, Duke University, 1997).

8. Hundreds of such institutions are included in William Edward Burghardt Du Bois, *Efforts for Social Betterment among Negro Americans* (Atlanta, GA: Atlanta University Press, 1909). ＼

9. Nannie Helen Burroughs' school still operates in Washington, D.C., and has been renamed for its founder. A street in that city also commemorates Burroughs. In Augusta, Lucy Laney's home has been restored and is now open as a museum and conference center.

10. Glenda Elizabeth Gilmore, *Gender and Jim Crow: Women and the Politics of White Supremacy, 1896–1920* (Chapel Hill: University of North Carolina Press, 1996).

11. In 1982, the Mary McLeod Bethune Council House in Washington, D.C., was designated a National Historic Site. The building had served as Bethune's home and as the headquarters for the National Council of Negro Women. It now houses the NCNW archives and museum.

12. Although there has been an outpouring of scholarship that examines the history of women and the built environment, very few sources focus specifically on African American women. One exception is Barbara A. Tagger, "Interpreting African American Women's History Through Historic Landscapes, Structures, and Commemorative Sites," *OAH Magazine of History* (Fall 1997): 17–19. Other essays that include several sites associated with black women are Darlene Roth, "Feminine Marks on the Landscape: An Atlanta Inventory," *Journal of American Culture,* 3 (Winter 1980): 673–685; and Elsa Barkley Brown and Gregg D. Kimball, "Mapping the Terrain of Black Richmond," *Journal of Urban History* 21 (March 1995): 298–346.

13. Department of Commerce, Bureau of the Census, *Negroes in the United States, 1920–1932* (Washington DC: Government Printing Office, 1935), 85.

14. The manuscript census is available for a period previous to the last 72 years.

15. The 1937 city directory for Durham incorrectly footnotes Moore's wife, Cottie, as white.

16. The census probably incorrectly recorded their language as Hebrew, rather than Yiddish.

17. Levi Branson, *Directory of the Businesses and Citizens of Durham City for 1887* (Raleigh, NC: Levi Branson, 1887); *Hill's Directory* (Durham, NC: Hill Directory Co., 1905–06); *Hill's Directory* (Durham, NC: Hill Directory Company, 1917); *Hill's Durham* (Durham, NC: Hill Directory Company, 1936–37).

18. Segregation patterns differed in every city, depending on its particular racial history and the nature of its economy. See Charles S. Johnson, *Patterns of Negro Segregation* (New York: Harper & Brothers, 1943).

19. Shotgun houses represent a style of architecture prevalent in the southern U.S. Possibly derived from a housing style found in west Africa, these long, narrow structures were homes to many low-income black and white families. Typically one room wide and with a front porch, these buildings were named to suggest that a bullet shot through the front door could be launched through the house in a straight line until it passed out the back door.

20. By 1924, the Sanborn Map Company had mapped approximately 11,000 towns and cities across the United States. For further information about fire insurance maps, see Walter W. Ristow, "United States Fire Insurance and Underwriters Maps, 1852–1968," *Quarterly Journal of the Library of Congress* 25(3): 195–217; and Diane L. Oswald, *Fire Insurance Maps: Their History and Applications* (College Station, TX: Lacewing Press, 1997).

21. Tera W. Hunter, *To 'Joy My Freedom: Black Women's Lives and Labors in the New South* (Cambridge, MA: Harvard University Press, 1997), 62–63.

22. Pauli Murray, *Proud Shoes: The Story of An American Family* (New York: Harper & Row, 1978), 26–27. Also see Murray, *The Autobiography of a Black Activist, Feminist, Lawyer, Priest, and Poet* (Knoxville: University of Tennessee Press, 1989), originally published as *Song in a Weary Throat* (New York: Harper & Row, 1987). A founder of the National Organization of Women, Murray was trained at Howard University in the 1940s as one of the coterie of what would become civil rights lawyers.

23. Gwendolyn M. Parker, *These Same Long Bones* (Boston: Houghton Mifflin, 1997), 58.

24. Murray, *Proud Shoes*, 234–236; Murray *The Autobiography*, 60; Pauli Murray to Alma Louise Fitzgerald Biggers, 14 June 1975, Folder 331, Box 12, Pauli Murray Papers, Schlesinger Library, Radcliffe College.

25. Annie Mack Barbee, Interview by Beverly Jones, 28 May 1979, interview H-190, transcript, Southern Oral History Program, Southern Historical Collection, University of North Carolina at Chapel Hill (hereinafter cited as SOHP/UNC). Tera Hunter argues that although the living conditions in black neighborhoods justified the concern for tuberculosis expressed by public health officials, these officials instead blamed the spread of that disease in white households on the deficiencies of black domestic workers. They thereby disregarded municipalities' responsibility for dangerous health conditions in black neighborhoods. Hunter, 186–218.

26. Mary E. Mebane, *Mary* (New York: Viking Press/Fawcett Juniper Books, 1981), 165–70.

27. Several excellent studies focus on black women's work in tobacco. See Delores Janiewski, *Sisterhood Denied: Race, Gender, and Class in a New South Community* (Philadelphia: Temple University Press, 1985); Beverly Washington Jones, "Race, Sex and Class: Black Female Tobacco Workers in Durham North

Carolina, 1920–1940, and the Development of Female Consciousness," *Feminist Studies* 10 (Fall 1984): 441–451; Carolyn Manning and Harriet A. Byrne, *The Effects on Women of Changing Conditions in the Cigar and Cigarette Industries,* Bulletin of the Women's Bureau, No. 100 (Washington, DC: Government Printing Office, 1932).

28. Dora Scott Miller, interview by Beverly Jones, 6 June 1979, interview H-211, SOHP/UNC; Blanche Scott, interview by Beverly Jones, 11 July 1979, interview H-229, SOHP/UNC; Barbee interview; Mebane, *Mary,* 173–76.

29. Barbee interview.

30. Department of Labor, Women's Bureau, *Negro Women in Industry,* (Washington, DC: Government Printing Office, 1922), 58.

31. Ella Parks Howerton (Whitted), "Remembering . . . 'The Meanderings of an Old Lady' [1900–1918]," Howerton Family Papers, Special Collections Library, Duke University (hereinafter cited as SCL/DU).

32. Mary Bailey, interview by Glenn Hinson, 26 January 1979, interview H-189, SOHP/UNC; Anderson, *Durham County,* 261; Emma Shields, "A Half-Century in the Tobacco Industry," *Southern Workman,* 51 (September 1922): 420; Raymond Gavins, "North Carolina Black Folklore and Song in the Age of Segregation: Toward Another Meaning of Survival," *North Carolina Historical Review* 66 (October 1989): 412–41.

33. Bailey interview.

34. Bailey interview; Scott interview; Miller interview; Jones, "Race, Sex, and Class," 450.

35. Department of Commerce, Bureau of the Census, *Fifteenth Census of the United States, Vol IV, Occupations* (Washington, DC: Government Printing Office, 1933), 425.

36. Miller interview; Maude Brown, interview by Beverly Jones, 3 August 1979, interview H-192, SOHP/UNC; Elizabeth Ross Haynes, "Negroes in Domestic Service in the United States," *Journal of Negro History* 8 (October 1923): 339–396. For first person accounts about household workers and their work, see: Susan Tucker, *Telling Memories Among Southern Women: Domestic Workers and Their Employers in the Segregated South* (Chapel Hill: University of North Carolina Press, 1988).

37. Murray, *Proud Shoes; The Autobiography.*

38. Robert J. Tyndall, statement before the Durham City Board of Education, Public School Hearing, Morehead Elementary School, 4 November 1974, Folder 272, Box 11, Pauli Murray Papers; Murray, *The Autobiography,* 17; Murray, interview by Genna Rae MacNeil, 13 February 1976, interview G-44, SOHP/UNC. Tyndall was the principal of Lyon Park School in 1974, the year the city closed the facility.

39. Murray, *Proud Shoes,* 270.

40. The Julius Rosenwald Fund contributed toward the building of African American schools. Local black communities provided supplies, building materials, labor, and an equal number of dollars toward the schools. For African

Americans, this amounted to a double tax, as they also paid taxes to support public schools which they could not attend.

41. Pauli Murray's aunts were an exception, having moved to the west side of Durham before it was a neighborhood. The family remained there as the area took shape. Most teachers lived in Hayti and traveled across town to work in schools in other neighborhoods.

42. Claudia Brown Roberts, *The Durham Architectural and Historic Inventory* (Durham, NC: City of Durham and the Historic Preservation Society of Durham, 1982), 117–118; Johnnie McLester, interview by Leslie Brown, 15 February 1991, Durham, tape recording in author's possession; Josephine Clement, interview by Leslie Brown, 15 February 1991, Durham, tape recording in author's possession; Addie Marie Faulk, interview by Leslie Brown, 27 October 1995, Durham, tape recording in author's possession.

43. Figures for women and men employees come from "A Report on a Survey Made Among the Home Office Clerks, The North Carolina Mutual Life Insurance Company," September 1924, in Asa T. Spaulding Papers, Box 178, SCL/DU.

44. R. McCants Andrews, *John Merrick: A Biographical Sketch* (Durham: Seeman Printery, 1920), 53–55; Walter B. Weare, *Black Business in the New South: A Social History of North Carolina Mutual Life Insurance Company* (Urbana: University of Illinois Press, 1973; reprint, Durham, NC: Duke University Press, 1990).

45. Viola R. Turner, interview by Walter B. Weare, 15 April 1979 and 17 April 1979, interview C-15 and C-16, SOHP/UNC.

46. On department stores as female space, see Susan Porter Benson, *Counter Cultures: Saleswomen, Managers, and Customers in American Department Stores, 1890–1940* (Urbana: University of Illinois Press, 1988).

47. The tradition of operating housing for single working women dates back into the nineteenth century, as organizations such as the YWCA and the Women's Christian Association established residences for female migrants to cities. Such establishments not only met women's practical need for affordable housing, but also appealed to middle-class reformers' desire to ensure that women maintained respectability by protecting them from prostitution or vice.

48. *The North Carolina Mutual Life Insurance Company,* promotional booklet, (Durham: NC Mutual Life Insurance Company, 1921), 20–21; *The Mechanics and Farmers Bank,* promotional booklet, (Durham, NC: Seeman Printery, 1921),15–16.

49. Turner interview; *Hill's Durham* (Hill Directory Company, 1936–37). Similar facilities existed in other cities, including the nurses' home associated with the Homer G. Phillips Hospital in St. Louis.

50. Stephanie J. Shaw, *What a Woman Ought to Be and to Do: Black Professional Women Workers During the Jim Crow Era* (Chicago: University of Chicago Press, 1996), 14–42 and 83.

51. Hazel V. Carby, "Policing the Black Woman's Body in an Urban Context," *Critical Inquiry* 18 (Summer 1992), 739.
52. Turner interview.
53. Julia Lucas, interview by Leslie Brown 21 September 1993, Behind the Veil Collection, John Hope Franklin Center for African and African American Documentary, SCL/DU (hereinafter cited as BTV); *The Mechanics and Farmers Bank* promotional booklet, 15–16.
54. Lucas interview; York D. Garrett, Sr., interview by Kara Miles, 3 June 1993, BTV; Julia Lucas and Charles Lucas, interview by Leslie Brown, 28 November 1993, notes in author's possession; "Hayti In Its Heyday: An Oral History Performance," Durham, NC: St. Joseph's Historical Foundation at the Hayti Heritage Center, 13 March 1991.

SUGGESTED READINGS

Elsa Barkley Brown, and Gregg D. Kimball. "Mapping the Terrain of Black Richmond." *Journal of Urban History* 21 (March 1995): 298–346. This study examines the efforts of African American residents of Richmond to claim and give meaning to public space from the end of the Civil War through the early years of the twentieth century. Brown and Kimball's sophisticated analysis considers the symbolic and actual use of public space as an arena of contest and conflict between black and white residents, as well as between men and women, and those of distinct socioeconomic classes. The study provides a model for how to investigate and uncover the meanings of space within a culture.

William H. Chafe, Raymond Gavins, and Robert Korstad, eds. *Remembering Jim Crow: African Americans Tell About Life in the Segregated South*. New York: New Press, 2001. This collection of oral testimony and photographs depicts the experiences of black southerners during segregation and describes the diverse regional, economic, social, and cultural lives of residents of the South. Drawn from the extensive Behind the Veil collection at Duke University, it provides its readers with access to a history that has remained in the purview of family stories.

Tera W. Hunter. *To 'Joy My Freedom: Southern Black Women's Lives and Labors After the Civil War*. Cambridge: Harvard University Press, 1997. This book examines women's migration to a New South urban center, Atlanta, in the postbellum era, and illustrates the value of women's labor to the development of black communities forged in freedom. Centering African American women as the subject of the book, Hunter draws out a history of resistance and struggle.

Jacqueline Jones. *Labor of Love, Labor of Sorrow: Black Women, Work, and the Family from Slavery to the Present*. New York: Basic Books, 1985. A classic survey of African American women's history, Jones' book provides insight into women's economic roles in both black communities and U.S. history. Offering a deep understanding of the dimensions of black women's work, it provides surprisingly abundant data drawn from census, governments studies, and other public documents.

Richard L. Mattson. "The Cultural Landscape of a Southern Black Community: East Wilson, North Carolina, 1890–1930." *Landscape Journal* 11 (Fall 1992): 144–159. Mattson describes the spatial patterns and architectural forms found in this southern black community. Although focused primarily on middle-class neighborhoods, this article surveys housing types found throughout the city, and provides information about the role of black and white architects and developers.

Stephanie J. Shaw. *What A Woman Ought to Be and To Do: Black Professional Women Workers During the Jim Crow Era*. Chicago: University of Chicago Press, 1996. A collective biography of middle-class African American women teachers and other professionals, this book provides an analysis of connections between gender, race work, and community status.

Deborah Gray White. *Too Heavy a Load: Black Women in Defense of Themselves, 1894–1994*. New York: W. W. Norton, 1999. Detailing black women's organized resistance to racial and gender oppression, this book also describes class differences and resulting conflicts among women reformers. A survey of national organizations that black women have formed, the book highlights women's contributions to community uplift and their perspectives on national politics.

Chapter 11

REINTERPRETING PUBLIC EVENTS: THE IMPACT OF WOMEN'S HISTORY ON PUBLIC CELEBRATIONS

Barbara J. Howe

Women have been part of public celebrations at least since Sarah Fulton helped organize the Boston Tea Party. In 1830, Sarah Josepha Hale organized a fund-raising campaign among women to finish the Bunker Hill Monument.[1] Residents of Grant Township in Lyon County, Iowa, especially praised pioneer women for "overcoming adversity" when writing their local history during the nation's centennial celebration in 1876.[2] During 1998–2000, California celebrated a three-year sesquicentennial of the events that began with James Marshall's discovery of gold on the American River on January 24, 1848, and ended when California became a state in 1850. At the opening event in January 1998, Kate Magruder portrayed Dame Shirley, who documented life in early mining camps in her writings.[3] JoAnn Levy ensured that women's history was part of the celebration by talking about "gold-rushing women." "Invariably," she found "audiences fascinated with their adventures and experiences."[4] "It's my window of opportunity to get people's attention," she told a reporter for the *Sacramento Bee*. "While they get a Gold Rush awareness, I'll give them a *gender* awareness."[5]

As organizers, legendary historical figures, or symbols, women have played numerous roles in local and national public celebrations since our nation began and have thereby helped shape our understanding of our history. It was only in the last decades of the twentieth century, however, that the burgeoning scholarship on women's history and the involvement of historians of women in public celebrations across the country began to make a significant impact on public celebrations, an impact that this chapter intends to reinforce and strengthen with suggestions for those planning future events.

The Bunker Hill, Grant Township, and Gold Rush commemorations also reflect the evolution of our understanding of women's history, following an agenda that Gerda Lerner set out in 1969. According to Lerner, feminist writers, not professional historians, first identified women and recognized their contributions. Hale's efforts at Bunker Hill might illustrate that stage of women's history. Next, Mary Beard traced "the positive achievements of women, their social role, and their con-

Figure 11-1. *When Anthony Met Stanton* on the bridge at Seneca Falls, NY, recreates the meeting of the famous team of Susan B. Anthony and Elizabeth Cady Stanton. Amelia Bloomer is shown introducing them in Ted Aube's sculpture. The statue was given to the Village of Seneca Falls by Gov. George E. Pataki on behalf of his commission honoring the achievements of women during the celebration of the 150th anniversary of the first women's rights convention. (*Photo by Eileen Eagan.*)

tributions to community life." Grant Township residents did this in 1876. Lerner thought the third stage should be a "new conceptual framework for dealing with the subject of women in American history" because "women themselves are as entitled as minority group members are to having 'their' history fully recorded."[6] JoAnn Levy tried to accomplish that goal with her Gold Rush programs. While Lerner set forth this agenda over three decades ago, it is still a useful benchmark to measure the level of sophistication one sees in public celebrations of women's history at both the national and local levels.

This increasing sophistication is particularly clear in the repeated celebrations of one landmark event in women's history—anniversaries of a hastily called meeting in Wesleyan Chapel in Seneca Falls, New York, in July 1848, at which Elizabeth Cady Stanton suggested that women should have the right to vote. Fifty years later, Stanton's daughter, Harriet Stanton Blatch, and members of the New York Women's Political Union marked the anniversary by putting a plaque on the Wesleyan Chapel—a public celebration of women's history with Mary Church Terrell as the main speaker.[7]

The Nineteenth Amendment to the U.S. Constitution, which gave women the right to vote, was finally ratified on August 26, 1920, when Tennessee's Harry Burns heeded his mother's command and cast the deciding vote in the state leg-

Figure 11-2. JoAnn Levy portrayed Eliza Farnham, a forty-niner, and the author of the first book on California by a woman. Levy, author of three books about women in the California Gold Rush, performed a Chautauqua program at the visitor center of the Marshall Gold Discovery State Historic Park at Coloma, California, where gold was discovered. This program took place during 1998, the year of California's sesquincentennial observance of the discovery of gold. (*Courtesy of JoAnn Levy.*)

islature to ratify the proposed amendment. The City of Nashville has marked the occasion with a silhouette of a suffrage leader outside the Hermitage Hotel, the suffrage headquarters in downtown Nashville near the capitol.

Seneca Falls continued to be "holy ground" for women's rights activists, who continued to celebrate anniversaries of the 1848 convention there. Local women ran the 1948 centennial, which drew a crowd of 2,000 speakers and featured a "new declaration, oriented toward world peace" in a world plunging deeper into the Cold War following World War II.[8]

By 1970, in the first years of what we now call the second wave of the women's rights movement, celebrations of that historic August 26 vote had spread far beyond Nashville and far beyond simply the anniversary of a vote. Women and men were beginning to recall an event that had been lost in the public consciousness by linking it to contemporary issues. Thus, on August 26, 1970, 50,000 people marched down New York City's Fifth Avenue, celebrating the fiftieth anniversary of the Tennessee legislature's vote with the first nationwide Women's Strike for Equality. This anniversary date has since become known as Women's Equality Day.[9] Since 1970, this has been a day to remember the past and press forward with demands for the future. To facilitate these celebrations, Gerri Gribi developed a World Wide Web site including suffrage song sheets and other ideas for celebrations at the local level.[10]

The 150th anniversary of the Seneca Falls convention, under the banner of Celebrate '98, was the most important public celebration of women's history at the end of the twentieth century. Celebrate '98 centered its activities around the convention anniversary and drew heavily on the scholarship of many prominent historians of women.[11] The chapel site and Elizabeth Cady Stanton's home, which became part of Women's Rights National Historical Park when the National Park Service created that park in 1982, became pilgrimage sites for those attending national conventions of the National Organization for Women, National Council of Women's Organizations, and Girls' International Forum, among others.[12] During the celebration days of July 10–20, 35,000 people visited the park, more than the total visitation for 1997 (28,000) and almost one-half of the total visitation for 1998 (75,000).[13] First Lady Hillary Rodham Clinton ended her "Save American's Treasures Tour" on July 16 at Seneca Falls, where she presided over anniversary activities.[14]

The greater significance of Celebrate '98 lies in the fact that, like the bicentennial of the American Revolution or the fiftieth anniversary of the end of World War II, commemorative events also took place across the country. Celebrate '98 allowed people who had never taken a course in women's history to understand events that, for too long, were barely mentioned in most United States history texts.

The National Women's History Museum compiled a list of events around the country that illustrate the range of anniversary events.[15] Gerri Gribi performed her original "A Musical Romp Through Women's History" in Des Moines, Iowa, on August 26. Concert-goers in St. Paul, Minnesota, heard the world premiere of Carol Barnett and Marisha Chamberlain's "Meeting at Seneca Falls," performed by the San Francisco Women's Philharmonic. Phoenix, Arizona, held a Spirit of Seneca Falls Celebration Event in October, while the Holley House Museum in Lakeville, Connecticut, had women's history exhibits during the summer of 1998, and the Georgia Women's History Initiative developed a women's history web site to celebrate in cyberspace.[16] United States military bases in Belgium and Germany sponsored events to link Americans living abroad with those celebrating at home.[17] West Virginia University incorporated the suffrage colors and a revised version of the Declaration of Sentiments into a retirement ceremony honoring the founding director of the women's studies program.[18]

Women's activism for suffrage culminated in 1920 with the adoption of the

Nineteenth Amendment, but celebrations in support of women's rights continued. The Worcester Women's History Project (WWHP) was founded in 1994 "for the purpose of raising awareness of the history of women in Worcester County" in Massachusetts. At the first national women's rights convention, held in Worcester in 1850, over 1,000 men and women, both white and black, called for "'Equality before the law, without distinction of sex or color'." In 1997, the WWHP celebrated the 150th anniversary of Lucy Stone's first public speech. *Women 2000,* in October 2000, included a national conference on women's rights as part of the convention's sesquicentennial celebration. During Women's History Month, 2002, they launched a Women's Heritage Trail.[19]

In days of instantaneous news coverage that could track millennial celebrations as the year turned to 2000 around the world, it is important to remember that Celebrate '98 focused on an event that only those in upstate New York knew about before it occurred and which involved very few people at the time.[20] Still, the anniversary resonated around the country in ways that historians will be interpreting and re-interpreting for years to come.

Apart from the fireworks and hoopla of that New Year's Eve, the nation's millennium celebration also reflected some of the impact of women's history scholarship on public celebrations. Celebrations included the best of historical scholarship, as well as reflecting popular culture. The White House celebrated the millennium with a theme of "Honor the Past—Imagine the Future." To encourage discussion of this theme, the White House Millennium Council hosted the "Sixth Millennium Evening at the White House: Women as Citizens: Vital Voices Through the Century" (on March 15, 1999) during Women's History Month. Historians Nancy Cott and Alice Kessler-Harris, and Ruth Simmons, president of Smith College, discussed "women as volunteers and reformers, women's struggle for rights, and women in public/civic life." The National Endowment for the Humanities sponsored the evening, with support from Sun Microsystems, and the discussion was broadcast by satellite around the world.[21] Internet web sites such as Lifetime Entertainment Services's "Lifetime Online: Women of the Twentieth Century," allowed people to vote for the most influential women of the twentieth century in the categories of "Screen Queens," "Creative Legacies," "She's Got Game," "Innovators," "Vox Populi," "Breaking the Glass Ceiling," "Teacher, Teacher," "Hearts of Gold," and "15 Minutes of Fame."[22]

The Seneca Falls sesquicentennial, with women's history specialists playing key roles throughout the celebration, and the various millennium "best of the century" events, were among the most public, and most original, of the public celebrations of women's history at the end of the twentieth century. However, other public celebrations, like the anniversaries of local and national events, can also include the history of women. Communities across the country frequently remember traditions, honor outstanding women, and celebrate anniversaries with varying recognition of women's history scholarship. It is important to look at how women's history can be incorporated into events that are less obviously focused on landmark events and on well-known pioneering women leaders.

Although there are many such real women to honor, community celebrations sometimes include women in ways that are more symbolic than real. The Grant Township women noted above were able to portray real pioneer women in 1876, but that was not the case in Des Moines, Iowa. On July 4 of that year, women represented "Columbia," "the Goddess Liberty," and the thirteen colonies. J. A. Hill's *Hill's Book of Tableaux* (1884) recommended that women "draped in classical garb" could have their "major opportunity to appear in public celebrations" by representing "abstract virtues of the state or nation" like "'Columbia,' 'Legislative Power,' 'Executive Power,' 'Judicial Power,' 'The Army,' 'The Navy,' and 'the Thirteen Original States'."[23] It would be interesting to know if anyone recognized the incongruity of women representing branches of the government and military service where they were not welcome when in modern dress.

In 1889, suffrage leaders Mary A. Livermore and Cora Scott Pound produced "The National Pageant and Dramatic Events in the History of Connecticut." Their seventeen "living, speaking, moving tableaux" included a scene about "Women's Sphere, 1800" (a colonial home full of parents, grandparents,and sixteen children), "Women's Crusade in 1873" (where members of the Women's Christian Temperance Union invaded a barroom), and "Women's Sphere, 1889." Women in business, law, the ministry, and medicine joined in a final procession across the stage to the strains of *The Battle Hymn of the Republic*. David Glassberg noted that "such a decidedly feminist emphasis" was not common in similar pageants, but did illustrate women's increasing authority in planning public celebrations. Not all women were content to portray "Justice" if they could represent real women instead.[24]

Symbolism and romanticized ideas of the past continue to be important in local pageants. Girls dress up in wooden shoes, caps, and aprons to portray Dutch girls during the annual May Tulip Festival, celebrating the city's Dutch heritage in Albany, New York. The girls ceremonially "act out scrubbing one of the main streets in the city," starting at State and Lodge Streets, in a "popular perception of the role of colonial Dutch women." The festival, which began in 1949, also includes the crowning of a Tulip Queen and a juried craft show at Pinksterfest.[25]

Wisconsin's clubwomen, in contrast, followed a feminist approach to honoring women during that state's 1948 centennial commission. Working through the Wisconsin Federation of Women's Clubs, members published a lengthy pamphlet on women's contributions to state history.[26] They also recreated the office of Rhoda Lavinia Goodell, the state's first woman lawyer and a prominent prison reformer, as their booth for the celebration.[27]

Historians of women can be very influential in moving celebration plans away from pageant traditions and symbolism and toward reality and substance. This is most often possible if, like the woman in Wisconsin, there are others who share common goals and knowledge, who are also willing to question stereotypes and assumptions of women's roles in these events. Far too often, though, members of celebration commissions have had little opportunity to learn about women's history in school. They, therefore, may not know how to ask questions about women's roles in a community or to find the answers to the historians' questions without assistance.

The bicentennial of the founding of Morgantown, West Virginia, illustrates the challenges and rewards of incorporating feminist historians' perspectives into an anniversary event. During the bicentennial year of 1985, a bicentennial commission accepted the responsibility for publishing a history of the community. With public history students as contributors, the commission successfully published a history that included photographs of an African American baseball team, members of the Carpatho-Russian Orthodox Greek Catholic Church, and a Lewis Hines photo of children working in a local glass factory. The commission honored outstanding citizens; celebrated and remembered the community's past at dinners; organized a huge street party and an interfaith religious event; and buried a time capsule.

A personal story points up the feminist issues that can occur during the planning for celebrations. The bicentennial commission members had only one major disagreement: whether or not to have a bicentennial queen. This was to be a high school girl who would, of course, be a good citizen and good student, with her beauty to be a distant consideration. Every surrounding community celebration and major annual festival had a queen, some of whom wore gorgeous gowns handmade by women who annually designed and sewed the perfect dress for the coronation. When discussion at one meeting turned to designing the gown for this young woman, I realized, as the most outspoken feminist on the bicentennial commission, that I was quickly reaching the end of my crusade to avoid choosing a bicentennial queen and needed to focus the committee's and community's attention away from seeing women only as beautiful objects dressed in gowns who presided over ceremonies. The commission chair reminded us all that beauty was not to be the only selection criteria. My retort—"Have you ever seen an ugly queen?"—went unanswered. I argued that, if we had a queen, we needed to have a king—a young man who was also a good student and good citizen. I pointed out there were many other ways of honoring outstanding young people in the community other than crowning one a queen. My friend, the public librarian, had far more influence than I did. When the vote took place, she quietly pointed out that selecting a queen was exploiting a young woman. I do not remember the margin of victory, but we did win. There was no bicentennial queen—or king.

Sometimes, anniversaries remember periods of conflict within a community, and not just the dim memories of brave ancestors conquering a wilderness. In 1997, Little Rock, Arkansas, marked the anniversary of Central High School's desegregation forty years earlier. Growing out of this commemoration, the following year the community celebrated the fortieth anniversary of the Women's Emergency Committee to Open Our Schools. This committee originated on September 16, 1958, when "a group of concerned women" organized in opposition to Governor Orval Faubus's decision to close Little Rock high schools to avoid desegregation. Until 1963, when it disbanded, the group had worked to elect school board members who would support integration and had sought actively "to defend public education by seeking and then assisting those Little Rock candidates for local and state offices who supported public schools."[28]

On a more on-going basis, some communities link women's history to heritage tourism. Superior, a small town in southeastern Nebraska, hosts the Lady Vestey Victorian Festival each year on Memorial Day weekend. Evelene Brodstone was born in Superior in 1875 and, after college, went to work for the London Vestey Packing Company, marrying her British husband, Lord Vestey, in 1924.[29] She was an important benefactor for Superior, providing funds for scholarships, a hospital, park repairs, and "anonymous gifts to needy families."[30] Linking heritage tourism with women's history, Superior honors who the town describes as the hometown "girl who became the highest paid woman business executive in the world. Her Cinderella story, beginning in this Victorian Capital of Nebraska, is featured in entertainment for the entire family." The town promotes the festival as "one of the Top Ten Festivals in the nation," and the Nebraska Department of

Figure 11-3. Beverly Beavers portrays Lady Vestey, whose portrait hangs at her left, at the annual Lady Vestey Victorian Festival in Superior, NE. Born Evelene Brodstone, Lady Vestey was a town benefactor. She became an executive at the Vestey Packing Company in London and married the owner, but she never forgot the needs of her home town. (*Courtesy of the Hastings Tribune. Photo by Beth Bohling.*)

Tourism and Nebraska Community Improvement Program have honored it as Nebraska's Outstanding Event. Beginning in 1997, Superior has used the festival as the opportunity to bestow a Gracious Lady Award on an "outstanding contemporary woman who has enriched the lives of those around her." The festival also includes tours of historic homes and sites, "A Visit With Lady Vestey" presentation, Victorian tea, antique show, and quilt show.[31]

Colleges and universities can also mark anniversaries by reexamining the role of women in their histories. Shortly after Morgantown's bicentennial celebration ended in late 1985, West Virginia University turned its attention to the centenary of women's education on campus, celebrating the arrival of the first ten women degree candidates in 1889 and the graduation of the first woman, a transfer student from Vassar, in 1891. The entire celebration was based on extensive research into the experiences of women as students, faculty, and staff. Using the theme of "Excellence through Equity," the committee also worked to recover the history of African Americans who wanted to attend a university that did not admit them as undergraduates until after the 1954 *Brown v. Board of Education* decision. Organizers gathered enormous amounts of information about the history of women at WVU, published a historical digest, held public events that celebrated women's accomplishments on campus, and dedicated a time capsule located near the Morgantown bicentennial time capsule. Unlike the bicentennial, a young woman who was a good student and good citizen, and attractive, became a central figure in the event—a central figure whose success was proclaimed whenever possible. This young woman was Natalie Tennant, the first (and, to date, only) woman to be chosen by the students to portray the university's mascot—the Mountaineer. Like the men before and since, she dressed in fringed pants and shirt, ran around carrying a rifle at football and basketball games, and represented WVU at many public events.[32]

Georgia College and State University and Simmons College also have recognized the history of women at their schools through celebrations. In 1988, Georgia College and State University began preparing for its centennial celebration. In researching the institution's history, Robin Harris discovered a few boxes in the library's Special Collections labeled "Julia Flisch." Those boxes led to Harris's important reinterpretation of the college's founding as she compared "the rhetoric of the founding" of what was then known as Georgia Normal and Industrial College with "the reality of the state-supported liberal arts education offered to women" there. Flisch, Harris found, "had begun writing in newspapers and speaking from public platforms" as early as 1882, "calling for Georgia to recognize and address the need for educational and vocational opportunities for women." When Flisch spoke at the cornerstone laying ceremony in 1890, this daughter of immigrants, then twenty-eight years old and unmarried, addressed "the plight of southern women caught between the rhetoric of southern womanhood and the realities of life in a region economically devastated by the War."[33]

Simmons College, a women's college in Boston which celebrated its centenary in 1999–2000, also included history in its celebrations. Simmons's charter was

Figure 11-4. Natalie Tennant was the first woman to hold the position of West Virginia University's mascot, the Mountaineer, an honor celebrating one hundred years of women at WVU. Dressed in fringed pants and shirt and carrying a rifle, she represented WVU at sports and other public events. (*Courtesy of West Virginia University Photographic Services.*)

signed on May 24, 1899, and the first students arrived on October 9, 1902.[34] In addition to promoting the college's history through the World Wide Web, Simmons's Office of Advancement took a Centennial Road Show to thirty-seven cities, from Cape Cod to San Francisco, from the fall of 1999 to the spring of 2000. Simmons conducted "history 'roundtables'" at many of these events, asking alumnae/i to share their college memories.[35]

SUGGESTIONS FOR INCORPORATING WOMEN'S HISTORY INTO PUBLIC CELEBRATIONS

Historians of women need to seek out opportunities to incorporate the perspectives of women's history into the plans and publications for public celebrations, beginning in the initial planning stages of these events. This will ensure that the history celebrated and remembered is, in fact, as inclusive as possible so that the audiences, whether the residents of the community or students and employees of a university, realize that history is incomplete if they ignore half the population. Fortunately, the scholarship about women in education is providing new models and resources for those examining their own schools.[36]

Historians of women explore more than women's roles as organizers of events or as pioneers who seem to disappear from any future roles in the community's history. Rather, historians of women working on public celebrations ask new questions about women's experiences and include the knowledge that results from those new questions in those celebrations. They work to document women as family members, students and teachers, wage-earners and business owners, community leaders and volunteers, athletes, environmentalists, voters and politicians, church members and clergy. They ask such questions as: what were women's working conditions? how did they organize during wartime to maintain their households while husbands were gone? how did they keep their families together during the Great Depression? when did girls start to play Little League baseball?

The National Women's History Project (NWHP) has many resources that can help organizers incorporate women's history into public celebrations. Their web site at <www.nwhp.org> includes a calendar of women's history events around the country. It was this organization that lobbied the United States Congress to designate March as Women's History Month. Information about the Women's History Month activities can be found on the NWHP web site. Thousands of children in grades six through twelve celebrate Women's History Month, for instance, with History Day projects that they present in their local communities and, perhaps, at the annual National History Day competition.[37]

The NWHP promoted intriguing"Y2K Party Ideas" for celebrating the millennium that can be adapted for any public celebration event. These include using the NWHP "An Extraordinary Century for Women" as an event theme, with NWHP buttons and small posters/placemats as souvenirs; inviting guests to portray outstanding twentieth-century women or male supporters of women's rights. Hosts could also hang a large sheet of paper on a wall so participants can list and comment on the contributions of twentieth century women. The NWHP also has a number of films that can be shown at public events, including "There's No Such Thing as Women's Work," "The Equal Rights Amendment: Unfinished Business for the Constitution," or a short film entitled "A Fine and Long Tradition."[38]

Further NWHP ideas for community organizations could easily be incorporated into the plans for public celebrations. These include working with the historical society to establish a Women's Hall of Fame to honor women who have made contributions to the community, including annual induction ceremonies to honor additional women; arranging for a special tribute at places of worship to the ongoing work done by women for the congregation and encouraging congregations to discuss women's contributions to religious life; sponsoring a "Real Woman" essay or poster competition in a school or throughout the community, focusing on women from history or women important in the lives of the community; and working with a local newspaper to develop articles about local historic and contemporary women.[39]

Monuments to women are discussed in Eileen Eagan's chapter elsewhere in this volume, but it is also important to note here that identifying monuments related to women, celebrating existing monuments, and erecting new monuments can be part of public celebrations that incorporate women's history. New York Governor George E. Pataki commissioned a statue, *When Anthony Met Stanton,* to commemorate the 150th anniversary of the Seneca Falls women's rights convention. Created by Ted Aube, the statue recreates the historic meeting of the two suffrage leaders. Lynn Sherr and Jurate Kazickas's *Susan B. Anthony Slept Here: A Guide to American Women's Landmarks* is an excellent reference to identify sites that already have monuments. State historic preservation offices, local landmarks commissions, and state-wide historic preservation organizations have references to sites related to women's history for those who wish to erect a monument that interprets women's history at a particular site as part of a celebration.

To ensure that a monument is not forgotten after a celebration, consider appointing "guardians" who will keep the story alive and feel an obligation to ensure periodic public notice of the person or events commemorated. West Virginia University's Center for Women's Studies, for instance, appointed a group of "keepers of the capsule," who are to reopen the women's centenary time capsule in 2016, add new items to mark women's history over the previous twenty-five years, and then appoint their successors, who will do the same in 2041 and on into the future. This is an excellent way to inculcate young people with responsibilities for the future of significant historic sites and to ensure that the women's history we have worked so hard to recover does not disappear.

Organizations of women historians, women's history museums, state humanities councils, public libraries, state museums and archives, and local colleges and universities archives and history departments can help celebration organizers identify scholars in women's history familiar with their area. The National Women's History Project includes a list of these organizations and museums that is constantly being updated. A few sample groups include the Association of Black Women Historians, Chicago Area Women's History Conference, Michigan Women's History Center, Southern Association of Women Historians, Western Association of Women Historians, Women Historians of the Midwest, Women's History Coalition of Kentucky. Resource centers include the General Federation of Women's Clubs Women's History and Resource Center, Jewish Women's Archive, Montana Women's History Project, Nevada Women's History Project, and Women in Military Service for America.[40] State humanities councils are affiliated with the National Endowment for the Humanities and provide funding for a wide variety of public history projects that can include brochures, speakers, exhibits, dramatic presentations, and special events. The National Endowment for the Humanities maintains a web site that gives links to each state's humanities council for further information.[41]

The published scholarship on women's history that can inform these public celebrations is so extensive that it is possible to include only a few publications that might provide insights and models for planners. Museum exhibit openings provide opportunities for public celebrations, and the accompanying catalogues are important references. For example, the Arkansas Women's History Institute (AWHI), organized in 1983, owed its inspiration to an exhibit entitled "Texas Women: A Celebration of History." The AWHI opened its traveling exhibit, entitled "Behold, Our Works Were Good" in the fall of 1984; the project received major funding from the Arkansas Endowment for the Humanities. Then, as Arkansas celebrated its sesquicentennial in 1986, the AWHI sponsored a "sanctioned Sequiscentennial event" by expanding the exhibit and displaying it in the Old State House in Little Rock for three weeks.[42] The Virginia Women's Cultural History Project sponsored an exhibit entitled "A Share of Honour: Virginia Women, 1600–1945," which opened at the Virginia Museum of Fine Arts in Richmond in November 1984. Suzanne Lebsock and Kym S. Rice collaborated on the exhibit catalogue of the same name.[43] The West Virginia Women's Cultural Heritage Project, under the leadership of the West Virginia Women's Commission and West Virginia Women's Foundation, used funding from the West Virginia Humanities Foundation and National Endowment for the Humanities to support its 1990 exhibit on "Traditions and Transitions."[44] There are also state-wide histories of women in Alabama, Kentucky, North Carolina, Oklahoma, Kentucky North Carolina, Tennessee, and Texas, among others. Local histories of women written by historians link local women and events to national themes and organizations.[45]

In spite of this explosion in publications, it will be the rare public celebration that will not require more research into the history of women in that place. State archives, public libraries, and college and university libraries contain manuscript collections, records of women's organizations, photographs, and oral histories that can provide the information researchers need to document the history of women in their communities for celebrations. The Florida and West Virginia state archives, for instance, maintain web sites on women's history in their states.[46] West Virginia's web site provides links to other state archives.[47]

Other sources will provide more information on research methodology and sources than on specific aspects of women's history. The books in the American Association for State and Local History Nearby History series and Krieger Publishing Company's Exploring Local History series, both edited by David Kyvig and Myron Marty, are excellent places to begin.[48] "Women's History, Local History, and Public History," by Barbara J. Howe and Helen M. Bannan provides information on sources for researching women's history in a community.[49] Publicizing the event and the quest for information may encourage people to search through closets and attics to uncover letters, diaries, and photographs documenting women's experiences. Collecting oral histories, with proper release forms giving permission to use the interviews, will take time but will also uncover women's stories previously considered unimportant.[50]

The nationwide interest in celebrating women's history, as reflected in the various endeavors noted above, culminated at the end of the millennium with the President's Commission on the Celebration of Women in American History. President Bill Clinton established this group by Executive Order 13090 dated 29 June 1998 "to make recommendations to the President . . . on ways to best acknowledge and celebrate the roles and accomplishments of women in American history. Recommendations may include, among other things, the feasibility of a focal point for women's history located in Washington, D.C., and the use of the latest technology to connect existing and planned women's history sites, museums, and libraries."[51] The commission invited groups to register their women's history projects that documented or honored "the lives or works of one or more women in your community or state." They were included in the commission's final report.[52]

NOTES

1. Gail Lee Dubrow, "Restoring a Female Presence: New Goals in Historic Preservation," in *Architecture: A Place for Women,* Ellen Perry Berkeley and Matilda McQuaid, eds. (Washington, DC: Smithsonian Institution Press, 1989), 159. See also, Polly Welts Kaufman, *National Parks and the Woman's Voice: A History* (Albuquerque: University of New Mexico Press, 1996), 44.
2. John Bodnar, *Remaking America: Public Memory, Commemoration, and Patriotism in the Twentieth Century* (Princeton, NJ: Princeton University Press, 1992), 34.
3. Peter Hecht, "Golden Moment in History Celebrated," *Sacramento Bee,* 25 January 1998, <http://www.calgoldrush.com/extra/cololma012598.html>.
4. JoAnn Levy, e-mail to Barbara J. Howe, 21 July 1999. Levy is the author of *They Saw the Elephant: Women in the California Gold Rush* (Oklahoma City: University of Oklahoma Press, 1992). Her website is at <http://www.goldrush. com/~joann/>.
5. Kathryn Dore Perkins, "As Good as Gold," *Sacramento Bee,* 18 January 1998, <http://www.calgoldrush.com/extra/levy.html>.
6. Gerda Lerner, "New Approaches to the Study of Women in American History," in Gerda Lerner, ed., *The Majority Finds Its Past: Placing Women in History* (New York: Oxford University Press, 1979), 3–14. The article originally appeared in *The Journal for Social History* 3 (Fall 1969): 53–62.
7. Louise Bernikow, "What Really Happened at Seneca Falls," *Ms.* 9 (July/August 1998): 65. See also, Kaufman, *National Parks and the Woman's Voice: A History,* 222.
8. Ibid.
9. Suzanne Levine and Harriet Lyons, *The Decade of Women: A Ms. History of the Seventies in Words and Pictures* (New York: Paragon Books, 1980), 6.
10. "Gerri Gribi: Celebrate Women's Equality Day, August 26," <http://www. dct.com/~gribi/equalityday.html>.
11. For reflections on Celebrate '98, see the following articles in *The Public Historian* 21 (Winter 1999): Shelley Bookspan, "Begetting Legacy," 7–10;

Vivien Ellen Rose, "Remembering Seneca Falls: A Roundtable on Commemorating the Sesquicentennial of the 1848 Seneca Falls Women's Rights Convention, 11–20; Paula Barnes, "Elizabeth Cady Who?," 21–26; Molly Murphy MacGregor, "Living the Legacy of the Women's Rights Movement," 27–34; Ann D. Gordon, "Who Replaces Stanton, Anthony, and Stone?," 35–40; and Ellen Carol DuBois, "Seneca Falls Goes Public," 41–48.

12. National Women's History Project, "Living the Legacy: The Women's Rights Movement, 1848–1898; Programs and Events," <http://www.legacy98.org/events.html>.

13. "The National Park Service. Women's Rights National Historical Park," <http://www.nps.gov/wori/.>.

14. "White House Millennium Council. 'Save America's Treasures Tour' with First Lady Hillary Rodham Clinton," <http://whitehouse.gov/WH/EOP/First_Lady/ html/treasures/>; and "White House Millennium Council, 'Save America's Treasures Tour' with First Lady Hillary Rodham Clinton, Follow the First Lady," <http://www.whitehouse.gov/WH/EOP/First_Lady/html/treasures/ follow.html.

15. This list may be found at <www.nmwh.org>.

17. "The Spirit of Seneca Falls: Events and Celebrations," *Ms.* 9 (July/August 1998): 78.

18. For a list of these events, and other international events during 1998, see National Women's History Project, "Living the Legacy . . . Programs and Events," <http://www.legacy98.org/events.html>.

18. West Virginia University Center for Women's Studies, *"No Turning Back: A Retirement Celebration Honoring Judith Gold Stitzel,* November 1, 1998," program.

19. "Worcester Women's History Project, Activities and Accomplishments" and "Fact Sheet on the Worcester Women's History Project," Worcester Women's History Project, Worcester, MA. For further information, see <http://assumption. edu/html/academic/history/WWHP/front.html>.

20. Amanda Ray, for instance, has looked at numerous newspapers published in western Virginia in the summer of 1848 to see what readers might have learned about the fledgling women's rights movement. She found no references to the Seneca Falls convention.

21. "White House Millennium Council: What is the Millennium Council?", <http:// www.whitehouse.gov/Initiatives/Millennium/what.html>; and "The Sixth Millennium Evening at the White House: Women as Citizens: Vital Voices Through the Century," <http://www.whitehouse.gov/Initiatives/Millennium/ mill_eve6.html>.

22. "Lifetime Online: It Wouldn't Have Happened Without Her: A Salute to Influential Women of the 20th Century," <http://www.lifetimetv.com/exclusives/ 20th_century/index.html>.

23. David Glassberg, *American Historical Pageantry: The Uses of Tradition in the Early Twentieth Century* (Chapel Hill: University of North Carolina Press, 1990), 18.

24. Ibid., 39.
25. Christine Kleinegger, New York State Museum, on H-NET Discussion List for Local and State History, 26 July 1999, archived at <http://www.h-net.msu.edu>; "*Yankee Magazine's* New England.Com Search Results: Selected Events in Neighboring New York." <http://www.newengland.com/nycan/eventsny.html>; "The Albany Tulip Festival." <wysiwyg://86/http://albany.mininegc . . . albany/library/weekly/aa050398.htm>
26. Ruth Miriam De Young Kohler, *The Story of Wisconsin Women* (n.p.: Committee on Wisconsin Women for the 1948 Wisconsin Centennial, [1948]).
27. E-mail, Genevieve G. McBride, 27 July 1999, H-Net List for Women's History.
28. "'The men have failed . . . It's time to call out the women'," brochure produced by Cranford Johnson Robinson Woods and Arkansas Graphics "to celebrate the Women's Emergency Committee's 40th Anniversary, with assistance from the University of Arkansas at Little Rock (UALR) Public History Program." Brochure courtesy of Johanna Miller Lewis at UALR.
29. For more information on Lady Vestey, see Elizabeth J. Tremain, *Evelene: The Troubleshooter was a Lady* (*Lincoln, NB: Foundation Books, 1985*). The festival web site is at http://www.superiorne.com.
30. "Lady Vestey Festival," <http://www.superiorne.com/spc/exp_auct.htm>.
31. Ibid.
32. For more on the West Virginia University centenary celebration, see Barbara J. Howe and Lillian J. Waugh, "Pursuing 'Excellence Through Equity': The Centenary of Women's Education at West Virginia University" *History News* 45 (March/April 1990): 14–16.
33. Robin Harris, e-mail to Barbara J. Howe, 27 July 1999.
34. Simmons Centennial, <http://centennial.simmons.edu/early_days/splash.html>.
35. "Simmons Centennial. What's New," <http://centennial.simmons.edu/whats_new/year.html>; "Simmons. Centennial. Road Show," <http://centennial.simmons.edu/road_show/roadshow.html>. Brown University celebrated the one hundredth anniversary of women students at Brown with a conference and a history. See Polly Welts Kaufman, ed., *The Search for Equity: Women at Brown University, 1891–1991* (Hanover, NH: University Press of New England, 1991).
36. See, for example, Ruth Bordin, *Women at Michigan: The "Dangerous Experiment," 1870s to the Present* (Ann Arbor: University of Michigan Press, 1999); and Kaufman, ed., *The Search for Equity.*
37. Jodi Vandenberg-Daves, e-mail to H-NET List for Women's History, 26 July 1999.
38. "National Women's History Project," <http://www.nwhp.org/progidea.html#y2k-party>.
39. "National Women's History Project," <http://www.nwhp.org/progidea.html#comm>.

40. "National Women's History Project," <http://www.nwhp.org/nhist-orgs.html>.
41. "National Women's History Project," <http://www.neh.gov/html/st_by_st. html>.
42. The Arkansas catalogue was "*Behold, Our Works Were Good.*" *A Handbook of Arkansas Women's History,* Elizabeth Jacoway, ed. (Little Rock: Arkansas Women's History Institute in association with August House, 1987), 7.
43. Suzanne Lebsock and Kym S. Rice, "*A Share of Honour*": *Virginia Women, 1600–1945* (Richmond: Virginia Women's Cultural History Project, 1984).
44. The "catalogue" for the West Virginia exhibit was the 1990 issue (vol. 49) of *West Virginia History,* which included essays by the historians involved in the exhibit planning.
45. See, for instance, League of Women Voters of Alabama, comp., *A Collection of Biographies of Women Who Made a Diference in Alabama,* Miriam Abigail Toffel, ed. (Birmingham, AL: The League, 1995); Eugenia K. Potter, *Kentucky Women: Two Centuries of Indomitable Spirit and Vision* (s.l.: Big Tree Press, 1997); Margaret Supplee Smith and Emily Herring Wilson, *North Carolina Women: Making History* (Chapel Hill: University of North Carolina Press, 1999); Melvena K. Thurman, ed., *Women in Oklahoma: A Century of Change* (Oklahoma City: Oklahoma Historical Society, 1983); Wilma Dykeman, *Tennessee Woman: An Infinite Variety* (Newport, TN: Wakestone Books, 1993); *Wilma Dykeman, Tennessee Women, Past and Present*; with selected additional material edited by Carol Lynn Yellin (s.l.: s.n., 1977); James M. Day et al., *Women of Texas* (Waco, TX: Texian Press, 1972). Suggestions for these books came from Genie K. Potter, e-mail comment on H-NET List for Women's History, 28 May 1999. See also Katharine T. Corbett, *In Her Place: A Guide To St. Louis Women's History.* (St. Louis: Missouri Historical Society, 1999).
46. "West Virginia Division of Culture and History," <http://www.wvlc.wvnet. edu/history/womhome.html; and "The Florida State Archives: Collections Pertaining to Women's History and Women's Issues," <http://dlis.dos.state. fl.us/barm/fsa/women'sguide.htm>.
47. "West Virginia Divsion of Culture and History," <http://www.wvlc.wvnet. edu/history/linkarch.html>.
48. The American Association for State and Local History series includes David Kyvig and Myron Marty, *Nearby History* (Nashville, TN: American Association for State and Local History, 1982); Barbara J. Howe, Dolores A. Fleming, Emory L. Kemp, and Ruth Ann Overbeck, *Houses and Homes: Exploring Their History* (Nashville, TN: AASLH, 1987); Ronald E. Butchart, *Local Schools: Exploring Their History* (Nashville, TN: AASLH, 1986); James P. Wind, *Places of Worship: Exploring Their History* (Nashville, TN: AASLH, 1990) and Gerald A. Danzer, *Public Places: Exploring Their History* (Nashville, TN: AASLH, 1987); K. Austin Kerr, Amos J. Loveday, Mansel G. Blackford, *Local Businesses: Exploring Their History* (Walnut Creek, CA: AltaMira, 1996). The Krieger series includes R. Douglas Hurt, *American Farms:*

Exploring Their History (Malabar, FL: Krieger, 1996); Karen J. Blair, *Joining Together: Exploring the History of Voluntary Organizations* (Malabar, FL: Krieger, 2000); Michael W. Homel, *Unlocking City Hall: Exploring the History of Local Government and Politics* (Malabar, FL: Krieger, 2000); Elizabeth B. Monroe, *Next Door: Exploring the Architectural and Social History of Neighborhoods* (Malabar, FL: Krieger, 2000).

49. Barbara J. Howe and Helen M. Bannan, "Women's History, Local History, and Public History," *History News* 50 (March/April 1995): 7–11.

50. There are many books on conducting oral histories, but one of the basics still remains Willa Baum, *Oral History for the Local Historical Society,* 3rd rev. ed. (Walnut Creek, CA: AltaMira/AASLH, 1995).

51. "Women's History Celebration: The President's Commission on the Celebration of Women in American History," <http://www.gsa.gov/staff/pa/whic.htm>; and William J. Clinton, "Executive Order 13090," <http://www.pub.whitehouse.gov/urires/12?urn;pdi://oma.eop.gov.us/1998/7/2/14.text.3>.

52. "Women Who Made It Happen: A Women's History Project," <http://gsa.gov/staff/pa/whcform.htm>.

SUGGESTED READINGS

J. D. Britton and Diane F. Britton, *History Outreach: Programs for Museums, Historical Organizations, and Academic History Departments.* Malabar, FL: Krieger 1994.

Encyclopedia Britannica On-Line. <www.eb.com>. This has keyword search capacity through all the articles. A search for "Jane Addams," for instance, turned up references in 342 articles.

Sara M. Evans, *Born For Liberty: A History of Women in America.* New York: Free Press, 1997.

Karen Greenspan, *The Timetables of Women's History: A Chronology of the Most Important People and Events in Women's History.* New York: Touchstone Books, 1996.

Dolores Hayden, *The Power of Place: Urban Landscapes as Public History.* Cambridge, MA: MIT Press, 1995.

Darlene Clark Hines, ed., *Black Women in America: An Historical Encyclopedia.* Brooklyn, NY: Carlson, 1993.

Glenda Riley, *Inventing the American Woman: An Inclusive History,* vols. 1 and 2, 3rd ed. Arlington Heights, IL: Harlan-Davidson, 2001.

Lynn Sherr and Jurate Kazickaas, *Susan B. Anthony Slept Here: A Guide to American Women's History.* New York: Times Books, 1994.

INDEX

A number in italics indicates an illustration.